$25.00

WITHDRAWN

WITHDRAWN

WITHDRAWN

D1295367

The Presidency of
BENJAMIN
HARRISON

AMERICAN PRESIDENCY SERIES

The Presidency of

BENJAMIN
HARRISON

Homer E. Socolofsky
and Allan B. Spetter

UNIVERSITY PRESS OF KANSAS

Published by the University Press of Kansas (Lawrence,
Kansas 66045), which was organized by the Kansas
Board of Regents and is operated and funded by Emporia
State University, Fort Hays State University,
Kansas State University, Pittsburg State University, the
University of Kansas, and Wichita State University

Library of Congress Cataloging-in-Publication Data

Socolofsky, Homer Edward, 1922–
The presidency of Benjamin Harrison.

(American presidency series)
Bibliography: p.
Includes index.
1. United States—Politics and government—1889–1893.
2. Harrison, Benjamin, 1833-1901.
I. Spetter, Allan B., 1939–   . II. Title.
III. Series.
E701.S62   1987   973.8′6′0924   86-32592
ISBN 0-7006-0320-4

British Library Cataloguing in Publication data is available.

Printed in the United States of America
10 9 8 7 6 5 4 3 2 1

CONTENTS

FOREWORD

The aim of the American Presidency Series is to present historians and the general reading public with interesting, scholarly assessments of the various presidential administrations. These interpretive surveys are intended to cover the broad ground between biographies, specialized monographs, and journalistic accounts. As such, each will be a comprehensive, synthetic work which will draw upon the best in pertinent secondary literature, yet leave room for the author's own analysis and interpretation.

Volumes in the series will present the data essential to understanding the administration under consideration. Particularly, each book will treat the then current problems facing the United States and its people and how the president and his associates felt about, thought about, and worked to cope with these problems. Attention will be given to how the office developed and operated during the president's tenure. Equally important will be consideration of the vital relationships between the president, his staff, the executive officers, Congress, foreign representatives, the judiciary, state officials, the public, political parties, the press, and influential private citizens. The series will also be concerned with how this unique American institution—the presidency—was viewed by the presidents, and with what results.

All this will be set, insofar as possible, in the context not only of contemporary politics but also of economics, international relations, law, morals, public administration, religion, and thought. Such a broad approach is necessary to understanding, for a presidential administration is more than the elected and appointed officers composing it, since its work so often reflects the major problems, anxieties, and glories of the nation. In short, the authors in the series will strive to recount and evaluate the record of each administration and to identify its distinctiveness and relationships to the past, its own time, and the future.

The General Editors

PREFACE

For about thirty years, until his death in 1957, Albert T. Volwiler struggled in vain to write the biography of President Benjamin Harrison. Meanwhile, the late Harry J. Sievers had launched his own twenty-year project, which produced an incredibly detailed life of Harrison—in three volumes. The last volume, which did not appear until 1968, covered the presidential years. Typically, Sievers then concentrated more on the day-by-day events in Harrison's life than on the significance of his presidency. Thus, Harrison has remained one of the least understood presidents, almost forgotten in the history of the nation's highest office.

Benjamin Harrison was a surprise nominee for president in 1888. As the second choice of most delegates at the Republican National Convention, he gained the prize and defeated incumbent Grover Cleveland in the election. Harrison's one term in the White House, which was sandwiched in between Cleveland's two separate administrations, was filled with problems that burdened his years there. His preparation for the presidency was scant compared to that of most presidents. He had a fine legal practice in Indianapolis, and he had been a fixture in Republican politics in Indiana. But his single term in the United States Senate and his service in a variety of minor posts in his home state provided neither administrative nor executive experience. Yet the self-contained Harrison knew he had the innate ability to handle the presidency without delegating authority or relying on close advisors. As a young lad not quite eight years of age, he had seen his grandfather leave for Washington to become the ninth president. That legacy created a unique perspective toward his own responsibilities as chief executive; he personally supervised the enormous task of appointing Republicans to every available office, and he provided significant input for each major decision in his administration.

General accounts of his period inaccurately treat Harrison as a cipher; they dwell more on apocryphal stories about his nomination, election, and subsequent difficult relationships with the colorful political leaders of the Gilded Age. Yet his first two years as president produced landmark legislation—including the Sherman Anti-Trust Act and the McKinley Tariff—that was comparable in impact to the first two years of the Lincoln and Wilson administrations. Harrison, although recognizing congressional supremacy in legislative matters, worked diligently from his White House office to fashion legislation that he could accept. Harrison threatened but seldom used the veto, he had White House visits with congressional leaders as well as other members of Congress, and he enunciated his program in annual messages to Congress and the nation. William McKinley, in his own way, would use Harrison as a role model for a meaningful presidential role in legislation and would establish the foundation for the power of twentieth-century presidents.

After devastating Republican losses in the election of 1890, which left the House of Representatives under Democratic control, the last half of the Harrison presidency concentrated on foreign-policy matters. Because Secretary of State James G. Blaine, the most charismatic political figure of the era, endured incapacitating illnesses during much of the Harrison administration, Harrison added to his own work load the personal direction of State Department affairs. Only in the past twenty years have historians recognized the importance of the Harrison administration—and of Harrison himself—in the new foreign policy of the late nineteenth century. This administration faced challenges throughout the hemisphere, in the Pacific, and in relations with the European powers, involvements that would be taken for granted in the twentieth century.

This analysis of the Benjamin Harrison presidency relies heavily on the relevant primary source materials, including the manuscript collections of many of Harrison's contemporaries and the State Department archives. The authors want to acknowledge the efforts of many other historians whose works have added to the total picture of Harrison. But we owe a special debt to both Albert T. Volwiler and Harry J. Sievers for our understanding of Harrison. We have shared equally in the preparation of this manuscript, although Socolofsky concentrated on domestic policy and Spetter on foreign affairs. The coauthors have been the primary critics of each other's work, and the cooperation has been productive.

It is impossible to thank all the librarians and archivists who helped us, but we owe special acknowledgment to the staffs of the Manuscript Division, Library of Congress; the National Archives; the Farrell Library, Kansas State University; the Wright State University library; the library of the Kansas State Historical Society; and the Lilly Library, Indiana University.

Grants from the Kansas State University Faculty Research Fund and the Wright State University College of Liberal Arts Research Fund have made possible research for this study and the final preparation of the manuscript, which was typed by Nedra Sylvis and Leslie Weismiller. Advice, information, criticism, and encouragement, for which we owe thanks, has come from Henry Blumenthal, Robert Ferrell, Walter T. K. Nugent, Lloyd Gardner, and Donald McCoy. Readers for the University Press of Kansas have contributed to the strength of the final product. Proofreading, patience, and good humor represent the major contributions by both Penny Socolofsky and Lois Spetter, and we thank them for their support.

Homer E. Socolofsky
Manhattan, Kansas

Allan B. Spetter
September 1986   *Dayton, Ohio*

1

★ ★ ★ ★ ★

TAKING OFFICE

Forty-eight years to the day after his grandfather had become president of the United States, Benjamin Harrison took the oath of office as the twenty-third president on 4 March 1889. Relentless rain had drenched Washington, D.C., for several days, and it continued as the inaugural ceremonies got under way. In 1841 the grandfather, William Henry Harrison, at the age of sixty-eight, had become the ninth president. He had delivered an unusually long Inaugural Address, become ill from exposure in the abominable weather, and died of pneumonia a month later.

At fifty-five, the mean age of previous presidents, Benjamin Harrison was the fourth to wear a full beard. His complexion was light, his hair was light brown, and his beard was tinged with red. Like most of his predecessors, he had blue eyes. At just over five feet six inches, Harrison was slightly taller than James Madison, the shortest of presidents, but was much heavier. In spite of his stature, Harrison always dressed in a fashionable manner. He followed only Lincoln in habitually wearing a turned-down collar. Like Lincoln, he had a high, soft voice. Harrison had married younger than any of his predecessors, and like most of them, he brought children to the White House. His Anglo-Saxon background and rural upbringing were also in agreement with those of most previous presidents. He was the fourteenth lawyer to become president and was the fifteenth with a single given name. Harrison had previous military experience, again similar to many of the earlier presidents.[1]

Benjamin Harrison, his head uncovered in the rain on an open inaugural stand on the terrace at the east front of the Capitol, took his oath as president from Chief Justice Melville Weston Fuller shortly after one o'clock on that auspicious day. He was the fourth Republican to be elected to the presidency since the Civil War. Seated around him were his family and other dignitaries, including the outgoing Democratic president, Grover Cleveland. A sea of black umbrellas sheltered an enormous crowd that stood in the vast open area around the Capitol, facing Harrison as he replaced his high silk hat and began his Inaugural Address. The neatly dressed new president wore a Prince Albert coat, tailored in his home town of Indianapolis, Indiana, from American-made black broadcloth. The audience could not see that under his formal clothes was underwear of chamois skin, which he wore to protect himself from the weather.[2]

Whereas his grandfather had recited United States history and development to 1841 in the longest presidential Inaugural Address, Benjamin Harrison, with a message only half as long, set forth his idea of the national needs of the moment. It was still far too wordy, especially in the driving rain that soaked thousands of loyal Republicans who were witnessing the return of the Republican party to power after four long years of Cleveland.[3] Harrison marveled at the "happy contrasts between our country as it steps over the threshold into its second century of organized existence under the Constitution, and that weak but wisely ordered young Nation that looked undauntedly down the first century, when all its years stretched out before it." A difference was drawn between "thirty-eight populous and prosperous States . . . [and] thirteen States, weak in everything except courage and the love of liberty." The remainder of the more than four-thousand-word address dealt with prospective new states, the justification for a protective tariff, his assertion that federal administration of law should be the same throughout the country, his proposal to amend naturalization laws, his opposition to trusts, his feeling that foreign affairs would assume a new importance bolstered by a strengthened navy and expanded merchant marine, support for increasing the size of pensions, and an argument that election laws for seats in Congress could easily come under the jurisdiction of the Constitution. Other lead sentences in this address provide something of the president's thinking. For instance, he said:

> It is not a departure, but a return, that we have visited. The protective policy had then its opponents. The argument was made, as now, that its benefits inured to particular classes or sections. If the question became in any sense, or at any time,

sectional, it was only because slavery existed in some of the States. . . . Shall the prejudices and paralysis of slavery continue to hang upon the skirts of progress? . . . I have altogether rejected the suggestion of a special executive policy for any section of our country. . . . If our great corporations would more scrupulously observe their legal obligations and duties they would have less cause to complain of the unlawful limitations of their rights or of violent interference with their operations. . . . We have happily maintained a policy of avoiding all interference with European affairs. . . . It must not be assumed, however, that our interests are so exclusively American that our entire inattention to any events that may transpire elsewhere can be taken for granted. . . . We shall neither fail to respect the flag of any friendly nation or the just rights of its citizens, nor to exact the like treatment for our own. . . . The duty devolved by law upon the President to nominate and, by and with the advice of the Senate, to appoint all public officers whose appointment is not otherwise provided for in the Constitution or by act of Congress has become very burdensome, and its wise and efficient discharge full of difficulty. . . . I have a right, I think, to insist that those who volunteer or are invited to give advice as to appointments shall exercise consideration and fidelity. . . . While a treasury surplus is not the greatest evil, it is a serious evil. . . . It is very gratifying to observe the general interest now being manifested in the reform of our election laws.

Harrison's summation asked his listeners to "exalt patriotism and moderate our party contentions," then finally, he said:

I do not mistrust the future. Dangers have been in frequent ambush along our path, but we have uncovered and vanquished them all. Passion has swept some of our communities, but only to give us a new demonstration that the great body of our people are stable, patriotic, and law-abiding. No political party can long pursue advantage at the expense of public honor or by rude and indecent methods, without protest and fatal disaffection in its own body. The peaceful agencies of commerce are more fully revealing the necessary unity of all our communities, and the increasing intercourse of our people is promoting mutual respect. We shall find unalloyed pleasure in the revelation which our next census will make of the swift development of the great resources of some of the States. Each State will bring its generous contribution to the great aggregate of the Nation's increase. And when the harvest from the fields,

3

the cattle from the hills, and the ores of the earth shall have been weighed, counted, and valued, we will turn from them all to crown with the highest honor the State that has most promoted education, virtue, justice, and patriotism among the people.[4]

President Harrison had devoted much effort to his Inaugural Address, and reports about it were generally complimentary. Former President Rutherford B. Hayes wrote an admiring letter, in which he stated that he had read the

inaugural address—first hurriedly, and then with care. Some of the paragraphs read several times. I congratulate you, and the party, and the Country upon it. It is throughout in substance and style altogether admirable. Excuse me for alluding to its style. Jefferson and Lincoln, by a long distance, excel all others in their inaugural addresses. Yours will take rank with theirs. It is golden![5]

Woodrow Wilson, although an ardent Democrat, came to Washington to observe the inaugural festivities, but the weather changed his plans. He wrote his wife a complaining letter about the rain ''for the last thirty-six hours'' but observed that ''it's fit enough weather, however, to mark the incoming of the Blaine Republicans to the control of the government.'' Wilson's father wrote to the future president in like manner: ''I hope that you went over to see that fourth rate politician inaugurated, . . . a sad sight to every true lover of his country: the induction into so high an office of a man of whose principles are prejudices and all of whose prejudices are obstanacies [sic]—a little man whose vision is not that of a patriot but the partisan.''[6]

Most news accounts of Harrison's Inaugural Address came far closer to Hayes's remarks than to those of the Wilsons. As might be expected, Democratic newspapers, such as the *Atlanta Constitution* and the *Charleston News and Courier,* were more critical than were Republican and Independent journals. These two southern papers noted ''that the Republican boa constrictor is to be on view for the next four years, and that it will require a large supply of provender to keep him quiet,'' and that the Republican party thrust millions of unfit voters upon the South. Northern Democratic newspapers such as the *Albany* (N.Y.) *Argus* either condemned the length of the address or, like the *Cincinnati Enquirer,* found that the best portion was the statement on foreign policy.[7]

Republican journals, such as the *New York Tribune,* the *St. Paul Press,* and the *Boston Journal,* emphasized the positive aspects of the address and the new president's able presentation. Journals of an Independent character, such as *Harper's Weekly* and the *New York Times*, adopted a wait-and-see attitude but noted the pattern of the address, with its balanced phrases and the use of recurring statements followed by qualification, and said that it contained no novel theories, just familiar old ideas. The foreign press was most interested in the absence of bombast and in that portion of the address dealing with foreign policy.[8]

Harrison had accumulated ideas and had started to write his Inaugural Address back home in Indiana. The final touches were completed in the Arlington Hotel in Washington, after the trip of the presidential party on 25/26 February. Portions or all of the address were read to prospective cabinet officers James Gillespie Blaine and William Windom. Both were greatly pleased, while Blaine suggested a slight amendment which Harrison readily adopted. Secretary Elijah W. Halford finished a complete typed version about midnight on 3 March. A close friend, Murat Halstead, editor of the *Cincinnati Gazette*, who was to become the administration's first casualty when the Senate denied its confirmation of a Harrison appointment, found the address to be a "document of extraordinary literary as well as political merit." He added that this was "the universal opinion; and a great number are at pains to say so in the most extravagant terms, who are not accustomed to enthusiasm."[9] In reply to Halstead's compliment, Harrison said, "From a literary standpoint I did not give much thought to any matters of expression" in the Inaugural Address.[10]

After the ceremonies at the Capitol, the president and his family headed for the White House, while Grover Cleveland's family departed for the railroad station and residency in New York City. A crowd estimated at more than forty thousand escorted the president, and his carriage moved slowly. After a luncheon that was delayed by the belated inaugural ceremonies, Harrison and his vice-president, Levi Parsons Morton of New York, reviewed a four-hour parade composed of military, business, civic, and political units from all parts of the country.[11]

That evening a crowd of ten to twelve thousand attended the Inaugural Ball, which was held in the large interior courtyard of the Pension Office. The area had been transformed "into a luxurious salon adorned with fresh flowers and rare plants" with an "acre of tile floor reserved for dancing." The Marine Corps band, under the direction of John Philip Sousa, was one of two bands that played continuously from a Japanese pagoda. President and Mrs. Harrison arrived at 10:30 P.M. and appeared on various balconies to satisfy protocol. At a signal from Sousa, they came down the long staircase to head the grand promenade. Later the tired president and his wife returned to their quarters in the White House, which because of its cramped space and antiquity was less fashionable than their home in Indianapolis.[12]

When Harrison began his presidency, the United States had a population of slightly more than sixty-one million persons, an increase of approximately 25 percent in the past decade. Immigrants accounted for one-third of the new numbers, while natural increase took care of the rest. White persons in the population were 87.8 percent of the total when the census was taken the next year; all others were listed under the category of colored. The center of population in 1890 was south and east of Harrison's home town, Indianapolis, Indiana. This middle position had moved 48 miles since 1880, when it was very near the place where Harrison was born, just a few miles west of Cincinnati, Ohio. The settled area of the country, around two million square miles, was about half of the United States including Alaska. Urban America, with one-third of the nation's population, was rapidly developing during this era; in 1890, twenty-nine cities had populations of more than one hundred thousand. Slightly more than one-third of all urban dwellings were owner-occupied. New, on-site assembly of homes, rather than on-site fabrication, made housing more affordable. It was a product of the housing industry in the 1880s. Central heating of homes was expected; indoor plumbing was considered a necessity.[13] Agriculture continued to be the most widespread enterprise, employing two-fifths of all workers. Other extractive industries, such as mining and lumbering, had grown remarkably. However, the capacity of American manufacturing had doubled since 1880, and for the first time its products had a total value higher than those from farms and ranches. Much of this new economic activity was generated by many new miles of railroad, which provided a national market for industrial output. Rail-track miles, about one-third of the world's mileage, totaled almost 170,000 when Harrison assumed office. Significantly, most of this roadway had been integrated physically, so that cars from one line could be easily transferred to the tracks of another line.

In his Inaugural Address, President Harrison indicated a pride in the United States and its contemporary greatness:

> Our growth has not been limited to territory, population, and aggregate wealth, marvellous [sic] as it has been in each of those directions. The masses of our people are better fed, clothed, and housed than their fathers were. The facilities for popular education have been vastly enlarged and more gener-ally diffused. The virtues of courage and patriotism have given

proof of their continued presence and increasing power in the hearts and over the lives of our people.

At the same time he noted advances in religion, "the sweet offices of charity," and the "virtue of temperance," while he recognized that the nation had not yet attained an ideal condition.[14]

The road to the White House had been a long and uncertain one for Benjamin Harrison. Before the National Republican Nominating Convention in 1888, Harrison believed his chances were so slight for the nomination that he failed to make arrangements with his banker to finance the unexpected new expenses that were brought on by visitors who streamed into his home in Indianapolis. One author said that "the Presidency overtook and surprised Harrison while he was going away from it rather than toward it."[15] Harrison was a compromise candidate; for most of the Republican delegates at the convention, he was second to some other favored candidate.

Harrison was born in Ohio on 20 August 1833. By 1854, after his graduation in 1852 from Miami University in Oxford, Ohio, and his marriage the next year to Caroline Lavinia Scott, he moved to Indianapolis to practice law. His strong religious commitment made him and Caroline leaders in the First Presbyterian Church in Indianapolis. Both Benjamin and Caroline had grown up in homes with a strong allegiance to the Presbyterian faith. Benjamin had wrestled with his choice of profession—ministry or law—before the law won. In Indianapolis he soon became a deacon in his church, and for almost forty years he served as an elder. He was a Sabbath School teacher of young men, and his voice was heard in regular prayer meetings. In the Harrison household, Saturdays were used in preparation for the Sabbath, when cooking and other duties were reduced to a minimum. Presbyterians of that era believed that their church was responsible for the conduct and moral behavior of its members, and Harrison agreed fully. The activities of the Harrison family revolved around their church and Benjamin's law practice. He also became involved in Republican party politics. Before the Civil War he served as city attorney, secretary of the Republican State Committee, and Supreme Court reporter for Indiana.

The future president entered the Union Army as a second lieutenant in July 1862; within a month he was the colonel and commanding officer of the Seventieth Indiana Regiment. Harrison made his reputation fighting under General William Tecumseh Sherman in Georgia in 1864; he was promoted to brevet brigadier general in February 1865. At the end of the war he went back home to his family in Indianapolis, ready to rebuild his legal career.[16]

By the early 1870s, many Republicans in Indiana wanted Harrison to run for governor. He repeatedly turned down opportunities to run for that position or for a congressional seat. In 1876, however, when the Republican candidate for governor was forced to withdraw because of alleged involvement in unsavory activities, the state committee picked Harrison to run—but did not do so until 4 August. The election followed too soon for Harrison to overcome the disadvantage of the situation: he lost by about five thousand votes but emerged with greatly enhanced prestige.[17]

President Hayes considered Harrison for a cabinet position that year. Even more important for Harrison was the death of Indiana's Senator Oliver Perry Morton in 1877, which removed a very powerful rival and left Harrison in control of the state party. In June 1879, Hayes appointed Harrison to the Mississippi River Commission, where he gained visibility on a national level. As chairman of the Indiana delegation to the Republican National Convention in 1880, Harrison cast twenty-seven votes for James A. Garfield on the thirty-fifth ballot. A grateful president-elect wanted Harrison in the cabinet, but Harrison opted to run for a seat in the Senate. With no significant opposition, he was elected to the Senate on 18 January 1881.[18]

As the decade progressed, Harrison's political fortunes took on a grander scale. A few dedicated Indiana friends began to work to put Harrison in the White House. They would not be discouraged by his failure to win a second Senate term in 1887. They were joined by Philadelphia banker Wharton Barker, an early booster of Garfield's candidacy, who decided that Harrison deserved to be president. Barker met with Harrison in March 1884, and the senator approved Barker's effort to build a Harrison organization. Louis T. Michener, Harrison's closest political friend in Indiana, became the key figure in a continuing campaign which would be crowned with success by 1888.[19]

Any potential Republican candidate for president between 1876 and 1892 had to contend with James G. Blaine. First elected to the House of Representatives from Maine in 1862, Blaine became Speaker in 1869, at the age of thirty-nine. Despite allegations of misconduct during the 1870s, Blaine was the leading candidate for the presidential nomination at the Republican National Convention of 1876. After the heartbreaking failure to win the nomination, the "Plumed Knight" was then appointed to a Senate seat and was elected to a full term in March 1877. Blaine dominated the politics of the 1880s, though he began to have recurrent problems with gout. In fact, he seemed to have a continual preoccupation with his health. Thoughts about his own health were constantly included in calculations about his political future.[20]

Blaine was the only candidate who could stop the movement in 1880 to nominate Ulysses S. Grant for an unprecedented third term as president. The opposing forces battled ballot after ballot; on the thirty-sixth ballot, with a switch of almost 250 Blaine delegates, the convention chose Garfield. Blaine then entered the cabinet as secretary of state; after the assassination of Garfield, Blaine resigned. On his third try for the presidential nomination in 1884, Blaine finally won, but he lost the election to Grover Cleveland, the first president elected by the Democrats after the Civil War.

Blaine kept a low profile after this defeat, and he left for a prolonged grand tour of Europe on 7 June 1887. Still in Europe, he may have decided Harrison's destiny when he wrote to Stephen Benton Elkins on 1 March 1888. Blaine, who was determined not to run again, told Elkins, who had consistently supported Blaine's presidential aspirations, that he ruled out all potential nominees but one. Blaine concluded, "The one man remaining who in my judgment can make the best run is Benjamin Harrison."[21]

Elkins and other members of Blaine's legion never gave up the hope that Blaine would change his mind, but the dream faded in late June when Andrew Carnegie telegraphed to Whitelaw Reid in code from Europe: Blaine had made up his mind; he could not be moved. While the Chicago convention was in progress, Andrew Carnegie also cabled to Stephen B. Elkins from Carnegie's estate in Scotland, where Blaine was visiting. The message was again in code and stated simply: "Too late Victor immovable. Take Trump and Star," which meant: "Blaine immovable. Take Harrison and Phelps." Finally, the convention accepted Harrison, a respectable choice on the eighth ballot, but turned against William Walter Phelps, a wealthy New Jersey resident and New York City entrepreneur who had served four terms as a congressman, "largely because of ridicule that he parted his hair in the middle and combed it over his forehead bang style." Instead, as the Republican vice-presidential candidate in 1888, the delegates selected Levi Morton, a New York banker who had served two terms in Congress and four years as minister to France. Morton, who had turned down a post in Garfield's cabinet, was "literally hairless—no eyebrows and a head as bald as a billiard ball."[22]

During the so-called Gilded Age, politics and elections were mass entertainment for most American citizens. Political parties were highly organized for the all-male voters of this period. Patronage was considered the oil that ran each political machine, and there was a highly partisan press. But none of these factors explains the extremely large voter turnout in the era's frequent elections. Voters simply thrived on frequent opportunities to take a stand. Blaine telegraphed Stephen B. Elkins: "There's one more President in 'Protection,' and Harrison is a master of it."[23] President Cleveland provided the opening for Blaine's prophecy to succeed: Cleveland asked for major changes in the tariff, a position that many contemporaries interpreted as free trade. Most Republicans declared for some kind of protective tariff as a means of enhancing domestic production and for the use of reciprocity in order to extend foreign trade. Thus the dominant issue in the campaign of 1888 was the tariff. Except for the states of New York, New Jersey, Connecticut, and Indiana, the Republican party was generally successful outside the South, which was solid Democratic turf. These four states were swing states and were about the only ones to shift their presidential vote from one party to another. Thus, a political party needed a substantial share of the electoral vote from these four states to attain victory. Other pivotal states, on occasion, were Illinois and Ohio, which, with Indiana, were major corn-producing states, creating the impression that King Corn was in the driver's seat, not King Cotton. Although party instability characterized the era, most of the states were remarkably consistent in their political allegiance. Only a few states changed their votes for president in late-nineteenth-century elections, and all of this limited number did not change in any one election.[24]

The Pendleton Civil Service Act of 1883 altered the way in which political campaigns were financed. No longer was it possible to levy on salaries of civil servants for most of the money needed to run the national campaign. Much of the organization of the Harrison campaign was in the hands of the New York and Pennsylvania Republican bosses—former Senator Thomas Collier Platt and Senator Matthew Stanley Quay—and James S. Clarkson of Iowa. More money was gathered for this campaign than ever had been before. A special liaison committee, headed by John Wanamaker, a Philadelphia merchant, was instrumental in tapping industrial support for the protariff campaign of the Republicans.[25]

Benjamin Harrison, from the doubtful state of Indiana, was a unity candidate. He had the backing of all factions of the Republican party, thus forestalling the divisions that had plagued Blaine's candidacy in 1884. Harrison was buoyed up by Blaine's private and confidential letter of 19 July, which let him know that Blaine, all along, had thought Harrison's nomination "was the best and wisest that we could make." Blaine analyzed the election with

> a strong degree of confidence that you will be elected. You can carry your own state—You cannot be beaten in Connecticut—

That is enough!——New Jersey is always hard ground. . . . In New York—for the only time in her history except in 1853 if I mistake not—the Democrats have the national and state patronage & also complete control of the municipal machinery in New York city & Brooklyn. That is a great advantage to any party & especially for the Democracy.[26]

In taking this advice and that of others, Harrison continued to be an intelligent and thoughtful supporter of protection; he carefully controlled his own campaign activities from his home in Indianapolis. In addition, the race in 1888 was the first time since Lincoln's campaign in 1860 that the Republicans were campaigning on the record of a party other than their own.[27]

In 1884 James G. Blaine had made a campaign tour of about six weeks' duration, thus putting an end to the tradition that presidential candidates did not go out and campaign for themselves. Four years earlier, Republican candidate James Abram Garfield, because his farm in Mentor, Ohio, was a mere eight miles from a station on a major railroad line, had responded to visiting delegations by speaking to them from his front porch. Harrison, in 1888, had recognized that his home in Indianapolis was so accessible that he could not discourage visitors, so he deliberately planned his campaign around many voter pilgrimages. Matthew Quay, chairman of the National Republican Committee, was aghast at the possibility of Harrison's stumbling in such an open-ended format. Quay had decided to haul down the bloody shirt of rebellion, which had been emphasized in Republican campaigns since the Civil War, and to replace it with an orderly campaign of education, featuring pamphlets and broadsides to be sent all over the country. Harrison's front-porch effort was watched, with one of his advisors agreeing categorically that he would stop Harrison's speech making if Quay objected. As it turned out, in this campaign Harrison wielded the greatest influence himself. Varied delegations from all over the country came to his Indianapolis home, where he gave ninety-four superb speeches in his stay-at-home campaign.[28] This format was in keeping with Harrison's known abilities. When information about a delegation that was due to arrive was presented to Harrison, he and his advisors would decide on the topic to be discussed; Harrison would make a few remarks, which would be taken down by stenographers; then after proper editing, they would be released to the press. His combination of timeliness and topics that were appropriate to each group of listeners attracted daily national comment.

Delegations first came to Benjamin Harrison's residence in Indianapolis on 25 June 1888, the day he was nominated for the presidency. The first out-of-town delegation was from Danville, Indiana, and Harrison responded briefly. A month later, after he had spoken to one or more groups almost every day, the John A. Logan Club of Edgar and Coles counties, Illinois, came with two thousand people, including eighty-two veterans of the William Henry Harrison campaign. Harrison talked to them about John Alexander Logan. On 25 August, Harrison was in the midst of a two-week vacation at Middle Bass Island, in Lake Erie, where he was a guest of former Governor Charles Foster of Ohio. By 25 September the campaign was attracting more interest, although President Cleveland did not do any campaigning himself, then or later. Harrison had carefully delineated his position on most political questions in his letter of acceptance of 11 September. A group of more than a thousand from Wabash County, Indiana, was the first delegation on 25 September; it was followed by another group from Parke County, Indiana, and then by three hundred school children. To the Wabash County delegation he spoke on the surplus in the Treasury and what he would do about it. On 25 October, Harrison reviewed a parade in Indianapolis, made up of ten thousand workingmen-voters. He responded to a speech by a member of the Typographical Union in a large auditorium in Indianapolis with one of the longest speeches and probably the most impressive one of his campaign. He said, in part:

There are two very plain facts that I have often stated—and others more forcibly than I—that it seems to me should be conclusive with the wage-earners of America. The policy of the Democratic party—the revision of our tariff laws as indicated by the Democratic party, a revenue-only tariff, or progressive free trade—means a vast and sudden increase of importations. Is there a man here so dull as not to know that this means diminished work in our American shops? If some one says that labor is not fully employed now, do you hope it will be more fully employed when you have transferred one-third of the work done in our shops to foreign workshops? If someone tells me that labor is not sufficiently rewarded here, does he hope to have its rewards increased by striking down our protective duties and compelling our workmen to compete with the underpaid labor of Europe?[29]

Benjamin Harrison had bet his political career on nationalism, tariff protection, sound currency, and fair benefits for veterans; and the year 1888 was his for the taking.[30]

Two extraordinary developments occurred in the closing days of the campaign. The overall Harrison effort was remarkably free of blunders, but not unexpectedly one came in Indiana. A Republican poll that was taken in Indiana sixty days before the election showed the Democrats ahead. The treasurer of the Republican National Committee was W. W. Dudley, of Indiana. He knew about the Indiana political traditions, where a vote could be bought; he also knew that the major parties had budgeted part of their treasuries at every election to buy these votes at prices ranging from two to fifteen dollars.[31] Dudley did not have any direct responsibility for party activities in Indiana; these were in the hands of a state committee. Supposedly, Dudley sent a circular letter, which was opened by a curious mail clerk, to Republican field workers, urging them "to make the Democrats pay highly for voters to exhaust their resources . . . [and to] prevent frauds in the ballot boxes. He wanted every Republican at the polls, and every suspicious voter challenged." The final sentence produced the political furor and the term "Blocks of Five Dudley," by which he became known in later years: "Divide the floaters into blocks of five and put a trusted man with the necessary funds in charge of these five and make him responsible that none get away and that all vote our ticket." Dudley swore that the published letter was a fraud, he sued the newspapers that printed it, and he also brought suit against the mail clerk. Harrison, who was not sure about Dudley's action, never did exonerate him and later would not speak to him.[32]

The other development was the letter written by Osgoodby (or Murchison) to the British minister to Washington, Sir Lionel Edward Sackville-West. Charles Osgoodby, an orange grower in Pomona, California, posing as an English citizen named Charles F. Murchison, wrote to the British minister early in September, inquiring which party was favored by the British government. Sir Lionel's rambling reply, received a week later, in effect told his correspondent that Cleveland should get his vote. Osgoodby did not do anything with the letter at first. Finally, he gave it to his lawyer, who passed it on to the owner of the *Los Angeles Times*, where it was published late in October. When the British minister was confronted by the story, he fully acknowledged that he had written the letter. He made other incredulous statements that were harmful to the Cleveland administration, and apparently glorying in the stir he had made, he repeatedly gave newspaper interviews. The time remaining before the election was less than two weeks, too short a period to get a recall from the Foreign Office in London, so Cleveland sent him packing on 30 October.[33]

There is no way of knowing whether Dudley's letter or Osgoodby's letter influenced the outcome of the election. The big issue was still the fight over the tariff, which Harrison had defined as "not a contest between schedules, but between wide-apart principles."[34] Military words were still being widely used in 1888, as in earlier nineteenth-century elections, so the public was expected to see reports of the line of battle, the first gun, or a rally around a battle-scarred veteran. But campaigning was changing, and new electioneering techniques were coming into use. Harrison's ability to appeal to groups was much underrated by his eastern managers, who kept him mainly near his Indianapolis home. Voters still responded to emotional appeals that were connected with the Civil War, now a generation in the past. Thus, President Cleveland's offer to return captured rebel flags; his use of Memorial Day for a fishing trip; the choice of Congressman Roger Q. Mills, a former Confederate colonel, to lead his tariff fight; and the prominence of southerners in the stable of Democratic campaign orators—all added to the emotional content of the election race. In retrospect, one contemporary described this election as the last of the great hoopla, the partisan clamor associated with the previous generation. During the 1890s, Americans lost their political zest for concentrating on long-winded oratory and parades with brass bands. Torchlights were no longer needed in an age of electric streetlights.[35]

Harrison voted early on 6 November; then he returned home to learn the results on specially installed telegraph wires. He stayed up until the early morning hours of Wednesday, when it was obvious that he had won Indiana. Two mornings later, former President Hayes heard a newsboy yelling, "All about the election of General Harrison" outside his Spiegel Grove estate. Half-dressed, he rushed out of his house to buy the paper. Light "mist covered his bare head and beard, he nodded: 'How good. How good.' "[36]

In a very close election, though Cleveland still had a slight majority of around one hundred thousand of the two-party vote nationwide because of his increased majorities in the one-party states of the South, Harrison won 233 electoral votes to 168 for Cleveland. Harrison's race failed to broaden the popular base of the Republican party. As predicted, the outcome was crucial in four states—New York, Indiana, New Jersey, and Connecticut; Harrison captured the first two and, with them, the election. Blaine's prediction was half right, but New York was a good trade-off for Connecticut in 1888. Moreover, in southern and border states the Republicans increased their membership by nineteen seats in the House of Representatives, which was significant for control because the Republican majority in the House was razor thin. With a holdover majority in the Senate and on the Supreme Court, Republicans would take complete control of the federal government for the first time in many years. Only two states changed their electoral vote from 1884: New York, with thirty-six electors, and Indiana, with fifteen. The outcome was determined by extremely narrow margins. In New York, Harrison won by 13,002 votes out of 1,315,409 cast. His vote in New York City, which was down from Blaine's total in 1884, was more than made up for by the upstate vote. Harrison's slim margin in his home state of Indiana, where he was not able to get a majority in his hometown, was 2,348 votes out of a total of 536,964. The Republican presidential electors in 1888 received a majority of the vote in 1,157 counties nationwide, which was slightly less than the 1,290 that voted for the Democrats. This county total was the Republican high point in the period from 1876 to 1900. None of these shifts in voting patterns was substantial. Neither the tariff issue, in spite of its dominance, nor any of the reputed blunders or breaks in this race produced any major realignments. Harrison's vote was less than 1 percent higher in New York and in Indiana than that received by Blaine when he lost these states in 1884.[37]

But Harrison's margin of victory could have been even larger. He lost Connecticut by only 336 votes, a mere .22 percent of the two-party vote. There he declined somewhat in industrial towns from 1884, but he received increased support in farming areas. New Jersey was lost by 7,149 votes; West Virginia, by 1,873; and Virgina, by 1,539. Public comment, after the 1888 election, frequently discussed a corrupt bargain in New York, which produced vote trading to damage Cleveland's race. There the Democratic candidate for governor won by more than nineteen thousand votes over his Republican rival. Apparently, a bargain to embarrass Cleveland was mere talk, based on suspicion that was produced by a lack of party regularity in that vote. The Democratic candidate who was most harmed by the New York outcome, Grover Cleveland, said many years later that he had ''no idea or impression that the Presidential ticket was the victim of treachery in New York in the election of 1888.''[38]

In the four months between the election and the inauguration, President-elect Harrison was deluged with unsolicited advice on appointments and the character that his administration should take. He began the slow, deliberate process of selecting persons to receive cabinet positions and other major appointments. Neither before the convention nor before or after the election would Harrison commit himself or bargain with anyone over potential appointments. Harrison's usual response to efforts to get him to name persons prematurely to public office before the election was, ''I can be defeated for the Presidency, but I cannot be dishonored.'' Through the years he had thought about the presidency, because his name was frequently mentioned in news stories about the office. But he had ''never lost any sleep over it.''[39] Another part of Harrison's character was becoming obvious with election. He was a loner; he always had been. His sound intellect and extemporaneous-speaking ability, which were so important during the campaign, were impaired later by lack of imagination, by the absence of personal magnetism, and by a reserved, icy, and aloof manner. They would handicap many of his efforts as president. In an introspective way, Harrison was self-contained. With only a single term as a United States senator, he knew he had the ability to handle the presidency. Yet one of his closest advisors was chilled to hear him say, when it was evident that he was elected, ''Now, I walk with God.''[40]

There was much to be done before the Harrison family could depart for Washington. The president-elect was besieged by bags of mail each day, and there were always visiting delegations to see him. Several secretaries were employed to help Harrison get through his daily obligations. Two thousand people came to the Harrison residence on New Year's Day 1889 for traditional New Year's greetings. Harrison still felt free to attend public lectures, Grand Army of the Republic meetings, and similar public gatherings. Most of the time he was asked to speak after it was known that he was in the crowd.

Arrangements for the inaugural run to Washington were made by the Pennsylvania Railroad. The Harrison family would occupy the company president's car. A second car would be reserved for relatives and friends, including their close friend James N. Huston; attorney-general-designate William Henry Harrison Miller; Harrison's private secretary, Elijah W. Halford; stenographer E. F. Tibbott, with his family; and stenographer Alice Sanger. Reporters would occupy a third car. Departure was set for the afternoon of Monday 25 February, one week before the inauguration. The governor of Indiana and the mayor of Indianapolis, accompanied by several thousand people, including a thousand members of the G.A.R., escorted the Harrisons to the railroad station. Thirty-two prominent citizens formed a hollow square around the Harrison carriage, as a bodyguard of honor, and the distance of slightly more than one mile was covered in nearly an hour. From the rear platform of the special train, Harrison greeted his friends and neighbors of Indianapolis, saying:

> I cannot trust myself to put in words what I feel at this time. . . . I love this city. It has been my own cherished

home. . . . Let me say farewell to all my Indiana friends. For the public honors that have come to me I am their grateful debtor. They have made a debt so large that I can never discharge it. There is a great sense of loneliness in the discharge of high public duties. The moment of decision is one of isolation.[41]

Cheers rose from Indiana friends as the train departed, and at several stops in Indiana, Ohio, and Pennsylvania there were large crowds. In Washington the Harrison party was taken off the train unexpectedly at a freight depot, where members of the Inaugural Committee provided the official greeting. A suite of rooms in the Arlington Hotel's Johnson House annex, located on Vermont Avenue, provided lodging for the Harrisons until after the inaugural ceremony.[42]

After the official count of the electoral votes, President Cleveland wrote his personal congratulations to Harrison, "to assure you of my readiness to do all in my power to make your accession to office easy and agreeable. I am led to suppose that you will spend a number of days here prior to your inauguration etc." Harrison provided an immediate reply in similar formal language. He also wrote, "My plan is to leave home on the afternoon of Monday, Feby. 25th, and the proposed schedule will bring us to Washington the next afternoon. I will call at the Executive Mansion to pay my respects to you at such time during the week as may be convenient to you, and will be glad then to confer with you about the matters you have in mind, and about some that have occured to me." Harrison made a brief formal call at the White House on the morning of 2 March, and Cleveland paid a return visit to Harrison's quarters at the Arlington that afternoon. During one of these exchanges, Harrison asked Cleveland to keep the Senate in session briefly after the inauguration.[43]

Harrison had decided on his cabinet, with the exception of one or two positions, by the time he arrived in Washington. Just about everything, except the weather, went as planned on Inauguration Day.

After a rainy weekend the Harrison presidency was under way, and the multigeneration Harrison family was installed in the White House. The oldest member of this four-generation family was the father of Caroline Harrison, the Rev. Dr. John W. Scott, who was almost ninety years of age. Grandchildren Benjamin Harrison McKee, a favorite, and Mary Lodge McKee, his sister, lived at the White House with their mother, Mary Harrison McKee, during most of the Harrison years. Benjamin and Caroline's son, Russell, with his wife, Mary, and their daughter, Marthena, spent part of these four years in the president's household.[44]

One of the big initial activities facing President-elect Harrison had been the selection of the cabinet and other high-ranking officials. Now that he was president, the task of organizing his official family became a major priority. Announcements of Harrison's appointments came periodically from the White House office or from confirmations made by the Senate. These appointments served as the first crucial test of Harrison's ability to manage the task for which he had been elected. He believed he could handle the job; his constituents were divided, and they were to remain divided, on their opinions of Harrison's suitability as president.

2

★ ★ ★ ★ ★

THE FORMATION
OF A CABINET

On the day after Benjamin Harrison was elected president, he received congratulations from the man who expected to become secretary of state for the second time—James G. Blaine.[1] For all intents and purposes, thus began a mad scramble that would continue throughout the four months before Harrison's inauguration and that was typical of cabinet formation in the Republican administrations of the late nineteenth century.

On 8 November 1888, Blaine informed Stephen B. Elkins of a definite desire to serve again as secretary of state: "I would be glad to take the State Department and think I assume little in thinking he will offer it to me."[2] Though closely identified with Blaine, Elkins may have reacted with mixed feelings. He just happened to have a desire of his own for a place in Harrison's cabinet. At times, it seemed as if every important Republican in the nation had similar aspirations. President-elect Harrison therefore faced an unusually complex challenge. He had to decide what to do about Blaine, he also had to consider Elkins and others who had remained loyal to Blaine through more than a decade of presidential politics, and he had to confront a variety of powerful Republicans whose only loyalty belonged to their respective state machines.

Blaine, clearly hoping for recognition in the form of an immediate announcement of his appointment as secretary of state, wrote to Harrison on 9 November to establish his interest in foreign policy: "The friendly, peaceful and honorable settlement of the Fishery question will give profound satisfaction to the People and great *eclat* to yourself. Such a settlement I know is practicable and easy and will put to shame the silly talk about difficulty with England."[3] Blaine felt confident that he could arrange a permanent settlement which would guarantee that fishing vessels from the United States would have access to Canada's Atlantic waters. But Harrison had every reason to take his time and to weigh carefully whether he wanted to provide Blaine with the opportunity to add to his reputation over the next four years. Blaine's son Walker, for instance, thought of Harrison as a mere caretaker. Walker Blaine confided to his mother in July 1888: "If Harrison is elected and makes a good President I want you to bear this in mind, that his title to a renomination with power and patronage at his back is good for nothing. There is no power or combination that can prevent the Republican partisans from nominating father if he keeps alive and silent."[4]

In the final analysis, Harrison could not ignore Blaine. Harrison's private secretary, Elijah W. Halford, recalled some thirty years later that the president-elect had come to a simple conclusion: "Brother Halford, you and I will not have so good a time in Washington with Mr. Blaine out of the Cabinet as with him in it."[5] Harrison, however, realized that a quick selection of Blaine would revive the image of the prime minister who had dominated the administration of President James A. Garfield in 1881. Harrison instead kept Blaine waiting for more than two months, until mid January, and organized the administration without him. At the same time, Harrison maintained control over various Blaine supporters in two ways: they dared not do anything to jeopardize the awaited choice of the "Plumed Knight" or their own anticipated rewards.

According to John Watson Foster, who succeeded Blaine as secretary of state in mid 1892, Harrison immediately established his strategy for dealing with Blaine. Clearly, Blaine had reason to be less than enthusiastic about the treatment he received:

> From the day of his election it had been the intention of Harrison to invite Blaine to become Secretary of State, but he was not in haste to send the invitation, and both Blaine and his friends became restless under the delay. . . . Mr. Blaine . . . frequently talked with me about the other Cabinet places, but I could give him no information as to the intention of the President-elect. He was keeping his own counsel, when Mr. Blaine was expecting to be consulted.[6]

Just three weeks after the election, Blaine was already feeling frustrated and left out. With no word from Harrison, Blaine turned for help to Whitelaw Reid and the *New York Tribune*. As Blaine explained it, Elkins had at one point assured Harrison that Blaine did not wish to enter the cabinet. Elkins may have been furthering his own ambitions. In any case, Blaine set the record straight: "I have thought . . . that a line from you simply stating that you knew I would accept the appointment . . . might be wise. P.S. What I have a real curiosity to find out is whether Harrison or his advisors think that the constantly augmented support I have had since 1876 is worth consulting in the organization of an Administration."[7] On the following day, Blaine gave Reid carte blanche: "I see no objection to you saying to anyone that I will take the Secretary of State-ship. . . . Perhaps Harrison's mind needs to be freed from impressions created by interested parties that I would not take the place."[8]

November gave way to December, and William Walter Phelps tried to reassure Blaine. He reported happily on 6 December that the Executive Committee of the party had endorsed Blaine for secretary of state by a unanimous vote and had "intimated they would take any practical step to make their opinion operative on Harrison."[9] Yet Blaine kept the pressure on the president-elect. Two weeks later, he offered Reid a contribution for the pages of the *Tribune*: "This article was suggested by me and drafted by Walker. . . . It is, I think a most excellent way of giving me a 'boost' as the boys say—far better than a direct endorsement. . . . I should feel much obligated if you would insert it as an editorial in Saturday's *Tribune*."[10]

Finally, Harrison offered Blaine the position of secretary of state in a letter of 17 January 1889. But in addition to outlining some of his plans for the foreign policy of the nation, Harrison made crystal clear why he had chosen Blaine: "I have another great purpose and duty with which I am sure you will cooperate . . . that is preserving harmony in the party. . . . Each member of my official family will have my full confidence and I expect his."[11] Four days later, Blaine indicated that he understood perfectly: "Only a spirit of confidence mutual and perfect can make my service in the Cabinet valuable to the administration. . . . I have no motive near or remote inconsistent with the greatest strength and highest interest of the administration and yourself as official and personal head."[12] The two statesmen seemingly were prepared to make the best of a difficult situation.

As it turned out, Harrison had not needed advice about Blaine, such as he received in December 1888 from Murat Halstead, editor of the *Cincinnati Commercial Gazette*. Halstead suggested that Blaine would not be *persona grata* as minister to Great Britain and could not be sent into elegant exile as minister to France. Halstead concluded: "The best assertion of your own purpose that the administration of which you are to be the head shall be your own administration, and not that of anybody else, will be to take Mr. Blaine into the Cabinet."[13]

Nor did Harrison need advice when he decided on an approach toward Republicans loyal to Blaine—including Elkins, Reid, Phelps, and others who sought either cabinet or ministerial positions. Many assumed that Blaine was now in a position to provide unlimited opportunities. For instance, Blaine's acceptance brought an emotional and imaginative reaction from the normally sophisticated John Milton Hay, who shared his feelings with Reid: "Of course the great news is old news to you. . . . Blaine is in fine spirits and he and Walter Phelps are scouring the town for a home big and dignified enough for a Prime Minister."[14] Harrison would thwart such great expectations by isolating Blaine *within* the administration.

Mrs. Blaine, who did not find it difficult to dislike Harrison, was a disgruntled observer in early February 1889, as Harrison's treatment of the "Blaine Legion" became obvious. She described the situation for her son James: "The idea apparently is that having given Blaine the head of the table, no distinctively personal friend shall also have a seat."[15] Before the end of February, Reid confirmed her observations, sharing his frustration with Phelps: "Elkins has written a strong letter on the notion which he feared was gaining a lodgement, that after Blaine's own appointment, what was called 'the Blaine element,' i.e., four-fifths of the party, should be ignored in the Cabinet in order to preserve its balance."[16]

Reid had ambitions of his own; he wanted the most prestigious diplomatic post of minister to Great Britain. But as Phelps put it in his reply to Reid: "Elkins says: . . . Harrison thinks Reid may be too Blainey."[17] Reid thus consoled himself by rationalizing Harrison's decision: "The President concluded . . . sending me to England would silence the *Tribune* on points on which, as he said, he and the Republican Party had the right to expect it to be active and aggressive . . . the Irish question, the fisheries, the Bering Sea question, etc."[18] Harrison instead chose Robert Todd Lincoln—son of the fallen president, a Harvard graduate, lawyer, and former secretary of war—as the minister to Great Britain. Reid settled for the post of minister to France. Phelps was not the first choice for minister to Germany—Harrison appointed his close friend Murat Halstead, who failed to win the Senate's confirmation. Elkins did not enter the cabinet as the secretary of war until December 1891.

Before Harrison took the oath of office, the cabinet was expanded in February 1889 to include an eighth position—a secretary of agriculture.

Thus, the president-elect had to find seven colleagues for Blaine; but not one of the seven men who joined Blaine in the cabinet had been identified closely with his wing of the party.

Unbelievably, Harrison also ignored almost every prominent Republican. In the process, he alienated those leaders who had hoped to be in the cabinet. Others endured a similar humiliation; they waited in vain for the president-elect either to seek or to abide by their recommendations. Without the Republican leaders, Harrison methodically formed what has been called a politically obscure cabinet.[19]

There is no question, however, that Harrison felt comfortable with the cabinet that he selected. The president—and every member of the cabinet—observed the Presbyterian faith, perhaps the single most important credential for Harrison. Again and again, Harrison's choices mirrored his own background—five had legal training. But Harrison had additional emotional ties to several members of his cabinet; he dipped repeatedly into the pool of those who had risen to the rank of brevet brigadier general in the Civil War and/or were native sons of Ohio. The supply seemed unlimited in the Republican party of the late nineteenth century.

The secretary of the Treasury usually emerged as the most visible member of the cabinet in the post–Civil War era, a central figure in the constant struggle over monetary policy. Typically, Harrison had to make a fundamental decision about his secretary of the Treasury: the position could be filled by a representative of the conservative eastern (New York) financial community; or Harrison could look to the more liberal Midwest. In many ways, Harrison found the ideal man for the job; William Windom, a former secretary of the Treasury, was a midwesterner who lived in New York. But it would not be that easy.

Thomas C. Platt, the boss of the New York political machine, firmly believed that because he had delivered the state's delegation at the national convention, he would be made secretary of the Treasury. There is evidence that Harrison never approved such a deal. Furthermore, even if Platt appeared to be a legitimate candidate for the cabinet, he was neutralized by Warner Miller, a bitter rival in the New York Republican organization.

In 1881, Platt and the legendary Roscoe Conkling had resigned dramatically from the United States Senate in a dispute with President Garfield over New York patronage. To their surprise, neither Platt nor Conkling would gain vindication by being returned to the Senate by the state legislature. Platt was replaced by Warner Miller, who moved up from the House of Representatives. But Platt returned the favor, leading the effort that denied Miller a second term in 1887. When Miller also lost the race for governor in 1888, he expected that the president-elect would provide compensation. Miller, too, wanted to be secretary of the Treasury.

Harrison faced a no-win situation in New York. The only solution required that he overlook both Platt and Miller. The subsequent compromise decision to recognize New York with another cabinet position—the selection of Benjamin Franklin Tracy as secretary of the navy—did not begin to satisfy Platt or Miller. Both felt betrayed and later would turn against Harrison.[20]

Unfortunately, the search for a secretary of the Treasury also produced dissatisfaction in Pennsyvlania. In this case, the situation was further complicated when Harrison decided that the political novice John Wanamaker would represent Pennsylvania in the cabinet as postmaster general. The net result, once again: Harrison alienated two important Republicans. The Philadelphia banker Wharton Barker, who discovered Harrison and worked hard to spread the word in the years preceding the national convention of 1888, reacted negatively to the proposed cabinet on two counts. First, Barker informed the president-elect in late January 1889 that the selection of the fellow Philadelphian John Wanamaker for postmaster general seemed "absolutely hostile to me and my friends."[21]

Barker's real concern quickly became apparent, however: Pennsylvania could not hope for a second place in the cabinet, and he was yet another candidate for secretary of the Treasury. Early in February, a disappointed Barker wrote to Harrison again: "I have concluded that you have no intention of asking me to take the Secretary of the Treasury . . . but I thought you would feel that your relation to me was such that you would want to do so."[22] Harrison, by then weary of the whole process, sent a less-than-satisfactory reply; it addressed the protest about Wanamaker, rather than Barker's real complaint: "I have . . . concluded that those friends who think somebody not friendly is being set over them must take my assurance that such would not be the case."[23]

Harrison may have been forced to sacrifice Barker, an outspoken opponent of United States Senator Matthew S. Quay, the boss of the Pennsylvania machine. Barker had sought the Senate seat that the state legislature had awarded to Quay in 1887. And Harrison owed a huge political debt to Quay, who served as national chairman of the party in the campaign of 1888 and continued in that capacity. Yet Quay was about as unhappy as Barker was when Wanamaker received Pennsylvania's seat in the cabinet; Quay feared that such national exposure might create another formidable rival for power in Pennsylvania.[24] It soon became obvious that Quay had many differences of opinion with Harrison—most often these related to patronage—and he would line up with Platt in open rebellion against the president.

Harrison's first choice for secretary of the Treasury was Ohio-born William Boyd Allison, a midwesterner who had represented Iowa in the Senate since 1873. Harrison had served with Allison in the Senate. Allison had also been a serious candidate for the presidential nomination—perhaps best described, after Harrison, as everyone's second choice. But Allison, who established his reputation on monetary policy with the Bland-Allison Act of 1878, had at the last minute refused the same offer from President-elect Garfield in 1881. He most definitely preferred the security of the Senate to what could have been a temporary position in the cabinet. Allison declined again, particularly because of the realities of Iowa politics: he did not want to open a place in the Senate for Governor William Larrabee, a foe of the railroads. Yet Harrison's attempt to bring Allison into the cabinet, combined with the selection of Wanamaker for postmaster general, embittered another very influential Iowa Republican. James S. Clarkson, the national vice-chairman of the Republican party, had assumed that he would represent Iowa in the cabinet as postmaster general.[25]

Harrison finally obtained the services of Ohio-born William Windom as secretary of the Treasury, just as President Garfield had done in 1881. With the selection of Windom, Harrison may have sent a message to Blaine. Windom had been Minnesota's favorite-son candidate at the Republican National Convention of 1880, where Blaine had failed for the second time to win the presidential nomination. As secretary of state–designate in the Garfield administration, Blaine had then opposed the choice of Windom for secretary of the Treasury.

Windom, at the age of sixty-one, was a veteran of more than a decade in each branch of Congress. He had sought his fortune on the frontier in the 1850s, as had Harrison, Allison, and many others. A promising young lawyer, Windom had been elected to the House of Representatives from the new state of Minnesota in 1858. He had moved up to the Senate in 1870 and had remained there until called upon for cabinet duty in 1881. The assassination of President Garfield had ended Windom's first brief term as secretary of the Treasury, and he had returned to the Senate. When he had lost a bid for another full term in 1883, Windom had given up on Minnesota. He had moved to New York to return to the practice of law and to serve as president of the Atlantic and Pacific Railway Company.[26] But the man who seemed to bridge the gap between the Midwest and New York died suddenly in January 1891, after less than two years in office.

Harrison appeared determined to have Wanamaker as postmaster general, perhaps as a reward for the latter's crucial fund-raising efforts during the national campaign. The fifty-year-old merchant prince, who had revolutionized retailing in the United States, provided the Republican party with its largest war chest to that time.

Ironically, however, national chairman Quay felt threatened by Wanamaker's ability to raise money. The Pennsylvania boss visited with President-elect Harrison in Indianapolis on 19 December 1888 and offered several specific suggestions about the cabinet. In every case, Harrison completely ignored Quay's wishes. Quay hoped that Wanamaker—and Blaine—would be sent into exile in the diplomatic service. As a Stalwart, Quay had at no time supported Blaine in his various bids for the presidential nomination. At the same time, Quay assumed that Boss Platt would be secretary of the Treasury. And Quay strongly recommended that James Clarkson, his deputy in the national organization, should be included in the cabinet.[27]

Disappointment among party leaders was not confined to New York, Pennsylvania, and Iowa. As was the case in New York, two prominent Wisconsin Republicans were seeking the same cabinet position—both wanted to be secretary of agriculture, a position that had assumed cabinet rank in the closing days of the Cleveland administration. On this occasion, however, Harrison picked one of the two candidates, Governor Jeremiah M. Rusk. The president-elect thus made an enemy of the other candidate, the chairman of the state Republican party, Henry Clay Payne.

Wisconsin seemed to have a legitimate claim to be represented in the cabinet. The state's delegation at the national convention backed Rusk as a favorite son through three ballots. On the fourth ballot, Wisconsin cast twenty of its twenty-two votes for Harrison, providing an important boost for the bandwagon. And in the election, Harrison carried Wisconsin by a solid margin. But who deserved the reward—Rusk or Payne?

The forty-five-year-old Payne had served as postmaster of Milwaukee for a decade, from 1876 to 1885. But even as the current state chairman, his credentials could not match those of the six-foot-three "Uncle Jerry" Rusk and his long, colorful career.

The Ohio-born Rusk, who was fifty-eight years old, was the classic example of a self-made man. With little formal education, he had joined the list of those who had moved west in the 1850s. Rusk had prospered as a farmer, a businessman, and a banker. He had begun a political career on the local and state level; then he had risen to the rank of brevet brigadier general in the Civil War. Rusk had served three terms in the

House of Representatives in the 1870s; in 1881, he had become governor for the next seven years. Based on age and experience, Rusk deserved the recognition from Harrison. Yet Payne proved to be no more understanding than did Platt or Clarkson.[28]

The remaining places in the cabinet, at least, were filled without controversy. On the other hand, none of the four men who were chosen added to the political strength of the administration in any meaningful way. Harrison did not take the opportunity to counteract the damage done by the selection of Windom, Wanamaker, and Rusk; he simply refused to play politics with the construction of his cabinet. No state boss would be admitted to his cabinet.

In fact, Secretary of the Interior–designate John Willock Noble had turned his back on a public career; beginning in 1870, he had concentrated instead on a lucrative private practice as a railroad attorney. But Noble, like Rusk and Harrison, was Ohio-born and had attained the rank of brevet brigadier general in the Civil War. Furthermore, he had established a unique reputation in the Gilded Age—he appeared to be incorruptible—the perfect man to deal with very sensitive issues that came under the jurisdiction of the Department of the Interior: namely, railroad land grants and pensions for Civil War veterans.

There were remarkable similarities in the lives of Noble and Harrison. The fifty-seven-year-old Noble had attended Miami University for three years, though he then had graduated from Yale with honors in 1851. Noble had returned to Ohio for a year of law school in Cincinnati, but he, too, had gone west in the 1850s. He had stayed briefly in Missouri, then had moved on to Iowa. Despite his youth, Noble quickly demonstrated outstanding ability as a lawyer. At the end of the Civil War, he returned to Missouri; in 1867, Noble became United States district attorney for the eastern district of the state, with offices in St. Louis. Over the next three years he vigorously prosecuted violations of the nation's internal-revenue laws. His efforts pointed to an obvious conclusion in the mid 1870s: St. Louis was the key location in the illegal nationwide operations of the Whiskey Ring.[29]

New York's seat in the cabinet went to another former brevet brigadier general, Benjamin Franklin Tracy. Even the bitter Boss Platt knew that Harrison had made an excellent choice for secretary of the navy. Platt and Tracy had been schoolmates during the late 1840s and had gone on to become close political allies.

Tracy, now aged fifty-eight, had launched his legal career during the 1850s and had served as a county district attorney for much of the decade. After a brief term in the state legislature, he had gone off to participate in the Civil War. Tracy's tour of duty had included an extremely difficult assignment as commandant of the compound for prisoners of war at Elmira, New York. Perhaps twenty-five hundred Confederates had died while he was in charge; so it was not until 1867 that Tracy had received the rank of brevet brigadier general, to date from the end of the war in 1865.

Meanwhile, Tracy had become United States district attorney for the eastern district of New York. He had continued in that capacity until 1873 and had carried on his own crusade against elements of the Whiskey Ring. Tracy then had practiced law through the 1870s, until he returned to public life as a justice of the New York State Court of Appeals at the beginning of the 1880s. But Tracy had remained on the court only one year; he retired to battle lingering ill health between 1883 and 1885. When Tracy resumed private practice, one of his law partners was none other than Frank H. Platt, Boss Platt's son.[30]

Only one of the men who was chosen for the cabinet had provided visible support for Harrison at the national convention of 1888. Redfield Proctor, who had led the Vermont delegation, had seconded Harrison's nomination and had cast a unanimous grand total of eight votes for the candidate on every ballot. A grateful Harrison selected Proctor to be secretary of war. A Dartmouth graduate, the fifty-seven-year-old Proctor had seen limited service during the Civil War because of a bout with tuberculosis. After the war he had practiced law and had served several terms in the state legislature. Increasingly, however, Proctor had been drawn toward the business world. Thus, while he had become lieutenant governor and governor in the late 1870s, Proctor was better known as president of the Vermont Marble Company, the largest of its kind in the world.[31]

The choice of Proctor may have disappointed Stephen Elkins. But the Ohio-born millionaire, who was only forty-seven, could afford to wait patiently for his turn. In fact, Elkins viewed a cabinet position as a stepping-stone to his real goal: he wanted to represent West Virginia in the United States Senate. Ironically, when Proctor resigned from the cabinet late in 1891 to enter the Senate, Harrison chose Elkins to replace him. And when the Republicans captured control of the West Virginia Legislature in the landslide of the 1894 elections, Elkins realized his ambition for a seat in the Senate.[32]

Aside from Blaine, Windom, and Wanamaker, not one of the other cabinet members had a reputation that crossed state lines. But Rusk, Noble, Tracy, and Proctor were not unknowns. The new attorney general, however, was indeed politically obscure; yet at the same time, he was the ultimate example of the relationship that Harrison hoped to have with his advisors.

William Henry Harrison Miller—even the name had to make the next president feel comfortable—was the youngest member of the cabinet, at forty-eight. The nation soon would learn of his most important qualification; since 1874, Miller had practiced law in Indianapolis as a partner of the president-elect. A native New Yorker and a graduate of Hamilton College, Miller had moved to Fort Wayne after the Civil War. Over the next decade, he had established a reputation in Indiana legal circles and had earned an invitation to join Harrison's firm. The two men then had become much more than business associates; in fact, they had toured the West together on a six-weeks' vacation in 1881. The *New York Times* accurately described Miller as Harrison's "most intimate and confidential friend."[33]

On 5 March 1889 the Senate adjourned after a brief twenty-three-minute session, in which it confirmed Harrison's eight cabinet appointments. There was no opposition, and these appointments were not referred to a committee. Precedent was followed, for the Senate had rarely taken exception to cabinet selections.

By any standard of evaluation, Harrison's cabinet must be divided in two. On one side was James G. Blaine—unique in so many ways. As for the rest, Harrison assembled a cabinet that represented—just as he did—the honest, decent, solid Republicans all across the nation. While Harrison, who had been a brevet brigadier general in the Civil War, chose to omit the reconstructed South from his cabinet, the four members from the Midwest (Windom, Rusk, Noble, and Miller) included a representative from the border state of Missouri. While Blaine really belonged to the nation at large, a group of three—Tracy, Wanamaker, and Proctor—specifically acknowledged the importance of New York, Pennsylvania, and New England. But beyond geographic or other considerations, each of the men in this cabinet would give the United States his best.

Yet Harrison had ignored the bosses. He would pay the political price in the presidential election of 1892. In fact, the bosses did not wait until 1892. They waged an immediate and continuing battle with the president over the spoils of victory—patronage.

3

★ ★ ★ ★ ★

PATRONAGE BACK
IN REPUBLICAN HANDS

President Benjamin Harrison easily agreed with former President Grover Cleveland on at least one thing. The onerous task of making appointments to the federal civil service during their presidential terms proved to be most time consuming and unrelenting, as well as the most disappointing, activity of each administration. During the first eighteen months in the Executive Mansion, Harrison spent four to six hours each day on appointment matters and named almost seventeen hundred men and women to the civil service.[1] Naturally, cabinet members who were identified immediately after the inauguration attracted attention, but some of Harrison's other appointments brought more complaint in the news media and from the general public than any other thing Harrison did. His handling of patronage also brought disaffection from noted Republican leaders.

Rumors and news stories insisted that Harrison had made deals to ensure his nomination and election. In letters that Harrison wrote at the time, he claimed otherwise. For example, he replied to an Ohio correspondent that "I was nominated at Chicago without the smallest promise of any sort relating to federal appointments and I am now absolutely without any promise or entanglements of any sort." No doubt, subordinates in the campaign organization gave promises to gain support, but Harrison would have none of that. As a former senator, Harrison was aware of senatorial courtesy in his appointment procedure, which recognized that a Republican senator had the right to veto appointments that were made within his own state. Also Harrison placed much emphasis on which geographical areas should be represented in his administration. However, if his own judgment differed from that of a senator, Harrison would make his own decision unexpectedly, without any effort to retain the senator's loyalty. His abrupt and frank behavior was humiliating to many senators who expected a minimum of calm courtesy from their party's leader. About five weeks before the inauguration, even though he had asked Blaine to be secretary of state, Harrison wrote to an Indiana friend that he had not yet "apportioned any of the offices to any state or to any individuals." Harrison's private secretary remembered years later that Harrison was extremely careful in avoiding "even a semblance of a bargain, for under no circumstances would he be bound by any promise, express or implied, either during the campaign or later."[2]

Throughout the presidential campaign of 1888, Harrison gained a reputation as a supporter of the merit system. Cleveland's reluctant response in enlarging the merit system was well known, and because of that, many reformers preferred Harrison. He dealt with the reform of the civil service in general terms in his famous front-porch speeches. Similarly, he impressed loyal Republicans as a person who would take advice from party leaders to eliminate party factionalism. Thus, he could appeal to the growing body of reformers and still retain his ties to elder statesmen within his party. Once elected, Harrison had to face the insurmountable issue of providing jobs for thousands of loyal, partisan Republicans who were consumed with the thought of replacing federal officeholders who had received their jobs from Cleveland. It was an impossible job for anyone who possessed characteristics like Harrison's.

In those first months in office, more than 60 percent of Harrison's mail and a large portion of his office time for visiting with constituents involved civil-service appointments. Each supplicant claimed that he was an original Harrison man or that his state had to be recognized in this appointment. Selecting officeholders was a serious, time-consuming task to Harrison. Russell B. Harrison assisted his father during these early months in sorting out appointments. To a Wisconsin applicant Russell wrote, "If you are urged by Secretary [of Agriculture, Jeremiah] Rusk, Senators and the Congressional Delegation, you will have very little trouble in securing some place in the consular service."[3]

Many letters of application reached the president indirectly, as they were mailed to a member of his family or to his private secretary. Other well-used conduits to the president were through Louis T. Michener, the attorney general of Indiana; Charles Foster of Ohio, a cabinet possibility; Governor Joseph Benson Foraker of Ohio; Stephen B. Elkins of New York and West Virginia, another cabinet possibility; and two old

Indiana friends, Judge R. S. Taylor and Clement Studebaker. Senator William B. Allison of Iowa responded to an oral request by writing, "in accordance with your suggestion this morning, I send you this list" of requested appointments.[4]

Similar influence on appointments came from other Republican senators. Particularly close to Harrison were Leland Stanford, characterized as California's supreme arbiter in the distribution of patronage; John C. Spooner of Wisconsin; and Preston B. Plumb of Kansas. But Republican senators from the large-population states or those who were recognized as strong state bosses, such as Matt Quay of Pennsylvania or Charles Benjamin Farwell of Illinois, were far less effective in gaining appointments for their favorite office seekers. Thomas C. Platt, a former senator and the state party boss of New York, lacked influence with Harrison. Quay's biographer wrote that even though Quay was chairman of the Republican National Committee, he learned quickly that he could not dictate appointments to Harrison and that he had to fight vigorously for everything he was able to get. Farwell sent to Harrison a plan for distributing the spoils that would work to the advantage of Illinois and to congressional Republicans. The other Illinois senator, Shelby M. Cullom, joined the scramble for federal appointments by forwarding to Harrison a long list of positions that he wanted filled with Illinoisans, including the first assistant postmaster general, the commissioner of pensions, and the commissioner of internal revenue. Included on Cullom's list were positions in the outgoing administration that were held by Illinois residents. Later Cullom said, "I suppose [Harrison] treated me about as well in the way of patronage as he did any other Senator; but whenever he did anything for me it was done so ungraciously that the concession tended to anger rather than please." Both Quay and Farwell expected Harrison to appoint their favorites with no questions asked. Harrison rejected these offers because he wanted to know about each appointment. In spite of his reasons, the action brought bitter opposition from these leaders within his party. The president's failure to satisfy these party wheel horses weakened his administration and delighted his political opponents, who kept track of almost every appointment as being either pro- or anti-Harrison.[5]

No doubt, Harrison considered the political implications of each and every appointment. His response to a suggestion that John Hay, Lincoln's private secretary, ought to get some office provides an indication of the logic used by this most logical of all presidents. He said, "That would be a fine appointment, . . . but there isn't any politics in it!"[6] By this, Harrison implied that John Hay was not a Republican leader in any geographical area and that he did not have a following. But neither did Harrison want among his list of appointees in public office those who had too much political power, such as state party bosses. The fine line that was drawn in his appointments was not always clear, but it helps to explain Harrison's actions during the early days of his administration. He was seeking a middle ground in the persons he placed in office. In inquiring about people whom he did not know, he would ask penetrating questions of a mutual friend, in an effort to weed out scandal-prone or shady characters.

After Harrison had been in office for six weeks, the *New York Times* described the visitors to the Executive Mansion as a continuing parade. A portion of this report said: "The patronage fair at the White House shows no sign of closing . . . the crowd of callers was so large that some were only able to shake hands with Gen. Harrison and walk out, while others were unable to get into the room at all, and had to postpone their pleas until to-morrow, when they will get to the White House early."[7]

Unfortunately, Harrison did not have it in himself to delegate the responsibility for filling federal offices, which was to him an annoyingly burdensome task. Arthur Wallace Dunn, a long-time friend, wrote years later that Harrison was a "pleasant man in the White House so long as his visitors left politics and appointments alone. When business of that kind was mentioned he congealed immediately." Harrison's cool and detached procedure for handling office seekers, who were almost always left standing while they were stating their case, tainted much of the accomplishments of his four years as president. He gained the reputation as the White House iceberg, with all the attractiveness of a dripping cave.[8]

Perhaps Harrison was torn between duty and his personal idea of the presidency. There just was not enough time for everything. In order to speed the process of screening job applicants, he hurried them through his office and impatiently drummed the desk with his fingers while they were stating their case. Apparently he was willing to see almost everyone who came to Washington seeking an appointment. One of his ardent supporters stated that he "had no disposition to turn office seekers away. He was generous, too generous, in hearing their plea." Harrison wrote later: "It is a rare piece of good fortune during the early months of an administration if the President gets one wholly uninterrupted hour at his desk each day. His time is so broken into bits that he is often driven to late night work, or to set up a desk in his bedroom when preparing a message or other paper requiring unbroken attention."[9]

First in drawing substantial criticism was Harrison's recommendation for his commissioner of pensions. He selected Cpl. James R.

Tanner, commander of New York's Grand Army of the Republic. Tanner, who had lost both legs at the second battle of Bull Run, was a hero to Union veterans. He accepted the task with the understanding that he would "be liberal to our boys," but he lasted for only six months. Pensions for Union veterans of the Civil War were of very great interest during the 1880s and 1890s. Party platforms devoted unusual attention to this issue because of the sizable block of voters it represented: there were an estimated one and one-third million survivors of the Civil War in 1890. In New York, Pennsylvania, Ohio, Indiana, and Illinois, these veterans constituted between 12 and 15 percent of all voters, but only one of every eight of them were receiving pensions.[10] Tanner, a leading advocate of pensions for everyone who had served, was an ardent Harrison campaigner during the presidential race in 1888. G.A.R. audiences loved Tanner, and his supporters believed that his campaign speaking tours in both New York and Indiana were responsible for Harrison's victory in these states. As a member of the G.A.R. Committee on Pensions, Tanner was considered to be well qualified for commissioner of the Bureau of Pensions. Harrison's mail showed much support for Tanner; it often came from influential and respected Republican leaders. Tanner also wrote to Harrison's private secretary on Inauguration Day, requesting appointment to office. Less than three weeks later, Tanner's nomination as commissioner of pensions was sent to the Senate with the president's blessing.

Tanner was well intentioned, awkward, outspoken, and good newspaper copy. Leading contemporaries recognized that "his unbridled tongue gave wide advertising to his purposes, increasing the embarrassment of his party," and hastened his forced resignation. In his most widely publicized speech, given in Columbia, Tennessee, Tanner stated that "for twenty years I have been able only to plead, but now I am thankful that at these finger tips there rests some power . . . though I may wring from the hearts of some the prayer, 'God help the surplus.'" Tanner's speech was sent all over the country by Associated Press, and he became the highly visible target of the opposition press. A friendly critic stated that Tanner's "worst enemy has always been his tongue," and there seemed to be no way to get him to act more responsibly. His relations deteriorated with Secretary of the Interior John W. Noble, the cabinet officer in charge of Tanner's bureau.[11]

Some of the employees in the Pension Bureau took advantage of Tanner's lack of administrative experience and gave each other higher pension ratings. Many new beneficiaries were influential politically, and some were given increased pensions without having applied or without having taken a medical examination. Large back payments were made, and the requirements to prove disability were greatly reduced. Secretary Noble, who was wary of the actions of his underling, directed that regular procedures for dealing with pensions were to be used, and he forbade forty-eight-hour decisions, except in emergency situations. When Tanner ignored this directive, Noble asked for an explanation. Tanner told him, in a multipage letter dated 11 July 1889 and marked unofficial, that the secretary's power to review pension cases was limited only to cases that had not been approved. In exasperation, Secretary Noble replied to Tanner on 24 July 1889 in a detailed twenty-four-page letter, citing statutory authority for his power over all subordinates in the Department of the Interior. In his cover letter for the copy sent to President Harrison, Noble stated: "I have made a plain argument in support of my official authority; and against the illegality of the Commissioners action; with an itemized statement of the cases and the payments objected to: with specific grounds of objection; and I noted the fact that these issues have been paid to employees of the Pension Bureau."[12]

Harrison also received many letters urging him to retain Tanner, at least until after the fall elections. At about the same time, Noble wrote to the president: "T. thinks from my talk that he has to go. . . . He is *not* supported in his conduct and it will be a relief . . . if he is let out quietly." Tanner would not curb his tongue or mend his ways. Harrison sought to quiet the clamor by paying more attention to the Grand Army of the Republic and to other Union veterans. He journeyed home to Indianapolis to participate in the cornerstone ceremonies on 22 August 1889 for the immense Soldiers' and Sailors' Monument. A crowd of forty thousand was present for the president's speech. Harrison used this opportunity also to attend a reunion of his old regiment. Finally, on 11 September 1889, less than two months before some elections, President Harrison sent the United States marshal for the District of Columbia, Dan Ransdell, a close friend of both Harrison's and Tanner's, to the latter's home at midnight to request his resignation, which Harrison accepted at once. The president did not question Tanner's honesty, and he agreed to provide him with a leave of absence until his successor was appointed.[13]

The Tanner affair cost the Republican party in close races in the fall elections. From Indiana, Harrison got word that disappointments there were not great, "except in so far as the Tanner matter caused some republican soldiers to vote the democratic ticket." Replacing Tanner as pension commissioner was more easily said than done. Harrison sought Missouri Congressman William Warner and then George Merrill of Massachusetts, both of whom had been national commanders in chief of the G.A.R. Warner declined because of business interests, and Merrill, who had the support of both Senator George F. Hoar and Congressman Henry Cabot Lodge, also refused. Both privately believed that they would be placed in an impossible position as Tanner's successor. After Merrill's refusal, the position was unfilled for more than a month, and there were many applicants. Eventually, Harrison named Green B. Raum, an Illinois veteran, as commissioner of pensions, thus quieting some of the clamor. Raum had been a brigadier general in the Civil War and had been wounded in action. The following year, Congress (almost unanimously in each house) approved the Dependent and Disability Pension Act, and on 27 June 1890 Harrison signed it into law. This action was more generous than even Tanner had anticipated, as it provided pension opportunities for widows, minors, and dependent parents. Annual expenditures for pensions increased from $81 million to $135 million during the rest of Harrison's administration. This entirely new system of pensions for Civil War veterans and dependents was the most expensive pension law up to that time.[14]

Receiving almost as much complaint as the Tanner affair was Harrison's appointment of James S. Clarkson, an Iowa Republican leader and vice-chairman of the Republican National Committee, as first assistant postmaster general. Clarkson had the assigned duty of filling with loyal Republicans more than fifty-five thousand offices that were held by fourth-class postmasters throughout the country. Clarkson stayed in the administration for a year and one-half, believing all the time that his duty had been performed expeditiously. He was never criticized publicly by the president for his handling of this job. Clarkson, a significant figure in the Republican national campaign of 1888, expected a cabinet appointment for his effort. However, in seeking cabinet officials, Harrison concentrated on another Iowan, Senator William B. Allison, for secretary of the Treasury. Allison had been a candidate for the presidential nomination in Chicago, and later he had labored in the Senate from August to October 1888 to oppose the Democratic plan for a tariff. But Clarkson was making his views known to Harrison through Louis Michener and others. He reported that the general comment about the president-elect is that ''all who worked, except Blaine, are to be ignored, and men who did not work, and who have no following in politics, [are] called in to take the honors of victory that they did not help to win.'' Undecided about his appointment from Iowa, Harrison was still providing some encouragement for Clarkson. Allison was officially offered the Treasury in a letter of 17 January 1889, but he waited until late January to decline. The president-elect tried to persuade him to reconsider when Allison made a twenty-seven-hour visit to Harrison's home in Indianapolis. Allison's biographer decided that

> Allison's sorry handling of Garfield's invitation to join his Cabinet in 1881, and this rejection of Harrison's offer in 1889, make one think that he is seeing the same show twice. . . . But this time there was an unfortunate element in the story that was not present in 1881. . . . This time his ineptness had disastrous results for his friend James S. Clarkson, who was eager for a Cabinet position, but had subordinated his claims while waiting to see what Allison would do. By the time Allison had made up his mind to say "no," it was too late for Clarkson to push his own case.

Harrison wrote to Quay about this time: "You will believe me, I am sure, when I say that I not only appreciate Mr. C. work, but I appreciate and very much like him. In arranging to comply with your wishes and those of the committee in another direction, I feel that I had used the only place that I could have offered to Mr. C."[15]

So, because the small number of cabinet positions were already filled or spoken for, Clarkson was persuaded by Harrison to take the position of first assistant postmaster general, as a representative of the national committee. In this position his salary was $4,000 per year, half the amount received by a cabinet officer. There Clarkson gained the reputation, recounted in almost every history of the period, for "decapitating a fourth-class postmaster every three minutes." After being on the job for only a few weeks, Clarkson wrote that he was "most anxious to get through with my task here and leave. I am simply on detail from the National Committee, to see that some of the men who fought with us splendidly last year are rewarded."[16] Clarkson resigned on 1 September 1890 to direct Republican congressional campaigns.

By 30 June 1890 there were 59,663 fourth-class post offices, an increase of almost four thousand in a year. First-, second-, and third-class post offices totaled only 2,738, and their postmasters were appointed by the president, usually for four-year terms. Fourth-class post offices were the most visible presence of the federal government in small communities all over the country. There were many partisan and nonpartisan complaints over changes in postmasters.

Probably because of widespread criticism, Postmaster General John Wanamaker included in his annual report of 1890 the statement that fourth-class postmasters held commissions at the discretion of the postmaster general. He also wrote, near the end of his term, that "at least twenty thousand offices could be abandoned that produce no revenue for the Department'' and that almost all of them were these smaller offices. At that time he justified Clarkson's role in rapidly changing fourth-class postmasters by making a complicated comparison between the current and the previous administration. Thus, there were 39,945 changes out of 51,250 post offices under Cleveland, a replacement of almost 78 percent. In a similar period, there were fewer than 75 percent changes under Harrison: 43,823 out of 58,623 post offices, or 1,869 fewer than a like proportion. Removals of postmasters under Cleveland were 27 percent, or 13,881 in 51,250 post offices. Harrison's removals were 0.5 percent lower: 15,605 in 58,623 post offices, certainly a large number but 273 fewer than an even proportion.[17]

President Harrison, in his Inaugural Address, reaffirmed his support for civil-service reform, by saying: "Heads of departments, bureaus, and all other public officers having any duty connected therewith, will be expected to enforce the Civil Service law fully and without evasion. Beyond this obvious duty I hope to do something more to advance the reform of the civil service." However, the time that Harrison devoted to appointing loyal party members to public jobs dominated the news coming from the presidential office. Civil-service reformers expected far more than Harrison was willing to provide, and they quickly became impatient and critical. In responding to their charges, the friendly *New York Tribune* editorialized:

> The opposition papers keep up a loud chorus of attacks upon the Civil Service Reform record of President Harrison. To read them one would suppose that the President was carrying on an orgy of decapitation, instead of having, in fact, moved in the matter of changes with marked caution and deliberateness. A little scrutiny of these attacks will show that many of them are based upon what it is said by unfriendly newspapers the President proposed to do, but which somehow he doesn't.[18]

Except for Harrison's appointment of two recognized proponents of civil-service reform to the Civil Service Commission, the first two years of his presidency were a disappointment to backers of reform. By that time, Harrison's only addition to the merit service had been accidental, a result of Cleveland's last classification order for personnel in the railway mail service. Action was incomplete when Harrison took office. This order was postponed until 1 May 1889, so that newly approved railway mail employees could be included, rather than Cleveland's appointees. After he was out of office, Harrison recognized the usefulness of the

Pendleton Act when he wrote: "The Civil Service Law has removed a large number of minor offices in the departments in Washington, and in the postal and other services, from the scramble of politics, and has given the President, the Cabinet officers and the Members of Congress great relief."[19]

The appointment of Theodore Roosevelt of New York and Hugh S. Thompson of South Carolina as members of the Civil Service Commission to serve with holdover member Charles Lyman, of Connecticut, redeemed Harrison's administration in the reformers' eyes. Thompson, a former Democratic governor of South Carolina, was appointed on 9 May 1889, and Roosevelt, a Republican state assemblyman for New York City and an active campaigner for Harrison, took his oath of office four days later. Roosevelt received the most notice of any commissioner, partly because of his flamboyant personality. More attention in later histories was paid to Roosevelt and his experiences on the Civil Service Commission, because his political positions by then were built on this appointment. Roosevelt had Henry Cabot Lodge seek a place for him in the State Department, but when interviewed by Harrison on 7 May, Roosevelt readily accepted the position that was offered.[20]

An active member of the National Civil Service Reform League, Roosevelt carried his reforming zeal into the new job. He was impatient with Harrison's delay in broadening the civil service, and he was critical of the public servants whom he investigated for the commission. Roosevelt was loyal to Harrison, but he realized before long that the president generally ignored Roosevelt's recommendations. Roosevelt's primary complaints were directed toward the Post Office Department and the activities of Postmaster General Wanamaker and his subordinate James Clarkson. Ironically, Wanamaker, who was interested in change, was known to reformers as a spoilsman. He was a challenge to the civil-service reformers because he promoted economy and efficiency in the postal service, the very same benefits that reformers were claiming for a merit system. Wanamaker, prompted by the president, also proposed a pattern of promotion for merit employees, with a board of promotion to oversee this activity from within the Post Office Department, not from the Civil Service Commission. Almost every time a dispute arose between Roosevelt and the postal service, Harrison sided with Wanamaker.[21]

Roosevelt said later that "the little grey man in the White House . . . treated him with cold and hesitating disapproval." Also, Roosevelt is reported to have said that "Harrison had never given the Commission one ounce of backing." Nevertheless, the energetic young thirty year old bombarded the Executive Office with letters and memorandums in support of the investigations that he carried out on behalf of the Civil Service Commission.[22]

Harrison also received complaints about Roosevelt's aggressive and offensive behavior from such valued informants as Louis T. Michener, who wrote: "It seems to me that he should be given to understand that it would be well for him to have less to say to newspapers. When he was here, he was positively insulting to the republicans he met and extremely agreeable to every interest hostile to the republican party." As was his style, Harrison never censured Roosevelt; instead, he let his appointee handle his assigned duties, an indication, according to Arthur Wallace Dunn, that Harrison truly and "sincerely favored reasonable adherence to reform." But Roosevelt was a difficult person to deal with, and one commentator observed that both Harrison and Cleveland wanted to be rid of him on the Civil Service Commission, but neither was willing to face the hostile criticism for such an action.[23]

As early as July 1889 the Indian Rights Association activist Herbert Welsh sought Theodore Roosevelt's advice on a plan for adding personnel in the Indian Bureau to the merit system. The massacre at Wounded Knee, in late 1890, brought renewed effort for advancing civil-service reform in the bureau. Finally, on 13 April 1891, Harrison granted civil-service classification for 626 teachers and administrators in the Indian schools; this was followed by 140 employees in the Fish Commission almost a year later. Harrison's action in the Indian Bureau recognized that these positions had little relation to party interests and that special skills or training were needed. New steps almost always involve compromise. Reformers and the Indian Rights Association got only part of what they were seeking. Roosevelt, for instance, was in favor of giving Indians preference for most of these jobs.[24] Nevertheless, it was considered an auspicious beginning for reform in the second half of the Harrison presidency.

Harrison's appointment of Thomas Jefferson Morgan as commissioner of Indian Affairs received criticism of a different kind from that directed towards Wanamaker, Clarkson, or Tanner. Morgan was variously described as being one of the most capable of all commissioners, as a man who was ambitious to provide education to produce the continuous assimilation of Indians, and as a religious bigot with a drastic policy of ending the federal contract schools. Contract schools, which were administered by religious denominations, had their beginning with Grant's Peace Policy. As much as three-fourths of the federal expenditure for contract schools during the late 1880s was in the hands of Roman Catholic schools. Morgan, a zealous Baptist minister turned educator from Rhode Island, and Dr. Daniel Dorchester, a Methodist preacher and Massachusetts legislator who had been named superintendent of Indian education, were harshly criticized once their appointments were announced.[25]

Harrison made no public statement throughout the early stages of this controversy. Then he wrote to the Catholic archbishop of St. Paul, Minnesota, the Reverend John Ireland, that he regretted ''an impression that there is any disposition in the Indian Bureau, or in any other department of the Government, to allow even the smallest proscription of our Catholic fellow citizens. I have not appointed any one to office because he was a member of any particular church communion, I do not intend that any one now in the public service shall be prejudiced by reason of religious beliefs.'' He also commented about ''Dr. Dorchester; that in twenty Indian schools which he visited, and about which he was called to advise, eight Catholics were dropped and eight Methodists. . . . He tells me that some other persons were dropped and some other appointments made . . . of persons whose denominational relations he does not know to this day.''[26]

On 20 November 1889, Harrison, with two cabinet members, received four prominent Catholic clergymen, including Ireland, who were seeking to keep Morgan's and Dorchester's names from being sent to the Senate for confirmation. Archbishop Ireland was more willing to accept Harrison's interpretation of this case than were his fellow clerics. Some Catholic publications continued their criticism by publishing attacks on the Indian Bureau. At the same time an anti-Catholic agency, the American Protective Association, was actively supporting the aspirations of Morgan and Dorchester. After their confirmation by the Senate, Congress provided Morgan and Dorchester with a mandatory-school-attendance law and permitted other reforms, similar to those being carried out in the public schools throughout the nation. The Indian Bureau had vital support at this time from the Indian Rights Association and from civil-service reformers. A leading Catholic historian wrote that Morgan and Dorchester, ''it is true, maintained a careful objectivity in their public acts, but the dominant atmosphere of Indian reform was hostile to government support for Catholic contract schools.'' In fact, all contract schools, not just Catholic ones, were closed down. Even after Morgan and Dorchester left office at the conclusion of Harrison's presidency, opposition to the contract schools was so widespread that all of them were phased out during the next few years.[27]

Harrison's policies on patronage were those that had been used during most of the years of the Republic. However, his own feeling of responsibility as the chief magistrate isolated him from many of the leaders in the Republican party. The party platform and his own letter of acceptance gave preference for territorial appointments to residents there, and Harrison rigidly adhered to that principle. Because of the nature of Indiana politics, he was deeply involved in appointments within his home state. When there was a local dispute, either in Indiana or elsewhere, between two or more candidates for a position, he asked the local leaders to work out a compromise. Because each Republican congressmen had only about 250 federal jobs to fill, but he received applications from about 1,700 persons, there were many unhappy constituents.[28]

No doubt, Harrison explained too much to applicants who were not favored with an appointment. His staff was very small, and because he would not delegate this responsibility, he did it himself. The job was galling to him, and he complained to one of his brothers about a cousin who was seeking a job. Of course, several dozen relatives, according to press reports, received appointments from Harrison. Ulysses S. Grant had been criticized also for giving jobs to relatives. Harrison knew that, but he also knew that he did not have the affection of his countrymen that Grant had had. To Indiana friends who sent a book of names of persons who were seeking appointments, Harrison said he would keep his eyes on the list. Frequently, he would respond to job applications by saying, ''I am necessarily scattering so many disappointments'' or ''I fear the provisions will not hold out'' or ''Embarrassments are very thick and offices are very thin.''[29]

The number of job openings that were available to a senator depended on the population of his state. This practice had institutional standing and was a recognized and carefully graded system. Positions provided by members of Congress were vital to the politics of the late nineteenth century to assure jobs for party workers and to recognize party leaders. Arthur Wallace Dunn, a contemporary observer, stated that Benjamin Harrison was ''one of those remarkable men who gave the country a good administration and yet was rejected by the people. Cold, austere, aloof, able, and fearless, with absolute confidence in himself, he yielded only when under great pressure. In matters of patronage he deferred to Senators because he had been a member of the Senate, but he often preferred his own judgment.'' Unlike many of his predecessors, Harrison did not use patronage to secure favored legislation. When he made an appointment that attracted widespread adverse comment, he increased his unpopularity with his party leaders. With all the problems that Harrison encountered in patronage and with the time that it demanded, it is no wonder that he seemed always to be suspicious of people. He rarely committed himself in conversation, and he often assumed a superior air, which exasperated his friends and antagonized many who were meeting him for the first time. Among all of his talents, Benjamin Harrison was least effective as a party leader. Some later comments about him were: "The conflicting impulses that contended for mastery in his enigmatic personality proved to be his undoing. He loved politics but disliked politicians; he possessed a fine sense of humor but kept it a carefully guarded secret; and he displayed a superb ability in the analysis of problems but none in the management of men."[30]

Closely related to Harrison's problems with patronage were his relations to western territories and the formation of new states. One of the last actions of President Cleveland on 3 March 1889 had been to sign an Indian appropriations bill, which contained a rider that provided for the opening of the unassigned lands in Oklahoma, almost two million acres in the center of the modern state of Oklahoma. Cleveland did not set the date when settlement could begin. Thus, President Harrison issued a proclamation on 23 March 1889, identifying eligible settlers and establishing noon on 22 April as the beginning of the land rush. The federal government surveyed the unassigned lands and laid out four town sites. In late April the nation watched the rush of the '89ers with interest, captivated by the idea that the last well-watered homesteads were being occupied by this most recent group of pioneers. Some writers called this first Oklahoma land rush "Harrison's Horse Race." The organization of Oklahoma Territory provided additional opportunities for Harrison to fill newly created federal positions in the area. Leading officials in the new territory were appointed by the president.

Another action of the lame-duck Congress of 1888/89 brought a quick response during the first year of Harrison's presidency with enabling legislation that provided for the four states of North Dakota, South Dakota, Washington, and Montana. Congress gave approval for constitutional conventions in these territories. No new states had been created since Colorado had gained statehood in 1876, a delay due to the political make-up of Congress. The Democratic party, which controlled the House of Representatives during most of this time, opposed the admission of new states, which might undermine its dominance.

As a matter of fact, Harrison as a senator had sponsored a bill for Dakota statehood, which passed the Senate in 1886. A Democratic-controlled House committee refused to take up the bill, although for a time there was a discussion of statehood for New Mexico to counterbalance Dakota. Dominant groups in Dakota Territory favored its being divided into two states, a goal that became attainable when Harrison was elected. President Harrison mentioned the prospects for new states in his Inaugural Address. He took a personal interest in these four territories, and he sought to strengthen local Republican parties by making appointments to federal offices, generally from resident citizens. Not to be outdone, the citizens of Wyoming and Idaho territories also held constitutional conventions without congressional approval. During a period of eight months in late 1889 and through mid 1890, six new states were admitted to the Union, the greatest concentration of new states during the administration of any president.[31]

The signing ceremony for the admission proclamation of the twin states of North and South Dakota came on 2 November 1889. A South Dakota historian explained that ''neither state can claim priority over the other, as President Harrison purposely shuffled the admission documents so that none might know which came first. By common agreement in later years North Dakota holds thirty-ninth and South Dakota fortieth rank among the states of the Union.'' The proclamation for Montana's statehood was signed on 8 November, and Washington gained its statehood on 10 November 1889. Idaho became a state on 3 July 1890, and a week later, on 10 July, statehood was official for Wyoming. Unexpectedly, all of the first congressional delegations from each of these six states were solidly Republican: an increase of twelve in the Senate and seven in the House, one for each state except for South Dakota, where the population justified two representatives.[32] However, the new members of Congress from these new states were destined to provide severe problems for Harrison before long. The delegations from the first four new western states arrived in Washington just in time to take part in the debates over the most ambitious legislative program of the late nineteenth century.

4

★ ★ ★ ★ ★

DOMESTIC PROGRAMS

Republican leaders interpreted the election of 1888, with their control of the presidency and of both houses of Congress, as a mandate for change. Thus, the lengthy 303-day first session of the Fifty-first Congress, during the first half of the Harrison administration, enacted into law virtually everything in the 1888 Republican platform. With almost reckless abandon the overconfident Republicans passed new laws. The extent of major legislation produced from 1889 through 1891 compares with two other active Congresses: the first two years of the Lincoln administration, 1861–63, and the first two years of the Wilson administration, 1913–15. This remarkable Congress, in the early part of Harrison's presidency, one of the most productive in all American history, has a record for constructive legislation that was not equaled for many years.[1] Naturally, new legislation and its enforcement did not necessarily go hand in hand in the Harrison administration or in other nineteenth-century presidencies.

Harrison was ever the Whig at heart, so he did not initiate legislation. Instead, in his Inaugural Address he echoed the Republican platform. Friction was expected between Congress and the president. However, Harrison's term as a United States senator had reinforced for him a feeling of total legislative supremacy. Moreover, he was advised by long-time Senator John Sherman, Republican of Ohio, that "the President should touch elbows with Congress. He should have no policy distinct from that of his party; and this is better represented in Congress than in the Executive."[2] However, Harrison would be sensitive about his executive and administrative authority as president and would not tolerate challenges to his power.

In spite of his Whiggish tendencies, Harrison did take a hand in the legislation of his administration, and he established new precedents for providing presidential input for bills while they were still in Congress. He held informal dinners or receptions for congressional leaders, and he let them know about specific items that he would need in order for him to sign certain bills. He used a threat of veto on some measures, although his actual vetoes were few. Later, Harrison wrote that his primary influence on legislation had come from his veto power. Sometimes, members of his cabinet carried instructions to Capitol Hill. William McKinley, a frequent visitor at the White House, would use these Harrison techniques when he became president.[3]

During the stalemated politics of the late nineteenth century, single-party control of both houses of Congress and the presidency was rare. Republicans controlled the Senate eight of ten times between 1875 and 1895; the House only twice; and the presidency except for the Cleveland years. Only in 1880 did the Republican presidential candidate receive a plurality of the popular vote, and never in any race did he receive a majority. The Democrats were less action oriented than were their Republican contemporaries; the Democrats invariably advocated a reduction in power of the central government, and they emphasized smaller budgets. When they gained control of both houses of Congress and the presidency in 1893, there was no comparable clamor for legislation.[4] In fact, some of the Republican-inspired statutes of the Harrison administration were repealed.

In 1889 the meager Republican majority in the Senate, 39 to 37, and in the House, 168 to 161, was augmented with the arrival of eight new Republican senators from the four states that were admitted that year, along with five new Republican representatives.[5] In addition, with the organization of the House and the election of Thomas Brackett Reed of Maine as Speaker, the question of a small number of disputed seats was settled in favor of the Republicans, thus solidifying their majority. Thus, soon after the convening of Congress in 1889, the Senate could count on 47 Republicans, a majority of 10. In the larger House, there were 173 Republicans, a slim majority of 12. The effective majority in each house was far less.

This slight Republican majority should have interpreted voters' response in 1888 as a policy of caution, but instead its members pushed hard for the whole Republican program. To oppose Republican dominance the Democratic minority in the House sought to strangle and delay legislation by using the silent or disappearing quorum —that is, by asking for a quorum call, then not answering to their names. "Czar" Reed countered with new rules for determining a quorum, and he efficiently pushed through Republican legislation. Partisan politics was dominant, perhaps more so than during any other era in United States history. Reed's rules were endorsed on 14 February 1890, and much new legislation was passed on a rigid party vote.[6] In the Senate, the Democrats used the threat of filibuster to impede legislation.

Republicans and Democrats could agree that the biggest issue in the election of 1888 was the tariff, but there was almost total disagreement over what to do about it. Statements in their party platforms should have left no doubt about intentions—the Democrats were for "tariff reduction," whereas the Republicans were "uncompromisingly in favor of the American system of protection." A quarter-century of publicity on the benefits to be gained from a high protective tariff had preceded this election. The existing tariff, along with other revenue measures, produced more income than was needed for the operation of the federal government at current levels. The surplus—the excess of revenues over expenditures—was regarded as a depressant on the economy. That surplus on 30 June 1889 was $105 million.[7] Republicans, for the most part, believed that the surplus should inspire new governmental programs and that revenues could be decreased also by adjusting the tariff. There were other major issues confronting Congress in that session: antitrust legislation, silver used in currency, a federal election law, federal support for education, pensions for war veterans, and revision of the land laws; but the tariff issue attracted the most attention throughout the country.

Actually, shifts in electoral patterns to produce a Republican victory in 1888 had been minor. The efficiency of the Harrison election organization, combined with the inefficiency of Cleveland's organization, produced the difference in a few crucial states. Harrison's series of more than ninety brief, thoughtful, and effective tariff speeches from his own front porch during the long hot summer of 1888 had shown his knowledgeable support for tariff revision, the need to protect certain American industries, and the notion that reciprocity was included in protection. In his Inaugural Address, Harrison spoke in general terms about tariff reform immediately after his introductory remarks.[8] With victory in the election, new tariff legislation was entrusted to William McKinley, chairman of the Ways and Means Committee in the House.

Leadership in the House of Representatives turned immediately to the tariff as Congress convened in December 1889. While the voter mandate in the election of 1888 could have meant make no change or either raise or lower the duties, McKinley, who had campaigned on the idea that the tariff could be revised properly only by its friends, was sure that voters favored protectionism. So with his Republican majority, he wrote a bill to increase tariff duties. To provide an acceptable compromise for wool growers and farmers, duties on raw wool were increased, and some agricultural products were placed on the duty list. Imported sugar would come in without paying a tariff, and domestic producers were compensated with a bounty for every pound of sugar they produced. The sugar provisions, alone, could have eliminated the surplus.[9]

When Secretary of State Blaine heard that hides would go on the duty list and that sugar could come in free, he sought to change the minds of McKinley's committee members, who still did not understand what reciprocity could do. Blaine had been participating in the Pan-American Conference, and he knew how these proposals would affect Latin American countries at a time when the United States was seeking increased trade in the Western Hemisphere. Freeing sugar from duties was, to Blaine, giving something to Cuba and to other countries without getting anything in return. He proposed reciprocity treaties with each trading partner, thus lowering duties to expand trade. He was able to get hides back on the free list, but no changes were made on sugar or wool. Blaine also turned to the Senate Finance Committee, where he did no better. At first he made little impact on either committee for his long-term objective to use reciprocity to expand trade.[10]

President Harrison publicly gave Blaine support by mid June in a message to Congress. At the same time, Senator Eugene Hale from Maine offered a quickly drafted amendment, prepared by Blaine, to the McKinley bill, which granted the president broad powers for making reciprocity treaties with many countries, including Canada.[11] Slowly, McKinley became convinced that reciprocity would open doors to United States trade abroad, and public support for reciprocity grew throughout the summer, partly because of a newspaper campaign waged by Blaine. A less ambitious amendment by Nelson Wilmarth Aldrich was introduced into the Senate in August. Harrison, who approved of Blaine's strategy, worked behind the scenes to develop an acceptable compromise which would add the reciprocity amendment to the McKinley Tariff bill. Key figures, working with Harrison, included McKinley, Reed, and Nelson Dingley from the House and Nelson Aldrich from the Senate. The new amendment provided exemptions for certain foodstuffs and agricultural products. If reciprocal concessions were not made, the president could reimpose duties promptly on these goods without awaiting congressional action.

The Senate passed the reciprocity amendment of the tariff bill on a party-line vote early in September, while the House delayed. Faced with the highest tariff rate up to that time in United States history, western senators dallied until the silver legislation had been passed and until Lodge's election bill had been tabled to the next session of Congress. Confronted by a determined administration and an unmoving group of Republican senators and under pressure from mounting public opinion, which favored tariff revision, House Republicans capitulated on 27 September, and Congress adjourned on 1 October, immediately after the Senate took action on the bill. Harrison signed the McKinley Tariff Act into law on the same day. More than four hundred amendments, most of which raised custom duties to an average of 49.5 percent, placed rates slightly higher than any previous tariff. The law was a compromise and did not fully please Blaine, but it was a beginning. An important consequence of the McKinley Tariff Act was a fractured Republican party.[12]

Seldom had a Congress been so generous in granting additional powers to the president as was permitted by this act. Harrison was allowed to negotiate trade conventions and to modify tariff duties without congressional oversight. Reciprocity had been welded to protectionism, and Congress was ready to go home. The fall elections were only five weeks away, and the Democratic opposition had protectionism as a key issue for these elections.[13]

The Harrison administration never was given a chance to test the full effects of the McKinley Tariff Act with its reciprocity features. However, Blaine was identified as the "Father of Reciprocity," and John Watson Foster was commissioned to negotiate the reciprocity treaties. More than a dozen reciprocal agreements were arranged, some with European countries. Tariffs were reimposed on three Latin American nations which failed to cooperate. Within the United States, peddlers went through many rural districts, offering tin goods at inflated prices and claiming that the high price was due to the new tariff. Rural women, the object of these sales efforts, influenced their husbands and fathers to vote against the Republicans in 1890. The disastrous results for Republicans in that election ended for some time their majority status in Congress. Still, President Harrison, in his annual message to Congress on 1 December 1890 and in subsequent years, voiced optimism about the benefits coming from the new law: "The misinformation as to the terms of the act which has been so widely disseminated at home and abroad will be corrected by experience, and the evil auguries as to its results confounded by the market reports, the savings banks, international trade balances, and the general prosperity of the people." The same optimism was shown in Harrison's letter to the Western States Commercial Congress, held in Kansas City, Missouri, on 14 April 1891. Harrison said that he had great confidence in "the completion of further reciprocal trade agreements, especially with the Central and South American states, as furnishing new and large markets for meats, breadstuffs, and an important line of manufactured products." Later that year the president's anxiety about success for the McKinley Tariff Act was shown when he wrote: "The facts disclosed in your letter of the 12th, and by the enclosed extracts from Brazilian newspapers, were very interesting and quite surprising to me. Can you furnish me any information as to what proportion of this increased trade is from this country and due to our reciprocity arrangement."[14]

Indeed, the McKinley Tariff Act suffered from much misrepresentation, and it did not last long enough to show what it could do. Coming, as it did, during a period of industrial expansion, it reflected that constituency. The tin-plate-manufacturing industry was established in the United States because of this law, and farmers were wedded to the new idea of agricultural protection through the tariff. However, the law's protective features were limited by the bounty on domestic sugar, the inclusion of a full agricultural schedule, its reciprocity features, and protection of the new infant tin industry. The free-sugar provision, along with lower excise taxes, helped to solve the surplus problem, and most increases in tariff rates were actually selective and minor. The public's impression was that the prices of everything had gone up. Even the reduction in the price of sugar, which was produced by the free-sugar provisions, did not occur until well after the elections: the timing of this law was a first-class political blunder. Republicans could have satisfied their platform pledges of 1888—to stabilize prices and reduce the surplus—without resorting to the complications of the McKinley Tariff Act, and some of them agreed in retrospect. The tariff reciprocity that was included in this act had long-range effects for later interest in agreements on reciprocal trade. Blaine developed the reciprocity ideal, kept it alive, and gained the support of such Republican leaders as Harrison and McKinley. All of them saw that the future of the nation was global and that reciprocity would help to enlarge United States markets overseas. To these men, reciprocity was a logical and rational step. It included grand designs for global interests, but it proved to be ironically risky for Republican members of Congress.[15]

While the tariff issue was vital and was filled with partisan bickering, there was a virtual bipartisan unanimity in support of some kind of antitrust legislation. Business combinations known as trusts—such as Standard Oil, which was formed in 1879—proliferated in the late nineteenth century and were claiming a larger and larger share of the market. Widespread opposition to trusts from all over the country was the rule. "Antimonopoly" was a slogan that most people could agree on; to them the phrase attacked the trusts, a perceived evil. The issue was a bipartisan one by 1888, as party platforms for both the Democrats and the Republicans criticized existing trusts and other combinations. According to the Democrats, "the people are betrayed when, by unnecessary taxation, trusts and combinations are permitted to exist which, while unduly enriching the few that combine, rob the body of our citizens by depriving them of the benefits of natural competition." The Republican statement was in "opposition to all combinations of capital, organized in trusts or otherwise, to control arbitrarily the condition of trade among our citizens."[16] The Union Labor party and the Prohibition party had similar planks in their 1888 platforms.

After the Republican National Convention, Harrison stated that he was in full agreement with the Republican antitrust plank. Thus, when Congress opened on 2 December 1889, Senator John Sherman filed a proposed antitrust measure as Senate Bill No. 1, and many other antitrust bills were dropped into the hoppers of both houses. Sherman and other members of Congress were responding in an overwhelming manner to the pent-up demand of their constituencies. The common law had long contained strong opposition to monopolistic enterprises, and many states had passed laws to regulate business combinations. But there was no federal statute to restrain interstate combinations. Sherman said he was anxious about the vast combinations of capital that were exerting tremendous control over production and trade. Harrison also urged antitrust legislation because he considered trusts to be dangerous conspiracies that opposed the public good. The Senate responded quickly, and the Sherman antitrust bill was approved overwhelmingly, 52 to 1, on 8 April and was sent to the House. There, after conference with the Senate, it was passed in the House on 20 June without dissent, although 85 members did not vote. Harrison signed the Sherman Antitrust Act on 2 July 1890; except for the Dependent Pension Act, it was the first major piece of legislation during his presidency and is one that remains on the books after almost a century. Although it bears Sherman's name, the statute was primarily the work of Senators George F. Edmunds of Vermont, who wrote most of the bill, and George F. Hoar of Massachusetts, both of whom were the president's close friends. It was the first federal law to regulate trusts, although the Interstate Commerce Act of 1887 had sought to deal with similar combinations in interstate transportation.[17]

Later there was criticism that the sponsors of the law were insincere and had deliberately produced a bill with vague and ambiguous language that lacked even the proper definitions for what was a trust, a monopoly, or restraint of trade. As a matter of fact, this legislation, as well as contemporary state laws, relied heavily on ideas that had crystallized from common law; all of them were vague about details, even though the ideas that they included were widespread. Moreover, the law did not discriminate; it attacked the legality of almost all forms of business combinations. Sherman defended the common-law language that was used, and he denied vigorously that the antitrust law, by its very nature, was antibusiness. Instead, it opposed unfair business practices. The full congressional debate on this bill and the complete newspaper coverage at that time generally concluded that it was a severe measure and not a sham. Federal courts and district attorneys could initiate suits, but the Department of Justice, with a small staff and a low budget, was not prepared to take action against violators of the law. Successful plaintiffs in a suit could get triple damages from the defendant, an amount that was considered proper for unfair practices. Contemporary evidence testified to the honest intentions of the framers of the antitrust laws—namely, that they were responding in good faith to the public clamor to do something tangible about the problem of trusts.

Once he had signed the antitrust act, there is no evidence that Harrison sought to enforce the law. He was not inclined to pioneer or to explore the possibilities that the antitrust act offered.[18] Instead, he was fully absorbed by other demands of the moment. Neither was there any reference to trusts in Harrison's writings after he had left the presidency.

Attorney General William Henry Harrison Miller had the responsibility for enforcing the Sherman Antitrust Act. With too much to do, he failed to send special instructions to all the United States district attorneys concerning this new law. Lacking an understanding of the complexity of the problem, Congress had not appropriated funds for use in investigating trusts. More than a year after the law was in force, Miller did provide directions for district attorneys in areas where some of the larger trusts were located, and a few of them responded to the charge.

Thus, in the thirty-two months remaining in the Harrison presidency, only seven antitrust cases (four civil and three criminal) were initiated, primarily as a result of a few active and vigorous district attorneys. Only three of these cases were concluded before Harrison left office, and only the first, a case involving a Tennessee coal company, was won by the government. Minnesota lumber dealers, who had been accused of price fixing, filed a "demurrer to the indictment," which was sustained by the federal court. The Whiskey Trust case, the best-known one during the Harrison years, was "quashed for insufficiency of evidence."[19] Common law had been important in numerous previous cases heard in federal courts, but when confronted with antitrust activity, federal judges chose to interpret the antitrust law narrowly, making it almost impossible for the government's attorneys to win their cases. A kind of legend developed that federal attorneys really did not wish to win these cases.

In his last annual report, Attorney General Miller noted the grim difficulties in enforcing this law. His successor in the office took little interest in the Sherman Antitrust Act, and neither President Cleveland, with eight new cases, nor President McKinley, with three, made much effort to change that prevailing attitude. Like Harrison, both presidents were attentive to other issues that arose in their administrations and demanded immediate attention; therefore, the antitrust question was almost forgotten. Except for the zeal of a small number of district attorneys, the antitrust act would not have been used during the late nineteenth century.[20]

In its long-term effect the Sherman Antitrust Act was probably the most important law passed by the Fifty-first Congress. The act established the United States as one of a handful of industrial countries that favored the regulation of business combinations. Although most of the early cases that were filed under this law brought adverse decisions for the government, the actions taken in 1890 shaped later antitrust policy. Also, there is evidence that business combinations tried to avoid appearances that would produce federal suits against them.[21]

There was bipartisan agreement on antitrust policy and disagreement on handling the tariff, but neither of these topics produced the turbulence for the Harrison presidency that was centered on the money question. Even then, most business transactions were carried out with paper money, checks, and bills of exchange. The amount of government money in circulation was not so important as the feeling that it was a stable standard of value, generally recognized by law. Silverites wanted silver to be included in full-bodied federal coinage, because this would bring a higher price for their product and greater prosperity for their communities. Surprisingly, the silver crusade won great popular support from diverse groups such as those who were seeking cheap money to help debtors and those who were seeking bimetallism if it was backed by an international agreement. Deflationary pressures accounted for the newly organized Peoples party, and westerners, in general, advocated the addition of large quantities of silver to the national currency. Public finance was a volatile and divisive issue during Harrison's presidency; but it became a big debate after, not during, the presidential election. More than any other issue of the time, it cut across party lines. Both of the major parties were controlled by opponents of freely introducing silver into the national currency. Cleveland, in 1888 and earlier, was an outspoken critic of silver. By contrast, Harrison seemed to be a friend of silver, although he had never committed himself to free coinage at a prearranged ratio to gold. The money question hardly entered at all into the election of 1888.

Long-time Nevada Senator William H. Stewart believed he had received assurances from Harrison prior to the Republican National Convention that Harrison would never veto a bill providing for the free coinage of silver. Many delegates from silver-mining states voted for his nomination because they thought he would support silver. The monetary plank in the Republican platform sounded favorable, and with victory, Harrison engaged in cordial correspondence with Henry Moore Teller, Colorado's strong-silver Republican senator. Although Harrison did not mention silver in his Inaugural Address, silverites viewed his appointment of William Windom of Minnesota as his secretary of the Treasury as another positive step.[22]

The Bland-Allison Act, which had been passed over President Hayes's veto in 1878, had remonetized silver. The government was required to purchase from $2 to $4 million worth of silver bullion each month and to coin silver dollars. Purchases by the government never did exceed the minimum amount, and most of what was minted as money was not in circulation but was retained in government vaults. The United States maintained an official gold standard, with limited use of silver. The Bland-Allison Act, like many congressional measures, was a compromise. As a partial solution it had not eased the currency problem as it had been expected to do. General deflation during the late 1880s brought many farmers and westerners to view the free coinage of silver as forced inflation, a panacea for better economic conditions.

The silver issue attracted more attention just before Congress assembled in 1889. One of Harrison's informants from Indiana was sure that Cleveland's wing of the Democratic party would try to capture the convention of silverites, who were meeting in St. Louis on 26 November. He also reported strong Democratic sentiment for free coinage. He requested that the president include in his annual message a statement of support for silver as provided in the Republican platform, which would bring approval from old Greenbackers as well as from a number of Democrats.[23]

Secretary of the Treasury William Windom devoted much space in his first annual report of December 1889 to the thorny question of silver. He offered a variety of proposals for solving the silver problem. From these he recommended a compromise plan which satisfied neither the silverites nor their adversaries. Windom wanted the federal government to purchase all silver bullion, foreign as well as domestic, at the market price and to pay for it with U.S. treasury notes. His plan alarmed the backers of the gold standard.[24]

Harrison, in his first annual message to Congress, may have been testing public response. He mentioned Windom's plan without supporting it, saying that he had not studied it. However, Harrison did set his boundaries on the money issue when he stated: "I think it is clear that if we should make the coinage of silver at the present ratio free, we must expect that the difference in the bullion values of the gold and silver dollars will be taken account of in commercial transactions and I fear the same result would follow any considerable increase of the present rate of coinage. . . . Any safe legislation upon this subject must secure the equality of the two coins in their commercial uses." He also wrote: "I have been an advocate of the use of silver in our currency. We are large producers of that metal, and should not discredit it."[25] Late in January 1890 a large number of silver bills, including Windom's scheme, were introduced into both houses of Congress.

Then Senator Teller visited with Harrison on an urgent mission—to get Harrison to oppose his secretary of the Treasury. Teller did not know until this visit that Harrison did not favor free coinage as Teller interpreted it. Harrison agreed that the Windom plan was not the best solution, but he wanted a Republican bill, and he would veto any measure that went too far and was unsound.[26] From that point, Harrison's interest in a protective tariff became a hostage to silver legislation, and Teller and other western members of Congress became unreliable supporters of major Republican issues that had the president's backing.

The silver bloc could depend on the votes of sixteen senators. Because silver states were low population areas, the silver bloc had only nine votes in the House. Nevada, Colorado, and the six new western states, all of which were promoting the sale of silver, with support at times coming from members of Congress from Nebraska and Kansas, enabled the silver bloc to amass more than 20 percent of the vote in the Senate. Thus, this group could and did affect legislative outcomes, often to the detriment of the Harrison presidency.[27]

President Harrison approached the silver issue in 1889 with more understanding of the currency problems than had President Grant during the 1870s. Harrison had a particular point of view; he wanted to satisfy as large a group as possible and to avoid, as he termed it, unsound money. Harrison was not a gold-standard man, since he would permit the expansion of paper currency backed by silver. Harrison interpreted his own position as bimetallism. His announced opposition to a free-coinage law, however, lost him the support of free-silver Republican senators from the West, who frequently were found in alliance with eastern Republican senators who had broken with Harrison over patronage.

The money issue, as represented by the dichotomy of free silver versus a gold standard, proved to be the significant domestic question during the Harrison presidency that lacked an acceptable solution. No matter what decision would be made, a substantial number of Republicans would be opposed, or at best cool, in their support. In this no-win situation, Congress and the president sought a compromise that would satisfy most of the constituency that was concerned with the money question. While Senator Teller was convinced about Harrison's position on silver, there was still doubt in the minds of many members of Congress as to where the president stood on the issue. Some believed that under certain conditions he might sign a free-coinage bill.

The long, drawn-out battle on a replacement for the Bland-Allison Act was a divisive one for the Republican party. A hoped-for short session was encumbered by this and other vital issues: the tariff, an antitrust measure, pensions, and a variety of bills on elections and education. Democratic members of Congress were ever watchful to contribute what they could to hasten a split in Republican ranks.

By 7 June 1890 the House had passed a bill to purchase 4.5 million ounces of silver each month. The Senate added a free-silver amendment on 17 June by a vote of 42 to 25. Speaker of the House Thomas B. Reed was ardently opposed to free coinage, and he effectively used parliamentary procedure to prolong debate and ultimately to defeat the measure 135 to 152. Reed was not sure about Harrison's attitude on this bill.[28] Reed's leadership in the House made it unnecessary for the president to actually commit himself by either signing or vetoing such a bill.

Finally, in early July 1890, a new version, a compromise bill, much like the one that had almost been approved a month earlier, passed both houses. Senator John Sherman was instrumental in getting the conference committee to agree on this bill. Although he did not favor everything in this measure, it became known as the Sherman Silver Purchase Act after President Harrison signed it on 14 July. Harrison personally appealed to free-silver senators for its support. Party managers in the Senate suggested that later a free-coinage bill would be offered to reward party regularity.[29] Some western senators voted for the Sherman bill because they were unsure about Harrison: he might feel compelled to veto the kind of free-silver bill that they preferred. In the House, strong support for this bill came from Reed, and it passed more easily than in the Senate.

The Sherman Silver Purchase Act appeared to be an inflationary measure. Each month the Treasury was required to purchase 4.5 million ounces of silver, virtually the entire output of American mines. Treasury certificates would be used to pay for the silver; these would be redeemable in either gold or silver coin, as determined by the secretary of the Treasury. Concessions that were made to backers of free silver proved to be more restricted than they had expected. Because the monthly purchase was stipulated in ounces, a decline in the price of silver would require fewer dollars. In addition, the secretary of the Treasury had the option of minting silver dollars, if he believed that silver coinage was needed to redeem silver treasury certificates. Finally, the law stipulated that the ratio between gold and silver could be the existing legal ratio or one provided by law. Both Presidents Harrison and Cleveland used only gold to redeem the treasury certificates, thereby limiting the inflationary characteristics of this law.[30]

Harrison sincerely believed that he would end all controversy by signing the Sherman Silver Purchase Act. His advisors—Secretary Windom and Senators Aldrich and Sherman—told him that it was a safe bill, one that would help the silver industry and would fulfill the Republican pledge in the national convention's platform. Silver prices had risen to $1.04 per ounce in July 1890 and to $1.21 on 3 September, then had dropped to 98 cents in December. The ratio of silver to gold was 19.76 to 1 in 1890, 20.92 to 1 in 1891, and 26.49 to 1 in 1893, whereas the contemporary political slogan called for 16 to 1.[31]

In April 1891, Harrison wrote that he had "always believed, and do now more than ever believe, in bimetallism, and favor the fullest use of silver in connection with our currency that is compatible with the maintenance of parity of gold and silver dollars in our commercial use." He indicated that legislation to support a single silver standard had retarded "the free use of silver by the commercial nations." He showed disappointment with the consequences of the Sherman Act, for he "was assured by leading advocates of free coinage—representatives of the silver states—[that it] would promptly and permanently bring silver to $1.29 per ounce and keep it there. That anticipation has not been realized."[32]

In 1907 a leading American historian declared: "No incident in our national history more forcibly illustrates the lack of determined statesmanship. If the president, supported by senators and representatives from the East, who were opposed to free coinage of silver without an international agreement, had fought the silver propositions at every step, it would have been impossible to pass the silver-purchase act." Opponents of free silver numbered more than one-third of the House, and they could have prevented the passage of a bill if it were vetoed by the president. Thus, the responsibility for the Sherman Silver Purchase Act was placed on President Harrison and his eastern political advisors.[33]

Supporters of silver fought for free silver during the next six years. Six months after the passage of the Sherman Silver Purchase Act, the Republican-controlled Senate agreed to buy an additional twelve million ounces of silver in 1891.[34] Shortly after Cleveland became president for a second time, the precipitous decline in all prices, brought on by the Panic of 1893, caused the new Congress to repeal the Sherman Act. In 1896 the national presidential race featured the "Battle of the Standards." Silverites captured the Democratic party, but their presidential candidate, William Jennings Bryan, who based his campaign on a fight for free silver, lost to William McKinley, the Republican candidate, who by then was a gold-standard man. By the end of the century, the expansion in the world supply of gold ended the long and bitter fight that had produced the compromise law known as the Sherman Silver Purchase Act of 1890.

There were other significant issues facing the Fifty-first Congress. One was voting rights for blacks, which to Benjamin Harrison was fundamentally and conscientiously a moral one. He had always supported the Fifteenth Amendment. Waving the bloody shirt of rebellion, which had been a fundamental part of Republican campaigns for many years, was less used in his presidential campaign than in other elections since the Civil War.[35]

However, the third paragraph of the Republican platform affirmed the "rights and liberties of citizens . . . rich or poor, native or foreign born, white or black, to cast one free ballot in public elections, and to have that ballot duly counted." It also strongly supported a "free and honest popular ballot, and the just and equal representation of all the people." Harrison echoed these sentiments both in the campaign and in his Inaugural Address, and he sought to link a protective tariff with full and equal rights for all citizens. Party leaders advised Harrison to emphasize the tariff to the exclusion of other issues. He rejected this advice; his campaign speeches touched on all topics and indicated pride in his party's moral tradition. He stressed the tariff issue, but still he insisted on discussing his party's commitment to civil rights. Later he wrote to Whitelaw Reid that he was unwilling "to purchase the Presidency by a compact of silence upon this question." In part of the new president's first official comments he asked, "Shall the prejudices and paralysis of slavery continue to hang upon the skirts of progress?" His remarks also urged election reform, and he said that if "the public security is thought to be threatened by ignorance among the electors, the obvious remedy is education."[36] Thus, in the president's mind, the measures that were known as the McKinley Tariff, the Lodge elections bill, and the Blair education bill were joined. In spite of his strong support, only the McKinley Tariff became law; on each of the others he went down to defeat.

Strenuous efforts of Republicans to revive their party in the South after the Civil War had brought bitter failure. Harrison, along with Senators George F. Hoar and William Eaton Chandler, was still convinced that Republicans had a responsibility and a concern for the southern Negro. Their beliefs were both opportunistic and idealistic. The "lily-white" policy of establishing Republican strength among southern whites had failed, whereas southern blacks were considered natural allies.[37]

As a natural result, President Harrison became interested in organizing an offensive against the restraint of black voters in the South, an action that violated the Fifteenth Amendment. The issue came up in his vacation retreat at Deer Park in 1889. Senator Preston B. Plumb casually remarked at the dinner table about the necessity of supporting Negro voting in the South; otherwise the party would be dead there. Advisor Louis T. Michener responded quickly when he went back home to Indiana. Michener met with leading blacks in Indianapolis and then endorsed rapid action, while presidential secretary Elijah Halford was more cautious and tended to downplay the issue.[38]

Soon after Harrison's inauguration, Senator Hoar, as chairman of the Committee on Privileges and Elections, began to work in Congress on a bill to provide for the supervision of elections of members of the House of Representatives. The election of senators was still in the hands of the state legislatures; this bill would not confront that constitutional issue. Later, Senator John Coit Spooner of Wisconsin drafted another bill that provided for "supervision of state registration and election procedures by federal court-appointed officers from both parties." After Hoar had consulted with every Republican senator, most of whom approved, he put his draft in the Senate hopper. Southern opposition was immediate, but before the bill could come to the floor of the Senate, there was a clamor in the House, where a special committee, headed by Henry Cabot Lodge, was drafting a similar bill. Lodge had long been a public champion of federal supervision for congressional elections. He, with his colleagues, was committed to an open, free ballot, and they claimed the responsibility for writing a statute to control the election of their own membership. A newspaperman-lobbyist, John P. Davenport, helped to work out a compromise. The Senate bill was held back, thus giving the House bill priority, and Lodge rewrote his bill to conform to the Senate version. Harrison's message to Congress of 3 December 1889 was a far sterner statement than any he had given earlier. He said:

> The colored people did not intrude themselves on us; they were brought here in chains and held in communities where they are now chiefly found, by a cruel slave code. . . .
> When and under what conditions is the black man to have a free ballot? When is he in fact to have those full civil rights which have so long been his in law? When is that equality of influence which our form of government was intended to secure to the electors to be restored?

Other Republican leaders developed a corresponding hard line on voting rights throughout the country.[39]

The Lodge elections bill, which provided for the federal supervision of all congressional races, narrowly passed the House on 2 July 1890, 155 to 149, with 24 abstaining. The slim Republican majority was secured through the use of strong party discipline and through the hearty endorsement of Speaker Reed. Only two Republicans voted against it. Sectional battles in Congress, the fiercest since Reconstruction, erupted over this issue.[40] The greatest impact of this legislation would be in the South, where voter participation was restricted by threats and intimidation. Democrats, fearing a challenge to their easy victories in many southern districts, labeled it a "Force Bill" in spite of its civil guarantees, and they added to the public image the visions that some part of the extremely small 28,000-man United States Army would be used to enforce the mandates of the law. Actually, there was no provision for calling in federal troops to supervise elections. The appearance of Lodge's bill in the Senate was complicated by its competition with two other measures that became law under the titles of the Sherman Silver Purchase Act and the Sherman Antitrust Act. Senate sponsor Hoar had been actively engaged in debate on each of these measures. Finally, on 7 August 1890, the elections bill was reported from his committee, in the face of hostile dissent from Senator Arthur Pue Gorman of Maryland and his Democratic colleagues.

Lodge's bill became identified as a "Force Bill" directed at the South, even though it applied to congressional districts throughout the country. As a safeguard, federal circuit courts—not the United States Army—were to arbitrate election procedures in congressional races only, not in state or local contests. Petitions for investigating election irregularities would originate within each election district. The language of the bill was restrained; its intent was clear. There was nothing about the use of either federal troops or marshals. But it was not as nonpartisan in 1890 as it appeared on the surface, since most federal judges were Republicans. The measure's identity as a "Force Bill" greatly exaggerated its contents. However, the label stuck, it was repeated relentlessly, and the Lodge bill was so identified in most twentieth-century general history accounts without its contents being investigated. What was said about the bill had a greater impact than what the bill actually said.[41]

As one hot, sultry August day followed another, many members of Congress were anxious to return home, to campaign for the elections coming up in November. Several Republican leaders, placing high priority on a new tariff law, realized that time was too short to gain action on each of these controversial measures. Senator Matthew S. Quay, a spokesman for a higher tariff, introduced a resolution on 12 August to concentrate on five bills before September adjournment, with the tariff leading the list and the elections bill conspicuously absent. Presumably, Quay had made an agreement with Gorman that McKinley's bill would be approved and that Lodge's bill would be passed over to the next session to eventual discard. However, Quay announced the next day that his sole object had been to protect American industry and that he had had no intention of defeating the elections bill.[42]

Senator Hoar did not give up without a fight. He spoke about the great importance of the elections bill as "it reclaimed the conscience of the party and the nation" and said that it worked against "fraud, intimidation, and bribery." Its only enemy was an illegal minority that was usurping governmental control. Finally, Hoar demanded from the Republican caucus a written pledge that Lodge's bill would have top priority four months later, in the next session. His written pledge, entitled "Senators Agreement as to Election Bill & proposed change of rule," was signed by all thirty-five senators who were present. Copies were sent to seven absent senators, and all of them signed it, except for Richard Franklin Pettigrew of South Dakota. All of the silver Republicans agreed to Hoar's demand, and he announced that he was fully satisfied.[43]

In his second annual message to Congress, President Harrison noted that there was resistance to the federal elections bill. He rejected comments that "this legislation will revive race animosities, and . . . when peaceful methods of fraud are made positively impossible, they may be supplanted by intimidation and violence." He pushed for the legislation again in his third annual message, and to the end of his administration he continued his support. Even in his letter of acceptance of his second nomination, in the summer of 1892, he "deplored fraudulent elections in the South." As much as any president in the nineteenth century, Harrison wrestled with the question of civil rights for blacks. He "was conscious of race and race prejudice in American life, North and South. He was rather lenient in his assessment of the status, hopes and aspirations of blacks and Indians." Harrison was direct and frank in his approach to racial problems. In him there was an "absence of the usual political hedging." He "exerted greater leadership in matters of race, no matter how unsuccessful than any of the post-Reconstruction Presidents, not excluding Theodore Roosevelt."[44]

After the disastrous elections for Republicans in November 1890, the Senate again took up the elections bill and was met, in January 1891, by a faintly disguised Democratic filibuster. Before the election, Blaine and other Republican leaders were reported as disliking the Lodge bill; however, Blaine informed a newsman that "he would stand by the election bill if he were in Congress at the moment." In reality, Blaine was cool to most noneconomic issues. There was no White House mutiny as reported; in fact, Harrison called recalcitrant Republican senators to the White House, where he urged that they "do all they possibly could to pass the Lodge bill."[45]

After almost a month of inaction, silver Republicans began to voice discontent, speculating that recent Republican congressional losses were signals for a stronger silver law. Thus on 5 January 1891, in temporary alliance with Democrats, the silver Republicans pushed through the Senate a resolution to take up a new coin-and-currency measure in place of the elections bill. Although the silver bloc succeeded in gaining Senate approval for this silver bill, the bill made no headway in the House.

Senator Hoar brought up consideration of the elections bill again on 16 January; discussion of it passed only because Vice-President Morton cast the tie-breaking vote. The reappearance of the bill brought on another filibuster, and efforts to gain cloture were unsuccessful. Finally, on 22 January 1891, a resolution to replace the elections bill with another measure was approved by a narrow vote of 35 to 34, and the elections bill was unceremoniously shoved aside in its final defeat. Friendships of many years were strained to the breaking point; party regularity was taken seriously, and this issue had personal overtones. For the second time the action of silver Republicans tipped the scales and permitted the defeat of the Lodge bill, although other Republicans aided in undermining party discipline. Vice-President Morton did not use his modest authority as presiding officer of the Senate to push this legislation. During the debates over the "Force Bill," he was described as ever the courteous and poised moderator, as if he were presiding "over a company of guests at their own table."[46]

Opposition to Lodge's elections bill came from a variety of places outside the South. Big-city-machine bosses questioned its application in their wards, and Senator Stewart, with Nevada in his pocket, was uninterested in supporting this legislation. Leaders of the Farmers Alliance feared Republican gains from the law, and even city reformers were uncertain about its consequences. Strong-tariff protectionists could easily sacrifice the elections bill to preserve their economic interests.[47]

This contest was the last time that sectional bitterness and anger exploded in the nineteenth century. It was the last significant attempt in that century to provide equal political rights for the American Negro. Civil-rights legislation of that era was abandoned, with no resuscitation of Negro political rights until the 1930s and later. Restrictive provisions in state constitutions and oppressive Jim Crow laws developed rapidly throughout the South; elsewhere there was apathy on the issue of Negro rights. Republican efforts to do something for the Negro suddenly and dramatically stopped. However, Harrison began a presidential tradition of making routine statements in opposition to lynching.[48]

Only President Harrison and a few of the senators, such as Hoar, Edmunds, and Chandler, "really cared about the plight of the party in the South or the fate of the Negro." To Senator George F. Hoar the defeat of Lodge's elections bill indicated that national will and duty had failed. A chance to settle the issue by peaceable means had been lost.[49]

Harrison also strongly supported the Blair education bill, which had even more difficulty than the Lodge elections bill. The two were frequently linked, as the intended primary beneficiaries were blacks in southern states. Through the 1880s, Henry W. Blair, a Republican senator from New Hampshire, persistently sought to combat illiteracy by introducing a bill providing for federal aid to education. The $7 to $15 million that was to be appropriated over a number of years in this measure was minuscule by later standards, but in the 1880s it was a sizable portion of the entire federal budget. Blair's bill evoked more widespread controversy and discussion in the South than it did in other parts of the country, showing the cleavage between the Bourbon faction of the Democratic party and the older, agrarian-based faction. Generally, the Bourbons supported Blair's plan, while the agrarians cited its unconstitutionality and extravagance as grounds for opposing it.[50]

Blair's education bill received much support from the time he first presented it to the Senate in December 1881. Sixty petitions and memorials asking for federal aid to public schools had been presented to the previous Congress, almost all of which had come from the South. Although favorably reported by committee, along with a bill, pushed by Senator Justin S. Morrill, calling for school aid from income provided by the sale of public lands, the Senate took no action that year. In 1883, Blair and Morrill clashed over whose bill had priority; as a result, neither was considered. In January 1884, another Blair education bill was reported to the Senate; this one provided almost complete state control over federal funds to be used for public schools. Full debate in the Senate produced changes, including one that was strongly favored by Senator Benjamin Harrison to place stiffer restrictions against racial discrimination in the use of these funds. Senator Harrison voted for this bill, which received two-thirds approval in the Senate but was not taken up in the House.[51]

For the second time, Blair's education bill passed the Senate on 5 March 1886. This measure was almost identical to the 1884 bill, and it received even stronger support in the Senate. Again the Democratic-dominated House Committee on Education did not respond, although resolutions were offered requiring the committee to report. By this time, the weekly magazine *Nation* had a new editorial writer, Edward P. Call, who feared complete federal control of education. He bitterly attacked the education bill and soon gained a reputation as ''The Blair Bill Editor.'' Blair's bill was reintroduced early in 1888; it passed the Senate for the third time, but it was not reported favorably for discussion in the House. Never in this period did the House take a formal vote on Blair's bill or on a comparable bill originating in the House. During the 1880s, southern support for the Blair bill, both in Congress and in public expression, seemed much stronger than the opposition. The general feeling existed that public endorsement was widespread, but still the bill could not get through Congress. Opponents of the bill said that accepting federal largess for public schools would make them less self-reliant, that they would be opening the door to centralization and federal control. Moreover, the constitutionality of the bill was questioned, and some opponents of the tariff claimed that this bill was pushed to use up the surplus that was generated from tariff rates that were already too high.[52]

A new dimension was added to the racial issue in its relation to the Blair bill in 1889 when the active development of the Afro-American League gained widespread attention in the national press. The *New York Tribune* expected this group to be the Negro equivalent of the Indian-activist Lake Mohonk Conferences. Although initially seeking to avoid partisan politics, the Afro-American League in its conference in Chicago of January 1890 endorsed the Blair bill. Later the Afro-American League dropped its nonpartisan stance and could not be distinguished from any of the many other black interest groups.[53]

In 1890 the Blair bill was introduced into the Senate of a fourth Congress just days after heated controversy had erupted over the Hoar version of the elections bill. This time the bill called for federal appropriations to public schools that would be stretched over a period of eight years. Each state would receive its share of federal funds, based on its proportionate share of all illiterates in the country above the age of ten. This bill obligated a state governor to file a statement with the secretary of the interior that no discrimination existed between white and colored school children. In 1890, no discrimination was not the equivalent of no segregation.[54]

For the first time in the history of this bill the Republican party claimed a majority in both the Senate and the House. Moreover, President Harrison announced his continued support, and many other Republican leaders were known to be in favor of this legislation. Federal aid to public schools was not specifically mentioned in the Republican platform of 1888, but there was a strong advocacy of free schools as "the promoter of that intelligence which is to preserve us as a free nation; therefore the State or nation, or both combined, should support free institutions of learning, sufficient to afford to every child growing up in the land the opportunity of a good common-school education." Harrison did not ask for federal aid to education in his Inaugural Address—there were too many other things to mention in this long presidential message; but he did endorse the ideas in Blair's bill in his first annual message to Congress on 3 December 1889.[55]

Based on its experience in the 1880s, the Blair bill in 1890 fared less well than might have been expected. Blair applied all the pressure he could muster by engaging in what he called a positive filibuster, and he kept his education bill before the Senate for more than a month, 5 February to 20 March 1890. Debate was lengthy and acrimonious. Blair kept close tabs on senatorial intentions, and he expected passage, with the vice-president casting the deciding vote. Perhaps the *Nation* editorials' opposition to the "Bill to Promote Mendicancy," as Call always termed it, had the desired effect. Belatedly, two senators switched their votes, and the measure lost, 36 to 42, with Blair also voting in the negative so that he could move a reconsideration of the issue.[56] But it never came up again.

Interest in federal support for public education, as represented by the Blair bill, peaked about 1886. In 1888 the Blair bill passed the Senate, with its majority reduced to ten. For the first time, in 1890 the Senate defeated the bill. The earlier interest in this measure was no longer there. Opposition from both Republican and Democratic senators grew during that decade, while the need to provide assistance for large numbers of illiterates still existed. A House committee reported favorably on a similar bill in 1890, but the full House never considered it.[57]

An analysis of the party vote in the Senate on the four Blair bills shows that more Democrats than Republicans voted nay, but the first two times that it came before Congress, a majority of both Democrats and Republicans were for it. Southern Democrats, who often came from one-party areas, as well as southern Republicans favored this measure. The bulk of the opposition was based on economic and constitutional considerations and came from Democrats in the border and northern states, where it could be used as a real issue against Republicans. Usually, its opponents did not question whether or not the schools would be segregated, not did they seem to fear federal control. The unsuccessful effort to pass the Blair education bill in 1890 ended for many years a congressional effort to improve education, in general, and its associated civil rights for southern blacks. In fact, the prophetic words of a congressman in 1883 were becoming a reality: ''Means will be found for subverting the citizen's right to vote if ignorance exists.'' Southern political leaders increasingly justified discriminatory laws against black voting by pointing out the high illiteracy rates among rural southern blacks. The lack of effort, after 1890, to develop legislation to carry on the tradition of the Blair education bill shows that northerners, also, were abandoning their efforts to aid Negro education through federal assistance.[58]

Professed reasons for opposing the Blair bill always cited the fear of centralization, the fear that federal control would follow and would threaten local initiative, and the fear that this was an extravagant and unconstitutional way of doing things. Behind the high-sounding terms lay the real reasons—racial prejudice and the concern that education might alleviate some of the problems being encountered by poor blacks. Some southerners were apprehensive that providing education for blacks would have dire consequences. Negroes would make their own decisions in elections and would therefore become less easily manipulated. These fears produced more opposition to this legislation than did all other factors combined.[59]

The expansion of southern educational facilities without the benefits that the Blair bill offered had to rely on private philanthropy, mostly from the North, and upon action within the impoverished southern states. The increasing opposition to this measure in the Senate came from a combination of northern senators, western silverites, and a majority of the senators from the South. Northern newspapers that commented on this issue rejoiced openly when it was defeated. By this time, following the lead of the *Nation* and Edward P. Call, Senator Blair was castigated by opposition northern newspapers for introducing this legislation. He was called a crank, and his bill was called nothing more than a humbug, described as one of the most mischievous measures ever received by Congress. Harrison's plea in 1889 for racial justice through the use of kindness and education rather than army bayonets was replaced in 1890 with apathy.[60]

Blair had the best of intentions with the bill that he placed in congressional debates during a period of a decade. His education bill had always fared best in the Senate. Curiously, the Lodge elections bill easily passed the House. Neither of these bills received serious consideration by the other chamber, and both failed to become law. The time was not ripe; other issues demanded and received time and attention. To certain southern states, congressional inaction on black civil rights signaled the opportunity to impose additional educational and suffrage restraints on their black citizens. While unable to agree on election and education questions, Congress was moving on other issues that had been problems for many years.

One of these problems found a solution in the long-overdue Land Revision Act of 1891. How the federal government would dispose of the public domain was a significant issue during the nineteenth century. Revenues derived from the sale of federal land constituted a major source of federal income through most of this period, second only to tariff duties. Most nineteenth-century Americans had contact with their federal government only because it owned the postal service and operated the mails, but a sizable number of Americans also shared in the federal largess through the acquisition of cheap or free land from the public domain. Throughout the 1880s, many bills were introduced into Congress to repeal or change a conglomeration of land laws that had accumulated over half a century. The first twenty-three sections of the Land Revision Act of 1891 repealed the Pre-emption Act of 1841 and the Timber Culture Act of 1873, amended the Desert Land Act of 1877, and brought procedural changes in many lesser land statutes. Of more significance in the long run, and the most important action taken by the Harrison administration in affecting the American West, was the unheralded last paragraph of this law, section 24, which created the national forests.

Party platforms in 1888 touched on the divisive character of recent land policy. The Democrats, primarily because of the performance of Cleveland's controversial General Land Office Commissioner A. J. Sparks, claimed a reversal of "the improvident and unwise policy of the Republican party touching the public domain, and . . . [reclamation] from corporations and syndicates, alien and domestic, and [restoration] to the people, nearly one hundred millions of acres of valuable land to be sacredly held as homesteads for our citizens." The Republican platform had a much stronger statement, which affirmed "the policy of appropriating the public lands . . . to be homesteads for American citizens and settlers, . . . which the Republican party established in 1862, against the persistent opposition of Democrats in Congress, and which brought our great Western domain into such magnificent development." The restoration to the public domain of land that had originally been granted to the railroads was claimed as a responsibility of both Republicans and Democrats. Finally, Cleveland's Democratic administration was charged with harassing "innocent settlers with spies and prosecutions under the false pretence of exposing frauds and vindicating the law." In spite of interparty sniping on land questions, there was much agreement on needed reforms. President Harrison's reference to land laws in his Inaugural Address was very general and consisted of a single sentence: "It is due to the settlers in the Territories who have availed themselves of the invitations of our land laws to make homes upon the public domain that their titles should be speedily adjusted and their honest entries confirmed by patent."[61]

Approved on 3 March 1891, in the final days of the Fifty-first Congress, the Land Revision Act received adequate but perfunctory attention from members of Congress. The law's statutory title, "An act to repeal timber-culture laws, and for other purposes," suggests the catchall nature of this legislation. There was strong enough evidence about the fraudulent use of the Timber Culture and the Desert Land laws, which produced a congressional demand for their repeal or alteration. Also, the Pre-emption Act seemed to be out of place in an era when arable public lands were in short supply. More than a hundred land bills were introduced into that Congress. Some had passed earlier in this session, and the rest were assembled into this bill. As the Congress neared adjournment, a seventeen-section land bill was under consideration by a joint conference committee. Under the control of midwestern conservationists and on the advice of the secretary of the interior, who was sitting with the committee, a significant new clause was added. When the bill emerged from the conference committee, it had twenty-four sections, the last of which favored forest reservations as a rider that had not been considered before in either house. Belatedly added to the 1891 law, it passed in violation of the usual congressional procedures, because it was not printed so that members of Congress could study it before it was approved. This sleeper in the new legislation provided for revolutionary changes in United States forest policy. Section 24 must have been written hurriedly, as it was an incomplete sentence, which stated:

> That the President of the United States may, from time to time, set apart and reserve, in any State or Territory having public land bearing forests, in any part of the public lands wholly or in part covered with timber or undergrowth, whether of commercial value or not, as public reservations, and the President shall, by public proclamation, declare the establishment of such reservations and the limits thereof.[62]

Details are lacking about how the forest-reserve proposal was added to the Land Revision Act of 1891, but certain actions tie Benjamin Harrison closely to the clause favoring the new national forests. For instance, in April 1890, representatives of the Law Committee of the American Forestry Congress (renamed the next year the American Forestry Association) presented a petition to President Harrison in which they described the necessity of protecting the nation's rich natural resources. As was his manner, the president made no direct reply to the petition, but he cordially received the committee from the American Forestry Congress and forwarded their petition to Congress. Later, members of this same committee met with Secretary of the Interior John W. Noble, and they memorialized Congress on the need to set aside forest reservations.

The chief of the Division of Forestry, Dr. Bernhard Eduard Fernow, remembered that Secretary Noble told the joint conference committee in the eleventh hour that he would not permit the president to sign the bill "unless the Reservation clause was inserted." Another contemporary observer stated that section 24 "was in the hands of western men to a large extent." Since Harrison and Noble were dissatisfied with the initial bill, "western Senators went back and forth to the White House during the night in an effort to have it shaped up so as to secure the Presidential approval."[63]

In a speech in 1908, John W. Noble remembered that the first impressive appeal for a forest-reservation policy came slightly earlier, on 20 January 1890, when Harrison responded to a letter submitted by Professor Thomas Corwin Mendenhall, president of the American Association for the Advancement of Science, who was also chairman of a committee to preserve the forests on the public domain. Harrison sent the memorial to Congress "and recommended that adequate steps be taken to prevent the rapid destruction of our great forest areas and the loss of our water supplies." Noble also described the night of 3 March 1891, when President Harrison waited in an anteroom near Congress to sign bills that had been approved. When the land-revision bill came for his signature, he asked Noble whether it was "as it should be, and being advised it was, because of the authority to make reservations was thereby given, he said 'Then I will sign it' and he did."[64]

Certainly, Fernow was one of the prime movers of the law, but there were also Noble, Edward A. Bowers of the General Land Office, Senators R. F. Pettigrew and Preston B. Plumb, and Robert Underwood Johnson of *Century* magazine—all of whom were claiming credit for the success of getting section 24 through Congress. Others, including the naturalist John Muir, who founded the Sierra Club, and numerous congressmen, deserved recognition, as the idea of national forests had been around for many years. Bowers was the probable author of the forest-reserves paragraph, which contained neither a purpose for the reserves nor a means of administering them.[65]

Before a month had passed, President Harrison had authorized the first forest reserve, to be located on public domain adjacent to Yellowstone Park, in Wyoming. It was enlarged later in the same year. Fourteen additional reserves in Alaska, in the territories of Arizona and New Mexico, and in the states of California, Colorado, Oregon, and Washington were established during the remainder of his term. The Alaskan reserve, on an island in the Kodiak group, was usually ignored in later accounts of these first national-forest reservations. With it, Harrison's proclamations brought the total area in national forests to more than twenty-two million acres, about 11.5 percent of the national-forest system in later years.[66] Near the end of Harrison's presidency, a *New York Times* editorial regarded the creation of the new forest reserves as a creditable act and gave unstinted commendation to Harrison and Noble. In a final paragraph the editorial stated:

> These facts will show the earnestness and success with which the policy of forest reservation has been carried out during the last two years. The value of the services thus

performed can hardly be overestimated. The benefit is both local and national—in securing the sources of water supply and thus insuring irrigation of bountiful crops and in preserving unimpaired the glories and beauties of natural scenery in the West.[67]

Some of the accounts of the "Forest Reserve Act" emphasize the fortuitous circumstances that brought the passage of this conservation program for the federal government when the Senate was historically opposed to such measures. Others believed that the withdrawals that were carried out by Harrison and others provoked bitter opposition in the western areas that were most involved. Scholarship in more recent years holds that section 24 was not thrust upon an unwilling Congress and that the West did not declare war upon the new forest reserves. In fact, the West, through the Harrison and the second Cleveland administrations, was just as supportive of section 24 as was Congress. Nor did western newspapers make a big issue out of the early forest reserves when they were created; there was almost no comment. The initiative for setting aside many areas as forest reservations came from petitions signed by area citizens. Later there was no move in Congress to deprive a president of the authority to set aside national forests or to cancel existing reserves. Gifford Pinchot, who became chief forester for a long time in later years, called section 24 "the most important legislation in the history of Forestry in America." In speaking for the whole Land Revision Act of 1891, Congressman Lewis E. Payson, a Republican of Illinois, stated that "ten years of continuous search has resulted in placing upon the statute books of this nation, to endure, I trust, as long as the nation shall endure, these two propositions: that not an acre of the public domain shall be taken by anybody except as a home of a poor man or for reclamation, where now there is only desert."[68]

The remaining domestic legislation was less all-embracing than the actions already discussed. However, much of it was important for that era. Early in Harrison's administration, the United States agreed to the validity of an international copyright, and the Weather Bureau was transferred from the War Department to the Department of Agriculture.[69]

Taking more of the president's time and that of Postmaster General John Wanamaker was the use of the mails by the Louisiana Lottery, which they regarded as a corrupt and degrading influence. Both Harrison and Wanamaker were religiously and morally opposed to lotteries, as being a form of gambling. In his message to Congress in December 1889, Harrison asked for stronger laws to restrict the use of the mails by promoters of lotteries. Corruption that was disclosed in regard to these lottery schemes included bribery of public officials in both Louisiana and in North Dakota and the theft of cash from the mails. These added to the concern of the president and the postmaster general. Lobbying efforts by the promoters of lotteries were effective, at first, in curbing restrictive federal legislation. Wanamaker's efforts to influence the Post Office Committee of the House to report a bill barring the use of the mails by lotteries proved fruitless. On three occasions, Harrison called committee members to the White House to get support for his project, but these personal conferences failed even when he threatened to send a message to Congress urging that it take immediate action against lotteries. Finally, on 29 July 1890, Harrison carried out his threat and intervened with a special message to Congress, where the additional publicity produced the results that he was seeking. Three weeks later, although Harrison was described by some newspapers as a meddler who was trying to interfere in private individual affairs, the House reported a bill, and the Senate endorsed it without amendment. This new law "barred all letters, postal cards, circulars, lists of drawings, tickets and other materials referring to lotteries from the mails." Such mail, even registered letters, would be returned to the sender unopened.[70] The maximum fine for violation of this new postal law was $500, but the possibility of a prison term made it a harsher penalty.

Less successful were the president's efforts to obtain a law to increase the safety of railroad employees. Every annual presidential message to Congress during the Harrison years included a request for action similar to that of 3 December 1889, when Harrison urged "better protection of the lives and limbs of those engaged in operating the great interstate freight lines of the country, especially the yard-men and brakemen." In 1891, for instance, he called attention to the deaths, while they were coupling railroad cars during the previous year, of 369 brakemen; 7,841 had been maimed. He reported that a total of 2,451 railroad employees had been killed during the year and 22,390 had been injured. He called this loss "a cruel and largely needless sacrifice," because the federal government had responded earlier with legislation for similar safety needs on steamships.[71] The Fifty-second Congress provided a partial solution for Harrison by mandating improved coupling devices on the cars. Generally, congressmen preferred not to interfere with railroad operations, and the toll of railroad employees continued for another decade.

During the campaign in 1888, Harrison was regarded by some California newspapers as the pro-Chinese candidate of the Republican party. Friends quickly advised him that an anti-Chinese-immigration position on the West Coast was almost as important as the tariff question or the remonetization of silver. So Harrison explained in his letter of acceptance of the Republican nomination that "the objections to Chinese immigration are distinctive and conclusive, and are now so generally accepted as such that the question has passed entirely beyond the stage of argument. . . . Such amendments or further legislation as may be necessary and proper to prevent evasions of the laws and to stop further Chinese immigration would also meet my approval."

As a matter of fact, Congress acted a few weeks later, on 1 October 1888, with the passage of the Scott Act to curb the reentrance of Chinese to America when they had left the country for any reason. Thus, the Chinese issue was not mentioned in the Inaugural Address, although stricter naturalization laws were requested. Later, Attorney General W. H. H. Miller directed federal agents on the West Coast to investigate and prosecute illegal Chinese immigrants who entered by way of British Columbia. In 1892 the Geary Act was passed, which renewed existing anti-Chinese legislation for ten years. Chinese in the United States were required to register and to obtain a certificate of residence.[72]

Compared to most other nineteenth-century presidents, Harrison fared very well during his first two years in his ability to work with Congress on new legislation. He ever remained the Republican organization man, he strongly backed his cabinet officers, and he had few qualms about enhancing the power of the executive. Like most of his presidential predecessors, he provided no basic institutional innovations for his administration.[73] But the results of the election of 1890 showed that much of the Republican legislation of Harrison's first two years had gone too far for voters to accept readily. With overwhelming Democratic power in the House of Representatives for the incoming Fifty-second Congress, the productive years for domestic legislation in the Harrison administration were over with the completion of half of his presidential term.

Congress passed no earthshaking legislation in 1892 and early 1893. Contemporary comment in a partisan manner evaluated the activity of the Democratic-dominated House, sitting in opposition to a Senate that had a slight Republican majority and to a Republican president. With massive control, the 235 Democrats in 1891, opposed by 88 Republicans and 10 Farmers' Alliance men, selected Charles Frederick Crisp of Georgia as Speaker of the House of Representatives. For chairman of the Way and Means committee, Crisp by-passed Roger Q. Mills of Texas in favor of William M. Springer of Illinois, who sought to embarrass the Senate and the president by passing numerous small changes in the tariff, the so-called popgun bills. None of these measures was ever approved by the Senate, so Harrison was not faced with signing them.

The effort of the Democratic House to repeal legislation passed by the Fifty-first Congress was generally unsuccessful. Important domestic bills that were passed, according to the *New York Times*, were far less significant than those of the Fifty-first Congress. These included laws that have previously been mentioned, as well as a national quarantine against cholera, more restrictive immigration laws, and many other laws of lesser magnitude. Another important topic that was discussed by that Congress was an antioption bill, which failed to pass.[74] Still, appropriations by the Fifty-second Congress exceeded those of the so-called billion-dollar Republican Congress, which the Democrats had accused of being profligate. One historian reported that Democratic congressmen "made ingenious explanations that the government had been committed to disbursements which they could not disown." This Congress passed far fewer private pension acts than had its predecessor, only 13 percent of those reported favorably by the Pension Bureau. Silverites almost got their wish for an unlimited-silver-coinage bill in July 1892, which the Senate passed 29 to 25 but which barely lost in the House, 136 to 154. Statehood bills for Arizona and New Mexico were also approved by the House, and on 28 January 1893 the House unanimously endorsed a joint resolution to amend the Constitution to provide for the popular election of United States senators. The Senate took no positive action on any of these bills.[75]

The two houses of Congress effectively worked at cross-purposes on legislation. By one accounting, during the first session of the Fifty-second Congress, the House passed 475 bills, 284 of which were approved by the Senate. The Senate passed 691 bills, many of which were private bills for pensions; and the House approved only 113 altogether. Thus, almost four hundred acts were added to the statute books.[76]

For the second half of the Harrison administration the principal attention was directed, not to domestic affairs, but to foreign relations. At the conclusion of his four years as president, Benjamin Harrison was recognized as the head of a good and clean administration, but his loss of political support in 1890 and his defeat in 1892 provided the impression that his domestic policy had not generally been successful.

5

★ ★ ★ ★ ★

PRESIDENT HARRISON
ON TRIAL

Halfway through his four-year term, President Benjamin Harrison was confronted by a series of crises which profoundly undermined his ability to provide the kind of leadership that was apparent earlier in the Republicans' domestic program. Part of the responsibility for creating the crises was Harrison's vow to be solely responsible for making appointments to the federal civil service. He consulted his cabinet officers on programs involving their departments, and he permitted them wide latitude within their own areas of administration. But he did not easily delegate power, and he was sure he had the intelligence to handle the presidential tasks. He did not take advice easily, so he drove the Republican elephant alone, and he antagonized well-known Republican political leaders in the process. Moreover, Harrison had denounced the use of a kitchen cabinet, or a small coterie of advisors, and he could tolerate neither an uncrowned king nor a power behind the throne.[1] Leading Republican politicians, who were denied what they wanted from Harrison, willingly would have been of service if they had been given the feeling that they had a share in Harrison's crusade. But Harrison could not unbend in the presidency; his way was to go it alone.

Nor did Harrison believe in being too communicative on patronage issues. His brusqueness and frank comments were regarded as insults. He could not be other than himself. His cool and imperturbable manner amazed and discomfited his associates. An apologist warned a visitor, "Don't feel insulted by anything he may do or say, . . . it is only his way." These negative qualities, unrecognized during the campaign of

1888, became a virtual plague for him as president. For instance, with a watch in his hand and a huge pile of reports on his desk, he greeted the governor of Ohio by saying, "I've got all these papers to look after, and I'm going fishing at two o'clock." Then Harrison opened his watch case and waited for the governor to ask his question. A one-armed veteran came all the way from Minnesota to visit the president to discuss political conditions in his home state, which he thought could be straightened out by the proper appointments. He had barely begun his remarks when the president said to him, "I know all about the political conditions up there much better than you," which ended the conversation quickly and turned a former ardent supporter into an anti-Harrison man. Others accused the president of being unwilling to listen and said that he usually did the right thing but in the wrong way. Though possessing outstanding qualities as an upright and able person, he lacked a gracious manner when dealing with individuals. He disdained a tactful reply; he preferred directness, simplicity, and unusual frankness; and he unnecessarily made enemies in the process. A long-time acquaintance believed that the cold and abrupt mannerisms went with Harrison's conception of the office of president.[2]

When persons sought an appointment for themselves or for friends but then dallied too long, Harrison would take command and quickly terminate the conversation. Patronage seekers were never invited to take a seat—otherwise the meeting might go on endlessly. Harrison had always been a loner, and he had strong personal friendships with relatively few people. His ardent views on most political matters offered the possibility for conflict and made him suspicious of state political bosses. He could not trust their motives, and he refused to meet them as equals. They received little from him, even if they had provided the necessary support to gain his nomination for the presidency. Much of the defection of Republican leaders from the president came over the issue of patronage. The coolness that party leaders received from Harrison when they proposed candidates for appointment became the grist for ill feelings that put them in the mood to sabotage Harrison's later efforts. Factionalism within Republican ranks, which Harrison had been able to avoid in 1888, was rife by the time that elections were held in 1890, and a multitude of local issues caused a loss of eighty seats in the House of Representatives that year. There was no chance after the election of 1890 to get the kind of extensive Republican legislation passed that had made the Fifty-first Congress so productive. Tom Reed spoke for many Republicans, when he was chided for his role in the "Billion-Dollar Congress," with the retort that it was a "Billion-Dollar Country!" Basic governmental operations continued, and there were few real places in which to curtail federal expenditures. Thus a budgetary analysis of appropriations made by the Fifty-second Congress shows that it was also a billion-dollar Congress—a term that was used as a label for what was called the wasteful and extravagant Fifty-first Congress.[3]

Strong Republican leaders who were soon at odds with Harrison included former Senator Thomas Platt of New York, Senator Matthew Quay of Pennsylvania, and Speaker of the House Thomas Reed of Maine. In each case, the initial dispute was over patronage. Platt, the New York Republican boss, claimed that he had Harrison's promise to make him secretary of the Treasury. Many years later, with the publication of the Platt papers, there was no evidence to support his earlier claim. In 1889, Harrison vigorously denied ever having made a promise, and in later years his private secretary stated that he had received direct evidence that even Platt did not think there had been a bargain. When the Platt papers were opened, John Wanamaker, one of the few intimate survivors at the time, also denied that there had been a deal. However, in the next few years, rumors of Harrison's reneging on the Treasury post for Platt were repeated and treated as facts. Many unverified remarks of this nature were incorporated into later historical accounts— they made interesting but untrue stories.[4]

Because Platt was unable to get a cabinet position and the patronage that he wanted, he joined a faction in the Republican party that was hostile to the president. There was a credibility gap between Platt and Harrison which was not closed until late in the election race of 1892, when vice-presidential candidate Whitelaw Reid intervened and brought the two antagonists together.[5]

Pennsylvania's Senator Matthew Quay, chairman of the Republican National Committee in 1888, had major responsibility for organizing the successful Republican election drive that year. Quay met Harrison for the first time after that election, and his initial impression was that of dealing with a political tenderfoot. While many people said Harrison dominated every conversation, Quay reported that "the President-elect was all ears and no tongue" and that he "turned a frigid and contemptuous shoulder" on Quay's suggestions for appointments. Later, at a time that provided him little opportunity to disagree, Quay was asked for approval of Wanamaker as Pennsylvania's representative in Harrison's cabinet. Quay had nothing to say, although he had many Pennsylvanians in mind for the cabinet, but not Wanamaker. Harrison spent an inordinate amount of time on his cabinet appointments. For other federal positions, prospects from larger Republican states were carefully scrutinized by Harrison, whereas for smaller states the president followed precedent by listening to the advice of Republican senatorial and congressional delegations. Harrison did not want to be accused of surrendering to the powerful bosses, so Quay and other big-state bosses had difficulty in getting positions for their own people. No doubt, Harrison's attitude that his election victory in 1888 was the work of the Lord was a devout personal feeling. It might have been an ingenious device to keep politicians away, but it caused numerous snide remarks, and Quay certainly supplied his quota.[6]

Speaker of the House Thomas B. Reed had provided strong support for Harrison's election. He was also a member of the presidential party on trips that were taken during Harrison's first year in office. Moreover, Harrison and Reed cooperated on a number of important bills in the Fifty-first Congress. Reed's action in establishing new parliamentary rules reduced some of the pressure on the president so that he did not have to veto any major piece of legislation. Reed was a commanding parliamentarian, the master of the quick repartee, and was known for his epigrams. A huge man, twice as heavy as the president, Reed quarreled with Harrison over patronage in 1890 when the president appointed Col. F. N. Dow to a federal position and pardoned one of Dow's relatives from a federal conviction. Reed's harsh comment was that he had only two personal enemies in his life. "One of these Mr. Harrison has pardoned out of the penitentiary and the other he has just appointed" to a high position in Maine. A Republican congressman from Illinois, Joseph Gurney Cannon, an observer of the Reed-Harrison feud, said that "Reed had the tongue of a wasp and Harrison distilled poison like an adder; the dislike was cordial and undisguised." Usually, Reed's denunciation of Benjamin Harrison was for private audiences, but such actions had a way of becoming public.[7]

During the early part of 1892, these three Republican leaders—Platt, Quay, and Reed—along with former First Assistant Postmaster General James S. Clarkson, had had enough. They quietly organized a grievance committee; their object was a dump-Harrison campaign. Clarkson was angry with Harrison because he believed he had been cheated out of a cabinet position, and he thought that Harrison had not adequately backed Lodge's elections bill in 1891. These anti-Harrison conspirators organized in a secret meeting in New York City and expected James G. Blaine, with all of his illnesses, to become their Republican candidate for president. Blaine declined any further campaigning in an open letter, published early in 1892. He would not cooperate with the Grievance Committee, and neither would many other disaffected Republicans, but the move was an ominous sign of unrest in the GOP. Such disaffection provided additional problems and frustrations for the president.[8]

As a matter of fact, the Grievance Committee forced Harrison's hand in an unexpected way. He had hoped to retire after a single term, but the public attacks of that Republican faction caused Harrison to believe he had only two options: to "become a candidate or 'forever wear the name of a political coward.'" He told Halford that "no Harrison has ever retreated in the presence of a foe without giving battle, and so I have determined to stand and fight." Thus, on 23 May 1892, he announced his decision to a few loyal supporters to become a candidate for the Republican nomination for president "in spite of his strong desire not to be one."[9] Caroline Harrison was unprepared for her husband's announcement. She looked away for a moment and quietly asked; "Why, General? Why, when it has been so hard for you."[10]

Harrison's early loss of support from Republican senators and congressmen from the new western states was chiefly over the president's attitude toward the money question. Perhaps Harrison was intentionally vague in his feeling toward free silver, or westerners were reading more into his statements than was actually there. In any case, when he voiced opposition to any money bill that he considered unsound, these Rocky Mountain members of Congress and others from the West became undependable and unreliable supporters of the McKinley Tariff and other Republican measures. By then the president had become so embittered by endless talk of silver that he remarked, "I wish this free coinage of senators would stop."[11]

Another kind of defection that faced President Harrison and the Republican party came when a Republican transferred his allegiance to Democratic ranks. Few such political moves attracted as much widespread comment as that of Charles William Eliot, president of Harvard College. In October 1889, barely six months into Harrison's presidency, Eliot gave a speech in which he said that his reasons for changing parties were prompted by three actions: the talk of a new Republican tariff, a comparison of Cleveland's and Harrison's records on civil service, and the handling of the pension issue.[12]

To counter these detractors there were strong supporters of the president. One of Harrison's contemporaries, Commissioner Thomas Jefferson Morgan of the Bureau of Indian Affairs, with partisan pride, wrote that "no one has ever filled the Presidency with more efficiency." He admired Harrison and stated that the president "met promptly and ably every demand . . . [he has been] industrious, painstaking, conscientious, he has devoted himself with unwearied zeal to the faithful performance of his official duties." Morgan also reported that Harrison had "about him a body of trained clerks and efficient helpers . . . [but he] is accustomed to doing his own writing, instead of dictating to a stenographer."[13]

Congress failed to provide nineteenth-century presidents with resources for adequate office personnel. In actuality, the president's staff was meager. Only through long, grinding hours every working day was Harrison able to get through his ceremonial duties, the official visits, and the mass of paper work that confronted him. The chain of routine was wearisome and never-ending to the president. Fortunately, Harrison could comprehend quickly the content of government documents; otherwise his administration would have lacked the kind of direction he provided. He would act only after he had complete information; so at times a presidential decision would be delayed. His White House office was well regulated; copies of correspondence were kept and filed, along with letters received. He "took just pride in this precision, but it was an unfortunate trait. He never learned to delegate authority, and sharpened his temper with overwork." It was no wonder that he looked forward to days or weeks when he felt impelled to get away from Washington. But even then, the duties of his office followed him, though without the usual hordes of patronage seekers. Postmaster General Wanamaker was constantly looking for ways to increase the efficiency of the postal service, but Harrison took little interest in improving administrative practices in his own office or elsewhere.[14]

President Harrison's right-hand man was Elijah Walker Halford, his executive secretary and confidant. Ten years younger than the president, Halford had known Harrison for a long time in Indianapolis. When Harrison was elected to the United States Senate in 1881, he secured an appointment for Halford as clerk in the Senate Subcommittee on Indian Affairs. Later, as editor of the *Indianapolis Journal*, Halford used every opportunity to advance Harrison's political career. Halford, who was generally called "Lige" or "Brother Halford" by the president, began working as Harrison's secretary in late November 1888 and went to Washington with him the week before the inauguration. The intense pressure and long hours of duty in the White House office caused Halford to collapse at his desk on 4 October 1889, exactly seven months into the Harrison presidency. His illness was never identified in the press, but he could not be moved from the White House. Two days later he underwent painful surgery in the executive mansion, and Mrs. Halford was provided quarters there until her husband had completely recovered three weeks later.[15]

Because the presidential family occupied the same building as the executive office, problems were produced for Halford and for Harrison and his family. Mrs. Harrison sought relief: she had an architect prepare preliminary plans for enlarging the White House so that the presidential family would be entirely separated from the executive office. Later, Harrison wrote: "There is only a door—one that is never locked— between the President's office and what are not very accurately called his private apartments. There should be an Executive Office building, not too far away, but wholly distinct from the dwellinghouse. For every one else in the public service there is an unroofed space between the bedroom and the desk." In 1891 Halford did not go on the western tour to the Pacific Coast because his wife was ill. She died shortly after the tour was under way, a tragedy that was all too typical of the Harrison years. The secretary of the Treasury died in office, the secretary of the navy lost his wife and daughter in a house fire, the secretary of state lost two grown sons and a daughter, and Caroline Harrison died shortly before the election of 1892. The illness of a cabinet member, in the Harrison years, often meant that the White House office had an overload of work. During this four-year period, there was one time when Harrison and Halford were engulfed with the extra work of four different incapacitated cabinet officers. When Harrison's bid for reelection failed in 1892, Halford, at the age of fifty, sought security, comfort, and companionship. So Harrison restored Halford's Civil War rank of major and had him assigned to duties as a paymaster in the army, where he served another fourteen years. Then he retired on his pension and engaged in religious and charitable activities. In retirement, Halford lived another thirty years.[16] Halford told reporters about his daily response to avoid Harrison's testy temper: "When I see him in the morning and he greets me with, 'Halford, how are you today?' I sit down by his desk for a pleasant talk about matters. When he greets me with 'Good Morning, Mr. Halford,' I bolt the door and wait until after lunch for the talk."[17]

Another efficient worker in Harrison's White House office was E. Frank Tibbott, an executive clerk who served as stenographer for the president. He traveled on several of the presidential journeys, especially when Halford could not go. Tibbott was an expert copyist in an era when machines were beginning to take over office work. Another staff member in the White House office was Alice Sanger, who served as Halford's stenographer. She had been a stenographer in Harrison's law office in Indianapolis. After Harrison's election, Sanger had traveled to Europe, arriving home in time to take up her new duties in Washington. Eventually, Harrison learned to dictate his correspondence, but letters in longhand were still considered superior to any others. Usually, Tibbott would write out "in longhand the letter to be sent, but also [he] made a typed copy for the files."[18]

Presidents used various rooms in the White House for their personal office. The large Oval Room, located above the Blue Room, was employed as an office by President Arthur and by Cleveland, in his first term, as well as by many twentieth-century presidents. That room had been used earlier as a library and as a private sitting room. The Cabinet Room served as the office for Presidents Grant, Hayes, and Garfield. The room just east of the Cabinet Room was used as an office by Harrison. It had been so used by Lincoln and generally by earlier presidents. The Cabinet Room, during the Harrison years, became a waiting room for those who wanted to see the president.[19]

Early in the Harrison presidency the White House office received an average of seven hundred letters a day, only a small portion of which ever reached the president. Two-thirds of this total should have been sent directly to one of the departments, not to the White House. There was no contingency fund to take care of extra staff or to handle emergencies in the president's office.[20]

Telephones were available in the White House, but in the Harrison years there was as yet no person with identified duties solely as the telephone operator. A telegraph operator, however, was assigned to the president. Messages were more often carried to the addressee by the four messengers on the White House staff. In addition, there were three other clerks, to help with general office work, and two doorkeepers on the office floor, one of whom was a twenty-year veteran named Loeffler. Sgt. E. S. Dinsmore was the doorkeeper in charge of the lower floor. Harrison also had a military aide and a naval aide, whose roles were largely ceremonial. The name of one of these aides was likely to appear on the list in the presidential party on a trip away from Washington. In total, this small staff was loyal to Harrison. They worked long hours without complaint, though seldom would they hear the president compliment them on a job well done. One contemporary said that Harrison, "in his contempt for flattery, . . . seldom indulged in praise."[21]

Benjamin Harrison lacked experience as an administrator and had had only six years in Washington as a United States senator by the time he became president. Thus, political observers concluded that he would defer on many issues to members of his cabinet who had been long in the public eye. Halfway through his presidency the skepticism about Harrison's ability to lead his own administration had changed. By then it was recognized that he was absolutely the head in his administration. Harrison was sure of his position. While he did not interfere in the departmental work of members of his cabinet, neither would he permit any encroachment on his overall presidential power.[22]

The White House office schedule, during the Harrison years, provided for two cabinet meetings each week. Harrison also held weekly meetings with each cabinet member. Usually, each of the eight cabinet officers was assigned to a particular afternoon, and he came accompanied by a messenger carrying "an armful or a basketful of papers—chiefly made up of petitions and letters relating to appointments." Before signing a bill passed by Congress, Harrison always consulted the cabinet member who was most likely to be involved. For example, the public letters of Benjamin Harrison include many from individual cabinet members responding to the president's request for a report of any objection to approval of a particular bill. Congressmen could call on the president between 11:00 A.M. and 12:30 P.M. every business day except Monday. Harrison later wrote that "unless the President is very early, he will find some callers waiting for him as he passes through the Cabinet room to his office." He did say that his own posted hours for persons having business with him were "for 9:30 or 10 A.M. until 1 P.M., except on Mondays; but the hours and the exception are very little regarded."[23]

Public receptions in the Harrison years started the day after the inauguration and continued almost unabated for the next two days. Before departing from Indianapolis, the Harrisons, not knowing what they would be confronted with, "suggested to their Hoosier neighbors and friends that when they were in [Washington] they should call, assuring one and all that the White House latchstring would always be out." The crush of visitors who wanted to greet the president was so great that a set time was provided for these public receptions. The common practice was to provide several hours each week to permit "curious citizens to come in and shake hands with their President." During the first year of the Harrison presidency, public receptions were held in the East Room at noon on Mondays, Wednesdays, and Saturdays. Secretary Halford's physical collapse caused them to be abandoned for a while; then they were eliminated altogether by Halford because of the pressure of business. Unfortunately, Harrison was further isolated from the general public and denied what Lincoln called his public-opinion baths, which he found so useful.[24]

While Harrison spent most of each day on the normal routine of his office, the schedule for the White House family was also tightly organized. Breakfast in the Executive Mansion came shortly after 8:00 A.M. The family would then gather in religious devotions and prayer, led by Harrison or by his father-in-law, the Reverend John W. Scott. A light lunch came at 1:30 P.M., and family dinner was at 6:30 P.M. If possible, Harrison sought to have some leisure time for exercise, riding or walking, late each afternoon, and Halford was usually his companion. Harrison thoroughly enjoyed his grandchildren. His special favorite was Benjamin Harrison McKee, whose highchair was pulled close to his grandfather at mealtime. Many a night, Harrison took a large portfolio of required reading into his private apartment. A normal working day for Secretary Halford and many other members of the White House office staff lasted from nine in the morning until midnight.[25]

Financing the necessary White House social duties on the budget provided by Congress was an impossibility for Harrison. He complained about the expense of White House entertainment. He went into the White House in debt, and he added to that indebtedness during his four years there. Caroline found it impossible to manage the hostess duties alone, so her daughter and sister and, after her sister's death, her niece became permanent White House residents and assisted the First Lady.[26]

A long-time intimate acquaintance of both Benjamin and Caroline Harrison was John A. Anderson, who served as a member of the House of Representatives from Kansas for six terms from 1879 to 1891; he added to another crisis in these four years. Like Harrison, Anderson had won as a Republican, except for 1886, when he was reelected as an Independent. He had been Harrison's roommate at Miami University in 1852, and he was present at the wedding of Benjamin and Caroline the following year. The correspondence between Anderson and Harrison through the years was voluminous. They had much to share, and they were in agreement on many issues. It was through Anderson that Harrison had close ties and understanding of the West, especially California and Kansas. After the death of Anderson's wife, Mrs. Nellie Anderson, in the mid 1880s, he had a standing invitation to eat Sunday dinner at the home of Senator Harrison. Thus, Anderson's appearance, in later years, at Sunday dinners at the White House was expected.

The subjects of intimate discussions between the president and his congressman-friend, who came almost every week, were never written down. Most of the letters that Anderson wrote to Harrison after the latter was nominated as a presidential candidate were highly complimentary, but with Anderson's personal biases. He advised that Harrison's acceptance letter take the "strong steep ground against trusts." He also wrote that "you did a mighty wise thing in not taking a Directors' car," and he alerted Harrison to the attitude in the Far West of strong opposition to Chinese immigration. Their correspondence during the Harrison presidency was limited because of their frequent face-to-face meetings. Then, in 1890, much like William McKinley, Joseph Cannon, and Robert La Follette, Anderson was a casualty of the political upheaval, thus giving victory to Democratic and Populist candidates.

But unlike this trio, Anderson was not well, and he lacked the initiative for a political comeback. Therefore, it was a surprise to Anderson, and to most everyone else, when Harrison appointed him as consul general to Egypt when his congressional term expired on 1 March 1891. Anderson, enfeebled by his illness, sailed for Cairo on 6 April. The next January, Harrison wrote Anderson that "you have been so quiet since you have been in Cairo and I have been so busy and full of worriment and care since last spring and winter that I have not opened the correspondence. I am sorry to hear . . . that you have been ill; but glad to know that your present condition is more promising." Several months later, Anderson decided to return home, but he became so ill in Liverpool, England, that he was placed in a hospital, where he died on 18 May 1892. His death added to the feeling of personal tragedy that Harrison had during his four years in the White House.[27]

Another difficulty that faced Harrison, which he treated as a crisis, was the illness of John W. Noble, secretary of the interior. Finally, after two years on the job, Noble wanted out. He wrote the president: "Today closes my second year of Service and it is not in me to do two years more of the labor this Department demands of its chief officer." Harrison persuaded Noble to take an extended leave of absence rather than to resign. Twelve weeks later, Noble telegraphed from Hot Springs, Arkansas: "If circumstances permit please return letter of March sixth last am quite well again please telegraph reply." Thus, Secretary Noble stayed in the Harrison cabinet throughout the full four years.[28]

However, Redfield Proctor was elected to the United States Senate from Vermont and therefore vacated his post as secretary of war. Stephen B. Elkins was his replacement, thereby enabling Harrison to repay one of his hardest-working supporters. Secretary of the Treasury William Windom died suddenly on 29 January 1891, shortly after giving a speech in New York City. Harrison was grieved at this loss; it seemed like a personal blow to him. He had more cordial relations with Windom than with any other cabinet member. Harrison assumed the responsibility for telling the sad news to Windom's widow, and he assisted her in making funeral arrangements. With Mrs. Windom, his cabinet, and other officials, Harrison met the train returning Windom's body, and as a group they attended Windom's funeral. Two weeks later, Harrison wrote to his brother Carter that "the anxiety connected with the three deaths in the official circle, [including General Sherman and Admiral Porter] have quite overwhelmed me; though I hope to hold out without any break now until rest comes." An Ohio merchant and former governor, Charles Foster, was appointed to the vacant position of secretary of the Treasury.[29]

During all the time that he was Harrison's secretary of state, James G. Blaine was in poor health. In fact, his health deteriorated so sharply that he was a confirmed invalid as early as 1887, and he took himself out of the race for the presidency in 1888. For long periods of time, Blaine was away from Washington, endeavoring to regain his health, thus causing Harrison to spend extra time on foreign affairs. Even though Blaine was almost incapacitated, he contributed much to the early Harrison years. He and the president were in major agreement on most issues, and Blaine's reputation and his manner of presenting policy gained support for the administration. However, midway in the Harrison administration, the recurrent rumors of enmity between Blaine and the president carried more force. This crisis had become serious by January 1892, but it waited until June to explode. Then, three days before the opening of the Republican National Convention of 1892 in Minneapolis, Blaine provided somewhat bizarre action by suddenly resigning as secretary of state. The day before, on Friday 3 June, Blaine had attended a cabinet meeting, to report on affairs of his department. Harrison was irked by rumors that Blaine was again a candidate for the presidential nomination. So that afternoon he sent Stephen B. Elkins, a friend of both Harrison's and Blaine's, to ask Blaine either to renounce his candidacy or to resign. At 1:00 P.M. on the next day, Harrison received Blaine's brief, formal resignation, and he said to Halford, "Well, the crisis has come." Halford, who delivered Harrison's equally curt reply to Blaine within a half-hour, heard Blaine say, "Well, I am no longer Secretary of State." Although both men acted in haste, they certainly knew what they were doing. Elijah Halford believed that Blaine had resigned in pique, while Whitelaw Reid thought that certain Republican bosses were wreaking revenge on Harrison through this action. Harrison's Indiana friend Louis Michener attributed Blaine's resignation to Mrs. Blaine, who drove her sick husband into resigning. Historian Edward Stanwood cited Blaine's weakened physical condition, his temporary delusions, and the failure of his mental and physical powers as being responsible, whereas Blaine's biographer David S. Muzzey gave credit to all of these factors but summed it up by saying, "It is doubtful whether the Secretary himself really knew what his own mind was on the matter." Harrison had forced the resignation. But so had age, misunderstanding, and infirmity. Blaine's successor was the experienced diplomat John W. Foster, who had successfully negotiated many of the reciprocity treaties that resulted from the McKinley Tariff Act.[30]

The outcome of the mid-term elections in 1890 produced a transitional character for Harrison's administration that the president was never able to overcome. Harrison had distanced himself from many of the Republican leaders who had helped him gain election in 1888. He had developed an active foreign policy since 1890, but with the political opposition of the new House of Representatives, there was little he could accomplish in domestic affairs.[31]

The loss of Republican congressional seats in 1890 was blamed on the actions of President Harrison and the Republican-controlled Congress and on the proliferation of legislation. However, this explanation is far too simple. As always, the party that was out of power could more easily argue that political discontent was a product of national action—in the case of the Fifty-first Congress, its centralization of government authority. Most members of the Democratic party in the nineteenth century strongly believed that government should be passive. They were against big government, and they opposed any extension of the role of the national government into people's lives. They opposed increasing the federal budget, no matter what issue was involved. The Republican party, on the other hand, was more responsive to reform or to innovations in government. Republicans, by and large, were also more inclined to regard their party as a tool of moral reform than were Democrats.

Thus, in many states and at the local level, the Republican party became locked in a divisive struggle, involving the ethnic background and religious commitments of voters, their attitude toward the use of English in public and parochial schools, a moralistic crusade on behalf of prohibition, and the strength of party loyalty. In many local areas the Republican party was engaged in a moralistic campaign. To some the party seemed to be endeavoring to act as a policeman restricting their personal lives and actions. For example, suggested state legislation in the six midwestern states of Illinois, Indiana, Iowa, Michigan, Ohio, and Wisconsin produced far greater political turmoil and more defection from party loyalty than did anything that took place in Washington. Personal loyalty to a political party in the late nineteenth century was the strongest of any time in American history, and the greatest percentage of eligible voters—85 to 95 percent in this region—cast their ballots in elections of that period. Each voter believed that he had an important stake in the outcome of an election, and political parties were able to generate widespread enthusiasm to get out the vote.[32]

Elections of 1889, 1890, and 1891 in these midwestern states show that national issues did not affect voter loyalty as much as did local events. For instance, in Iowa and other midwestern areas, the effort to prohibit the liquor traffic split voters along ethnic and religious lines. Not since the formation of the Republican party had Iowa given control of its legislature, its congressional delegation, or its governor's office to other than the Republican party; but the election of 1889 was decidedly different. The prohibition issue of that year, along with support for Sunday closing laws, brought defection of Republicans from liturgical religious groups such as Catholics and Lutherans. Recent immigrants also left the Republican party in droves to vote for the Democratic candidate, who won the governor's office in both 1889 and 1891. In Chicago, Democrats regained control of city hall because of similar local issues. In Wisconsin, where immigrant groups outnumbered Yankees, the divisive issue was a law requiring that English be used as the language of instruction in all schools. A similar law in Illinois was equally disastrous for the Republican party. The race for governor in Ohio was won by a Democrat in 1889. The 1890 election resulted in the loss of thirty-three Republican congressmen in these six states alone— seven in Illinois, one in Indiana, six in Michigan, six in Wisconsin, nine in Ohio, and four in Iowa.[33]

National issues, such as the McKinley Tariff or the Sherman Silver Purchase Act, were significant, and no doubt they had some impact on the election in these six midwestern states. For instance, the McKinley Tariff went into effect shortly before the election of 1890, and there was not enough time for Republicans to discount rumors of its evil influence. James G. Blaine, with a prescience born of long-time political experience, had advised Harrison to call a special session of Congress to pass the tariff law in 1889, rather than waiting until 1890, shortly before the mid-term election.[34] Harrison was interested; therefore he had the experiences of several presidents who had called special sessions investigated and then decided against doing it. The silver issue was not as important in these six midwestern states as it was farther west, and it had even less effect on voter outcome in other areas east of the Mississippi River. As demonstrated in six states, these national issues could not move people from one party to another as completely as did local issues. Local and state party leaders soon learned to avoid issues that tended to split their regular constituency. Prohibition and English in all schools was downgraded as a featured stance of the Republican party in these areas. In years subsequent to those of the Harrison administration, the Republicans regained their dominant position in these six states.

Populism burst on the scene as a new third party in the election of 1890. Harrison had been warned about farmer agitation and unrest by western members of Congress, but he had concerned himself little with this new People's party, the cross-fertilization of agrarian grievances in the 1870s and 1880s, and the reform thought and energies of small third parties of that era. Changes that were taking place with the passing of the frontier, the collapse of the latest in a series of booms in 1887, and the rapid industrialization of American enterprise had influence on the plight of many farmers who were handicapped by low prices and an unfavorable weather cycle. They sought a political solution to their problems, and they appealed for support from organized labor and small-town businessmen.

Initially, the movement that became the People's party had operated through organizations of the Farmers' Alliance, which had formed in various parts of the country in an attempt to control political power at the state level by electing Farmers' Alliance–endorsed candidates from either the Republican or the Democratic party. The northern branch of the Farmers' Alliance, along with third-party men, were a force to be reckoned with in Kansas, Nebraska, South Dakota, and Minnesota. In the South the Alliance-endorsed candidates won the governorship in North Carolina, South Carolina, and Georgia, as well as the control of eight southern legislatures. Thus, the Fifty-second Congress contained two new senators who carried the new Populist label, in addition to as many as forty-four congressmen in the Alliance camp.

Actually, the national People's party was not created until 1891, and it held its first national nominating convention in Omaha in July 1892. James Baird Weaver, a former brigadier general in the Union Army, whose party background included Democratic, Republican, and Greenbacker, became the third party's candidate for president. In an effort to eliminate the political schism between North and South, the Populists selected a former Confederate major as their vice-presidential candidate. Espousing the protection of the weak from the oppressions of the strong and supporting expansion in the power of the government, the Populists polled more than a million votes in the presidential race in 1892 and became the first third party since the Civil War to win electoral votes.

In reality, success for the People's party in consecutive elections depended on fusion with the Democrats in the North and West and with the Republicans in the South. Internal dissension in the party and the inability to conclude fusion arrangements in most elections relegated the People's party to a minority status from which it could not rise. In the short run, the People's party lost, but its major ideas lived. The major parties responded to the reform ferment found in the People's party and in other reform movements by incorporating some of these ideas into party platforms. Ultimately, supporting legislation that could have been endorsed by Populists of the 1890s was enacted.

Truly, the number of governors, congressmen, and United States senators from the People's party was small. However, their elections substantially reduced the ability of the Republicans, during the last half of the Harrison administration, to continue their active legislating and added to the crises facing President Benjamin Harrison.

The major natural disaster during Harrison's presidency came in late May and June 1889, when there was severe flood damage and when lives that were lost at Johnstown, Pennsylvania, and in neighboring areas attracted the attention of the whole nation. Harrison treated this as a crisis of major proportions. He grieved for the people who were caught in the flood, and he showed his concern to the governor of Pennsylvania by offering federal assistance. To gain specific information, Harrison sent the supervising surgeon general, Dr. John B. Hamilton, on oral orders, to investigate the disaster. Also, through the Washington City Relief Commission, Harrison gave a personal check for $300 to flood sufferers.[35]

A series of crises for Harrison involved federal programs for American Indians, which we mentioned earlier. His Indian policy was a mixture of humanitarian considerations along with pragmatic politics, and Thomas J. Morgan, his commissioner of Indian affairs, was picked to fulfill that goal. Reaction to the president's program for Indians may have had an adverse bearing on Harrison's election effort in 1892. Nevertheless, Harrison was proud that much had happened in the Indian service during his first three years as president. The Indian was being educated ''for the intelligent exercise of his new citizenship,'' and twenty-three million acres of former Indian lands were opened for settlement. He believed the policy for the Sioux tribe was succeeding, even though dreadful mistakes had been made at Wounded Knee. Harrison's views toward the Indian problem were much like those of the Indian Rights Association, which had a strong advocate in Commissioner Morgan.

By late 1891, Harrison was cutting down on all invitations outside Washington. Extra burdens in the executive office required longer hours, Caroline's health was a grave concern, and his other activities consumed all of his energy. His response to an invitation to attend the annual dinner of the New England Society in New York City was: ''I am tired out. Never before have I understood what the old proverb of the last straw on the camel's back meant but I now have a full realization of it.'' He continued the onerous duties of the president, but the fire was no longer there. To a former senator friend, Harrison wrote: ''The sudden death of Senator Plumb, who had been in my office in apparent

fullness of health a day or two ago, has thrown a gloom over all of us."
Most of the president's correspondence at this time was pessimistic.[36]

Much of Harrison's domestic program during his last two years as
president languished, but it could not be repealed as long as the Senate
was in Republican hands. The times were no longer working to his
advantage. The series of crises that affected his administration, in
combination with the resignation of Blaine and the problems that came
after his renomination in 1892, left him a distant and aloof leader of the
Republican party. Because of his small presidential staff and his personal
characteristic of managing his own affairs, he had one crisis after
another. He did not have time to be a crisis manager; his only option
was to solve in some way his current problem. Too frequently, crises
overwhelmed Harrison's administration and reduced its effectiveness.
These crises did not adversely affect the functioning of the navy and the
army. In spite of his worn-out condition, Harrison could take justifiable
pride in the accomplishments of his administration in increasing the
readiness of the armed forces.

6

★ ★ ★ ★ ★

THE STEEL NAVY
AND THE NEW ARMY

The census of 1890 would indicate that the United States had a population of almost sixty-three million living in some three million square miles of territory. Yet, as the nation entered the 1890s, it had neither a regular army nor a navy capable of defending the vast territory and the rapidly growing population against any of the great powers. The status of the United States as a naval power, at least, already was in the process of changing dramatically. But a very small army which seemed to have only two duties—fighting Indians and preserving public order in certain instances of labor unrest—remained unchanged as a nonexistent factor in world affairs over the quarter-century preceding the Spanish-American War.

The United States had made the decision to build a modern navy in 1883. Not until the early 1880s had Congress come to grips with the post–Civil War deterioration of the fleet. The United States had no warships worthy of the name and had too many naval officers with no assigned duty. By 1882 the navy had one officer for every four enlisted men. The first step, then, was to set a limit on the number of officers at each rank—including only one vice-admiral and one admiral—in August 1882. With the retirement of Vice-Adm. Stephen C. Rowan at the age of eighty in 1889 and with the death of Adm. David Dixon Porter at the age of seventy-seven in 1891, the top two ranks were abolished for the immediate future.

The navy had been allowed to stagnate during the 1870s, while a few lonely voices in Congress argued that a modern naval force was essential for the implementation of foreign-policy objectives. During the 1880s, however, the nation rediscovered both the commercial and the strategic potential of a modern fleet. A consensus did not yet exist on the need for an offensive force including battleships, but more Americans had been persuaded that without a powerful navy, the nation could not flourish in the competitive world atmosphere of the decade.

Much of the credit for the revival of interest in a modern fleet must go to those junior officers who linked their careers to the status of the navy and conducted a very successful educational campaign throughout the 1880s. They "aggressively strove to change the attitude of Congress and the public regarding the part the Navy played in national life." Their campaign stressed the role of the navy in developing business opportunities abroad—but they did not hesitate to talk as well about the need to control the seas. Naval officers agreed about the importance in particular of the Pacific and any future Central American canal.

The junior officers quickly found support from those in the upper echelons of the navy's command structure. And the most eloquent spokesman for the cause of naval expansion, Capt. Alfred Thayer Mahan, had established his reputation by 1890 with the publication of a classic study, *The Influence of Sea Power upon History, 1660-1783*. This brilliant naval historian emphasized the absolute necessity of constructing an isthmian canal—and a navy large enough to protect such a canal. According to Mahan, the canal—and the navy—would then require the acquisition of bases in the Caribbean and the annexation of Hawaii. Mahan predicted that the international rivalry for markets and raw materials would prove the need for adequate sea power. Mahan's ideas received the enthusiastic endorsement of the Harrison administration. The result: "By 1890 . . . America began to demand a place in the sun." That objective could not be fulfilled without a modern navy.

Congress first responded in March 1883, authorizing the construction of the first three steel cruisers—the *Atlanta*, the *Boston*, and the *Chicago*. The *Chicago* was the largest of the ships, at just forty-five-hundred-tons displacement—but the three small vessels became the nucleus of the new navy. Another important turning point soon followed with the opening of the Naval War College—a postgraduate school for naval officers—at Newport, Rhode Island, in October 1884. Congress also approved the construction of five additional similar-sized cruisers, two larger cruisers, and two second-class battleships beginning in 1885.[1] But the new navy was barely off the drawing board when the Harrison administration came into office. By the time Harrison left the White House, the United States was well on its way toward naval stature in world affairs. The contributions of the Harrison administration cannot be exaggerated.

As of 4 March 1889 the new navy consisted only of the *Atlanta* and the *Boston* in commission. In his Inaugural Address, Harrison immediately called for much more—a commitment to become a naval power: the "construction of a sufficient number of modern warships and of their necessary armament should progress as rapidly as is consistent with care and perfection."[2] Less than two weeks later, the nation was stunned by the loss of three ships of the old navy—almost 10 percent of all ships available—in a devastating storm that hit Samoa. Casualties numbered fifty men and officers, and the navy lost its only important vessel built before the 1880s—the *Trenton.* At thirty-nine-hundred-tons displacement, the iron-hulled cruiser had been commissioned in 1879.[3] Its loss seemed to prove how fragile was the nation's navy on the eve of the 1890s.

Republican leaders clearly began to shape public opinion in support of building a formidable fleet. For many, it was an idea whose time had come, as well as an undertaking that could eliminate the embarrassing surplus in the federal budget. William Walter Phelps, who served Harrison as minister to Germany, used the occasion of his Phi Beta Kappa address at Harvard on 6 July 1889 to declare a national goal in no uncertain terms: "A navy should be created that would leave nothing to fear from any other naval power."[4]

The key figure in molding a national consensus on the issue was Harrison's secretary of the navy, Bvt. Brig. Gen. Benjamin Franklin Tracy. The secretary provided dynamic leadership; he also put in place a team that played a vital role in establishing an atmosphere conducive to the development of a powerful navy. The first step came in August 1889, when Tracy indicated his enthusiastic support for the Naval War College by restoring Captain Mahan to the presidency of that institution. Mahan had been president between 1886 and 1888, when the future of the Naval War College was very uncertain.[5]

Tracy wasted no time. He quickly gave those in favor of naval expansion something to work with. The *Chicago* at last became available in 1889, and he immediately joined it to the *Atlanta* and the *Boston* to create the symbolically designated Squadron of Evolution. The ships sailed as a unit for the first time in November and were on display all along the Atlantic coast. Before the end of the year, Rear Adm. John G. Walker, in command, informed Tracy about a typical reception: "The visit of the Squadron to Boston was most gratifying. From all sources were heard expressions of satisfaction that the United States has again taken a position as a naval power."[6]

As the squadron sailed on its maiden voyage, Tracy presented his first annual report to the nation. It had historic impact. He warned that the completion of all current naval construction would still leave the United States with the twelfth-ranked navy in the world. Tracy therefore insisted that the nation had to begin building battleships. He maintained that the United States needed no less than twenty such ships to protect both the Atlantic-Gulf and Pacific coasts. In December, as though on cue, Senator Eugene Hale introduced a bill providing for the construction of eight battleships.[7] This set the stage for a year filled with both triumph and tragedy for the secretary of the navy.

In January 1890, Tracy began a vigorous campaign to win broad support for what would be a massive undertaking in naval construction. To enthusiastic applause, Tracy told an audience in his home base of Brooklyn, New York: "Battleships can protect cities and pursue and punish the enemy. The only navy that can protect us from war is a navy capable of waging war."[8] At the very same time, however, the Naval Policy Board, which had been set up by Tracy, recommended a building program that shocked even the secretary of the navy. If accepted, the board's recommendations would have given the United States a navy second in rank only to that of Great Britain.[9] Publicity surrounding the proposals produced a potentially serious setback to Tracy's ambitions at the worst possible time.

The *New York Tribune* reported on 4 February about a devastating fire that had swept Tracy's home in Washington. The fire caused the deaths of Mrs. Tracy, their younger daughter, and a maid; the secretary of the navy barely survived. He suffered burns and required artificial respiration, which the president helped administer to the stricken member of his cabinet. Harrison then had Tracy moved into the White House to begin a long convalescence.[10]

Meanwhile, the chairman of the House Naval Affairs Committee, Charles Boutelle, was forced to compromise on the number of battleships. He faced formidable opposition, fueled by the recommendations of the Policy Board, to the concept of a navy that would have other than defensive purposes. Thus, Boutelle proposed that just three coastline battleships be constructed and emphasized their defensive nature. Republican control of both the House and the Senate then assured quick passage of the Naval Act of 1890 on 30 June.

As it turned out, Congress had approved three battleships that compared favorably with any ships afloat in the world at the time. The *Indiana,* the *Massachusetts,* and the *Oregon,* at more than ten-thousand-tons displacement, opened an entirely new era in naval construction. Congress also authorized another large cruiser, the *Columbia,* at seventy-three-hundred-tons displacement.[11] Passage of the legislation proved excellent medicine for the recovering secretary of the navy, but he now had to resolve a lingering problem which hampered the entire building program.

During Tracy's first year in office, two more cruisers, the *Baltimore* and the *Charleston*, joined the fleet. And he would have two more, the *Philadelphia* and the *San Francisco*, to work with before the end of 1890. But the total of seven small cruisers that were then in service represented the absolute potential of the new navy, unless Tracy could obtain armor in the quantity needed to complete the larger ships that had been authorized since 1886. For instance, of the two second-class battleships, at sixty-six-hundred-tons displacement, approved in 1886, the doomed *Maine* was not launched until November 1890; the *Texas* would not be launched until June 1892.[12] The two small battleships would not be commissioned until the mid 1890s.

In June 1887, Bethlehem Steel had agreed to provide fourteen thousand tons of armor for the new ships. Production had not yet started by the end of 1889. When Bethlehem did begin deliveries in 1890, neither the quantity nor the quality of the armor satisfied the secretary of the navy. Technology was advancing at a very rapid rate. First, Tracy learned that the British were developing armor made of a nickel-steel alloy. This was soon followed by a major breakthrough: the manufacture of hardened, or Harvey-ized (named for inventor of the process, Augustus Harvey), nickel-steel.

Increasingly desperate, Tracy turned to the Republican stalwart Andrew Carnegie, who appeared to be totally uninterested in what was an experimental situation involving great risk. Perhaps Tracy managed to kindle the steel magnate's patriotism. If so, the terms, worked out in lengthy negotiations, were at least as important for Carnegie. The end result was an oral agreement with Carnegie in August 1890, which was put in writing in November. Carnegie promised to deliver six thousand tons of armor. He then went to work with characteristic energy. By March 1891, Carnegie could boast to his close friend Secretary of State James G. Blaine: "Yesterday's tests of our armor-plate at Annapolis will no doubt receive the earnest consideration of the foreign ministers at Washington. The results . . . are without parallel in the history of armor . . . nickel plate with hardened face containing 50 per cent . . . carbon proved invulnerable."[13]

Despite the lingering effects of the tragic fire, Tracy had prevented a serious interruption in naval construction. Meanwhile, the definitive justification of the naval revolution in progress appeared in mid 1890 with publication of Captain Mahan's study *The Influence of Sea Power upon History, 1660–1783.* Those who favored naval expansion seemed to be gaining momentum. At about the same time, Tracy added another eloquent voice to the expansionist team. Because Tracy was not yet back to full strength, he told the president that he needed an assistant secretary of the navy. Harrison agreed, and Congress funded the position for the first time since the Civil War.

Tracy then chose an outstanding academic, Prof. James R. Soley, then only thirty-nine years old, who had graduated from Harvard in 1870 and had started teaching at the Naval Academy the following year, when barely twenty-one years old. He soon became chairman of English, history, and law at Annapolis and also held a commission in the naval corps of professors of mathematics. When the Naval War College opened in the mid 1880s, Soley joined the faculty to teach international law. He added to his impressive credentials by obtaining a law degree in 1890, as he was preparing to make a significant contribution to the cause of naval expansion.[14] He could not have imagined how quickly the cause would seem to be in danger of complete collapse.

When Tracy issued his second annual report at the end of 1890, he may have surprised some readers by insisting that twelve battleships, a significant decrease from the twenty that he asked for just one year before, would be enough to defend the interests of the United States.[15] But the report came out in the aftermath of the debacle of the 1890 congressional elections. While the fate of the new navy was not strictly a partisan issue, Tracy and other naval expansionists had feared that the Democrats would gain control of the House of Representatives in 1890. If that happened, the building program might be curtailed or even brought to a halt. Their worst-case scenario then developed, a landslide that left only 88 Republicans in the next Congress, to face 235 Democrats and 10 Populists.

A letter, written by Charles Henry Davis of the Office of Naval Intelligence in February 1891, perfectly expressed the gloomy outlook of the naval expansionists for the immediate future: "I myself believe that the naval boom in this country is at an end or nearly so. The next Congress which is Democratic is hardly likely to authorize anything more than a few 'gunboats' . . . and if the Farmers' Alliance people get on top good-bye to the Navy and everything else which makes the country decent and creditable."[16] Indeed, all signs pointed to a rather abrupt end to naval expansion.

Only one more small cruiser, the *Newark*, joined the new navy in 1891. As it turned out, it was the last cruiser to be commissioned during Harrison's administration. The navy, which included less than 10,000 enlisted men and officers when Harrison took office in 1889, was reduced to about 9,250 personnel by 1891. Meanwhile, in the two years between June 1890 and July 1892, Congress authorized the construction of only one cruiser, the *Minneapolis*. This sister ship to the *Columbia* was approved by the outgoing Congress on 2 March 1891 and did represent an important addition to the new navy.[17] However, the secretary of the navy, of course, wanted much more.

Tracy therefore launched another campaign in 1891, speaking and writing about the ships under construction in an effort to put pressure on Congress. In April he spoke to the Republican Club of Massachusetts, predicting that the battleships would be ready for duty in three years, but his message concentrated on the larger cruisers. Tracy boasted that the not-yet-completed *New York*, which had been approved in the late 1880s as the largest and most powerful cruiser in the new navy at eighty-two-hundred-tons displacement, would have enough speed to overtake 95 percent of the ships in existence. He pointed with pride to the two cruisers approved during the Harrison administration— the *Columbia* and the *Minneapolis*, which would have an effective range of some twenty-five thousand miles. It was estimated they could stay at sea for about 103 days. In June, Tracy contributed an article on the new navy to the *North American Review*. He emphasized the unique qualities—the power, range, and speed—of the battleships and cruisers that had been approved during Harrison's administration.[18] The message was obvious: the revolution must not be terminated.

Tracy then presented his third annual report at the end of 1891. He called on Congress to authorize two more battleships and a cruiser as powerful as the *New York*. The president heartily endorsed Tracy's request. In his third annual message in December, Harrison urged: "There should be no hesitation in promptly completing a navy of the best modern type large enough to enable this country to display its flag in all seas."[19]

Tracy did not let up. Early in 1892, while speaking to the Young Men's Republican Club in Providence, Rhode Island, he regretted that Congress had not yet authorized a cruiser similar to the *New York*. He warned that if the current Congress did not act, no new ships could be authorized until at least mid 1894.[20]

The Senate, which was still under Republican control by a comfortable margin, finally prevailed over the reluctant House of Representatives in July 1892. Congress approved only two ships, but those represented yet-another major breakthrough in naval construction. The first seagoing battleship was the *Iowa*, at eleven-thousand-four-hundred-tons displacement, which could no longer be disguised as primarily defensive in purpose. To complement this formidable warship and to add to the offensive power of the new navy, Congress authorized the construction of a cruiser even larger than the *New York*. Tracy had to feel special satisfaction; at ninety-three-hundred-tons displacement, appropriately, it was named the *Brooklyn*.[21]

The Harrison administration left the nation a naval legacy. Before the Spanish-American War in 1898, ten truly modern warships turned the United States into a legitimate naval power. Seven of those—four battleships and three large cruisers—were authorized during Harrison's administration. And three—the *Maine*, the *Texas*, and the *New York*—might never have been completed without Tracy's determination to maintain the momentum of naval construction. Thanks largely to the efforts of Tracy, the nation's navy had advanced a generation almost overnight. By the standards of the new navy in 1893, the *Atlanta*, the *Boston*, and the *Chicago* already seemed to be antiques.

Captain Mahan, who enhanced his reputation with two important publications in 1892—a biography, *Admiral Farragut*, and a two-volume study, *The Influence of Sea Power upon the French Revolution and Empire, 1793–1812*—took the time to acknowledge his personal debt to Secretary of the Navy Tracy. In October 1892, Mahan wrote to Tracy: "I send you my 'Life of Farragut' just published. If I have succeeded in a competent military biography, I owe the power to do so to my study of the past few years and to my prolonged connection with the [Naval War] college. For both I have to thank you." Less than two months later, Mahan added: "My publisher sent you a copy of my forthcoming book on the French Revolutionary period. That I have been able to complete it is due wholly to your support . . . I may say even to your protection."[22]

Both Tracy and Harrison did their best to keep the building program alive in the years to come. In his final annual report at the end of 1892, Tracy specifically called on Congress to approve another seagoing battleship. And Harrison stirred the patriotism of the nation with an eloquent plea in his fourth annual message:

> I earnestly express the hope that a work which has made such noble progress may not now be stayed. The wholesome influence for peace and the increased sense of security which our citizens . . . in other lands feel when these magnificent ships . . . appear is already most gratefully apparent. The ships from our Navy which will appear in the great naval parade next April in . . . New York will be a convincing demonstration . . . that the United States is again a naval power.[23]

After a brief delay caused by the devastating depression in 1893/94, Congress approved the construction of five more seagoing battleships—

the *Kearsarge,* the *Kentucky,* the *Alabama,* the *Illinois,* and the *Wisconsin*—in 1895/96. Then, after the destruction of the *Maine* in February 1898, Congress authorized the construction of three even-more-powerful battleships at twelve-thousand-five-hundred-tons displacement—the *Missouri,* the *Ohio,* and a second *Maine.* At the end of 1889, Tracy had warned that the United States would remain the twelfth-ranked naval power in the world unless it built battleships. Before the end of the century, with a new empire to defend, the United States already had the sixth-most-powerful navy, behind Great Britain, France, Russia, Italy, and Germany.[24] In the early twentieth century, amidst increasing concern about the intentions of both Germany and Japan, the navy of the United States was soon vying with France and Germany for second place behind Great Britain, thereby fulfilling the outrageous recommendations made in 1890 by Tracy's Naval Policy Board.

The memoirs of John M. Schofield, who became commanding general of the army in 1888 and continued in that capacity throughout the Harrison administration, provide revealing details on the status of the army as late as 1886. According to Schofield, there were sixty-six posts in the Division of the Atlantic, stretching from the Canadian border to the Gulf of Mexico. Only twenty-seven of the posts had garrisons, and fifteen of those had no armaments. Furthermore, the existing armaments were muzzleloaders, and artillery practice was held on a regular basis at only three posts. Schofield himself symbolized the declining prestige of the late-nineteenth-century army. When William Tecumseh Sherman had become commanding general in 1869, he had received a fourth star. His successor, Philip H. Sheridan, had taken command in 1883 but had remained a lieutenant general—with three stars. He did not receive the fourth star until just before his death in 1888. Schofield was commanding as a major general—with only two stars; he did not receive a third star until he was ready to retire in 1895.[25]

The trend seemed clear: the United States, unconcerned about outside enemies, had dismantled its army as quickly as possible after the Civil War. Who would have imagined, however, that the army that had been established in 1866 at an authorized strength of less than fifty-five thousand officers and men would be only half that size twenty-five years later? The new, leaner army was, nevertheless, unique in several ways. Four of the forty-five infantry regiments and two of the ten cavalry regiments that had been established in 1866 were reserved for black soldiers. At the same time, Congress had approved the use of one thousand Indian scouts. The organization of the army, including five

103

artillery regiments, remained basically the same even as it dwindled in size.

First, Congress sharply reduced the number of infantry regiments to twenty-five in 1869, including the consolidation of the four black regiments into two; then, in 1874, the size of the army was set at just twenty-five thousand enlisted men plus officers. The massacre of George Armstrong Custer and his entire command in 1876 led Congress to authorize a temporary increase of twenty-five hundred in the cavalry. The number of Indian scouts, which had been cut to three hundred in 1874, briefly was increased to one thousand again, then was cut back to three hundred in 1877. But more typical of Congress was the failure to renew the budget of the army before funds ran out in both 1877 and 1879.

The irony, of course, in the numbers game is that the army never reached its authorized strength. With a starting pay of just thirteen dollars per month as of June 1871, which had been reduced from sixteen dollars per month, many privates soon reconsidered their five-year enlistments. Huge numbers deserted the army in the late nineteenth century—three-quarters doing so during their first year of service.[26]

Through it all, the army continued the inexorable campaign against the Indians. Resistance on the southern plains—the area of the Texas panhandle and Oklahoma—had ended by 1874. At about the same time, however, the Indians prepared for a long last stand farther north, in the Dakotas, Montana, Wyoming, and Idaho, and in the Southwest—Arizona and New Mexico. During the late 1870s, the army encountered and forced into submission a series of legends—Crazy Horse, Sitting Bull, and Chief Joseph—in the vast expanse of the northern plains and the intermountain West. As the nation moved into the 1880s, only the elusive Apaches—first under Victorio, then under their own legend, Geronimo—remained at large in the Southwest. They routinely used Mexico as a refuge, and the army just as routinely crossed into Mexican territory.[27]

Finally, in the 1880s, the army began to effect changes that would have long-range impact. In 1881, new recruits were required to go through four months of formal basic training, while specialized training for infantry and cavalry was offered at Fort Leavenworth. At the other end of the spectrum, something had to be done with an aging officer corps, dating back to the Civil War, which stifled the ambitions of younger colleagues. A start was made in 1882, when all officers were forced to retire at the age of sixty-four.[28]

Meanwhile, after the surrender of Sitting Bull in 1881, only Geronimo was causing any problems by the mid 1880s. He, too, surrendered in March 1884, though he left the reservation again in May 1885 and eluded the army until September 1886. The era of the Indian wars at last seemed to be over.

During the Harrison administration, then, the time had come to concentrate on a fundamental change in the army—the focus was on the enlisted man. For the record, the army still had only 27,759 officers and men in 1889. That figure may have appeared more than adequate, however, because the number of forts in the West had declined from 111, in 1880, to 82, in 1889, and would be down to 62 by 1891. The increased mobility of forces, made possible by the rapid development of the railroads in the West, rendered many forts obsolete. For instance, when Harrison responded to urgent calls for Regular Army units to help restore order in the Coeur d'Alene mining district of Idaho in July 1892, the army was able to rush about eight hundred men—both infantry and cavalry—by rail from Montana and Washington within a day or two. Some three thousand striking miners, who had been locked out for more than three months, had attempted to drive out the scabs. The presence of troops, however, quickly broke the back of the strike—a typical outcome of late-nineteenth-century labor disputes. But with 25,582 enlisted men, the army's desertion rate in 1889 remained high, at 11.1 percent.[29]

Secretary of War Redfield Proctor, who had served as a colonel in the Civil War, remained in Harrison's cabinet until November 1891. At the end of his term, a contemporary observed: ''Perhaps no epoch in the history of the army has been so fraught with innovations as the past two years.'' Indeed, ''no secretary of war had done as much as he to better the living conditions of the soldiery.'' With the full support of Bvt. Brig. Gen. Benjamin Harrison, Proctor began immediately to revise the entire approach toward the enlisted man. Clearly, one thrust was to improve the quality of personnel. Beginning in October 1889, the army instituted a six-day probation period for recruits—time for an extensive background check to weed out undesirables. At the same time, the administration supported legislation that would have created two additional artillery regiments. The bill failed, as it did again in 1890, perhaps because the army intended to include black soldiers in at least one of the regiments.[30]

While rumblings about a religious revival on the northern plains— the most visible evidence of which was the ''Ghost Dance''—revived memories of the Indian wars in 1889/90, Congress was extremely cooperative in effecting a variety of fundamental reforms for enlisted personnel in June 1890. A significant improvement in diet was designed to make army life more attractive. At the same time, new regulations made it possible for an enlisted man to buy his way out of the army after one year of service, an offer that made it even more difficult to maintain the army at full strength. After three years, any soldier was entitled to a three-months' furlough—and discharge, if he so desired. Congress also paved the way for the most important single improvement in late-nineteenth-century army life. In September 1890, it authorized the president to put limits on the harsh sentences that were routinely being handed down by military courts for peacetime infractions.

Even before a new code had gone into effect, the desertion rate had dropped to 9.3 percent in 1890. But with the number of enlisted personnel down to 25,205 and continuing to decline, Congress offered an experimental solution to a possible shortage of manpower. In what might be considered a conciliatory gesture toward the Indians, or a symbol of a new enlightened attitude in the 1890s, Indians could now enlist in the army and were no longer limited to the special status of scout. The experiment proved to be short-lived, however, and all Indians had been released by 1897.[31]

Change came to the officer corps as well. Beginning in 1890, to make it easier for younger officers to move up, promotions were awarded within the branch of service (infantry, cavalry, artillery), and not on a regimental basis. Furthermore, all promotions through the rank of major would depend on more than the right connections; candidates had to pass required examinations. Finally, Congress endorsed an important change in the War Department itself, creating the position of assistant secretary of war. Proctor then made an excellent choice in April 1890—a fellow Vermont native, Lewis Addison Grant, a twice-wounded hero who had earned the rank of brevet major general during the Civil War. He was to receive the Congressional Medal of Honor in 1893.[32] The choice seemed to be an obvious bid to appease the top commanders of the army, who could never reconcile themselves to taking orders from the typical civilians at the War Department.

In December 1890, almost halfway through the Harrison administration, the Battle (or Massacre) of Wounded Knee revived painful memories of the Indian wars. In 1890 the Teton Sioux turned militant under the influence of the "Ghost Dance." By November, about six hundred troops were on the Pine Ridge and Rosebud reservations in South Dakota; the stage was set for one last tragedy of the Indian wars. December brought the death of Sitting Bull in a clash with authorities on the Standing Rock reservation. Then Big Foot and his followers left the Cheyenne River reservation for Pine Ridge. They camped about twenty miles from the Pine Ridge agency, and the inevitable battle took place on 29 December. At least 146 Indians were killed, including 44 women and

18 children, while 25 soldiers died, ironically from the same Seventh Cavalry that Custer had led to slaughter.[33]

Harrison was concerned and quickly sought information. The commanding general told Maj. Gen. Nelson Miles in South Dakota that the president had "heard with great regret of the failure of your efforts to secure the settlement of the Sioux difficulties without bloodshed. . . . He hopes that the report of the killing of women and children in the affair at Wounded Knee is unfounded, and directs that you cause an immediate inquiry to be made and report the result to the [War] Department. If there was any unsoldierly conduct, you will relieve responsible officers, and so use the troops engaged there as to avoid its repetition."[34] General Miles responded with an explanation that satisfied the president.

Soon there were some thirty-five hundred soldiers concentrated in the area, with two thousand more ready to move in if necessary. Complete pacification was achieved in mid January 1891. An era had ended. On 19 January 1891, Harrison described the affair at Wounded Knee as "very bloody" and declared that he had followed it "very closely, and kept a pretty strong hand on the Indian matter. It is a great gratification to know that it has been closed so speedily."[35] The Indians were now helpless, however, and were totally dependent on the federal government. A short time later, Harrison received information from the War Department that General Miles was opposed to "permitting the Indians from Fort Sheridan to leave the country with Mr. W. F. Cody." The primary concern was that the extravaganza known as Buffalo Bill's Wild West would exploit the Indians and leave them stranded in a foreign land.[36]

The momentum of army reform had not been interrupted. At the end of February 1891, Harrison issued the new code of regulations for peacetime courts-martial to go into effect in thirty days. The emphasis was clear: with the exception of repeat offenders, leniency proved to be the order of the day. As an example, the absolute maximum sentence for desertion—if the soldier had been involved in a conspiracy or had deserted during an Indian uprising—would be five years in prison at hard labor. For up to twenty-four hours of absence without leave, punishment consisted only of a fine. The maximum punishment for an AWOL offense—one that lasted more than ninety days—was three months of hard labor and a dishonorable discharge.[37]

The new code had a dramatic effect in 1891 as the desertion rate dropped to 6.2 percent; the number of enlisted personnel, however, was down to 24,411. Thus, while the reform movement continued in 1892 under the new secretary of war, Stephen B. Elkins, there was a simultaneous move to prevent the further erosion of an army that was already below the strength established back in the mid 1870s. A significant incentive for a few enlisted personnel stipulated that a bachelor under the age of thirty, with two years of service, could now apply to be considered for a commission. Some of those who had no such ambitions, however, undoubtedly were dismayed to learn that they no longer could buy their way out of the army after one year; the option was raised to a year and a half.

In 1892, enlisted strength crept back up to 25,050; and the desertion rate—5.5 percent—was less than half of what it had been when the Harrison administration came into office. But then came a shock for the relatively small number of enlisted men who made the army a career: Redfield Proctor, who left the cabinet to represent Vermont in the Senate, introduced an amendment to the army budget in February 1893 to develop an army of younger, presumably more physically fit, fighting men. The amendment applied only to peacetime but said, for instance, that the army would not accept any enlistees over the age of thirty (the age limit had previously been thirty-five). The section that had the most impact, however, dealt with reenlistments. Unless a private had been in the army for at least twenty years, hoping to retire after thirty years, he could not reenlist after ten years of service or if he was over the age of thirty-five.

Many felt betrayed. And when the army then completely abandoned the experiment of allowing soldiers to buy their way out, there was only one alternative for those soldiers. While the enlisted strength of the army climbed above what it had been in 1889—to 25,672—the desertion rate rose to 6.6 percent. Because of the obviously negative impact of the Proctor amendment, Congress rescinded it in 1894.[38]

Despite its good intentions, the Harrison administration had done little more than to preserve the status quo of the late-nineteenth-century army. There was no pressure to do more: the next military challenge for the United States—in Cuba and the Philippines—was still five years away. Meanwhile, the "new navy," which would bring Spain to its knees in 1898, had become the symbol of the nation's might.

7

★ ★ ★ ★ ★

BLAINE AND THE
STATE DEPARTMENT

After an interruption of about seven years, James G. Blaine became secretary of state for the second time in March 1889. His presence provided President Harrison with a unique challenge, though Blaine had surprisingly little impact on the nation's foreign policy during the early 1890s.

Historians still debate what Blaine had accomplished—or had not accomplished—while secretary of state for President James A. Garfield in 1881. His influence extended beyond foreign policy during a first brief stint as head of the State Department. By appointing Blaine, Garfield hoped that he had found a premier for his administration. During his short-lived presidency, then, Garfield had developed a very close relationship with Blaine. David Pletcher, however, in the definitive work on the foreign policy of the early 1880s, has made it clear that Blaine's important initiatives all took place after he had become a lame duck with the death of Garfield on 19 September 1881. Until that time, Blaine had brought little glory to the nation or to his own reputation.

Charles S. Campbell has defended the traditional view of Blaine as being one of the most significant figures in the transformation of American foreign relations in the late nineteenth century. Campbell insists that Blaine, as early as 1881, had the vision of an American system—revolving around a Central American canal—that would include the Central American nations, the Caribbean, and Hawaii. Such an evaluation must be balanced against a recent study of the administrations of Presidents Garfield and Chester A. Arthur, which, while concentrating particularly on Blaine's various attempts to intervene in Latin American affairs, severely criticized his diplomacy: "It is difficult to conceive of more clumsy statecraft. His tenure in office was marked by showmanship and demagoguery, evincing little of the maturity needed for any 'large policy.' "[1]

Blaine may have been trying to reestablish his influence in the Republican party and to set himself up for the presidential nomination in 1884 when, in 1881, he made the moves that established his enduring reputation in the diplomatic history of the nation. On 19 November he made it clear to Great Britain that the United States was no longer satisfied with the Clayton-Bulwer Treaty, which covered the joint construction of a Central American canal. Blaine then issued invitations on 29 November for the first modern Pan-American Conference; on 2 December he launched a new initiative in an attempt to end the War of the Pacific, which was turning into a great victory for Chile over Peru and Bolivia; he concluded the three-weeks' flurry of activity with an unprecedented declaration on 10 December about the relationship between the United States and Hawaii. Blaine was out of office by 19 December.[2]

During the 1880s, Chile remained estranged because of Blaine's hostile interference in the War of the Pacific. On a more positive note, however, there was a legacy of continuing interest in a Central American canal, a Pan-American conference, and the status of Hawaii. Every one of these issues then confronted the Harrison administration. It has been easy, therefore, to discuss Blaine's foreign policy during the early 1890s. But this was the *Harrison* administration—and there was no premier.

When Harrison and Blaine took office, they had gone through Blaine's long wait to receive the notification of his appointment and an additional difference of opinion, which hit very close to home for the secretary of state. Blaine wanted his son Walker, who had been third assistant secretary of state in 1881, to serve as first assistant secretary of state. There is no existing record of exactly how the president refused Blaine's request, though obviously he did. Harrison may have decided that the State Department should not be turned into a family affair. In any case, Walker Blaine would not be first assistant secretary of state, as Whitelaw Reid would not be minister to Great Britain. Walker had to settle for a lesser post as examiner of claims in the State Department, from which he served as his father's right-hand man anyway.[3]

It was possible at that stage of his career for Blaine to ignore both developments. From all accounts, however, Mrs. Blaine would never either forgive or forget. She clearly did not accept the fact that Harrison had made it to the White House, while her husband had been deprived of the honor. Harrison had then insulted her son as well. It is difficult to comprehend the depth of her animosity toward the president. Both the memoirs of John Foster, who succeeded Blaine as secretary of state, and David S. Muzzey's classic biography of Blaine dealt with her bitter feelings for Harrison. But Albert T. Volwiler, who had talked to various contemporaries of the principals, faulted Muzzey for not coming to grips with the importance of Mrs. Blaine's jealousy and antipathy in regard to Harrison.[4] Before Harrison completed his term in office, Mrs. Blaine would feel that the president had wronged yet another member of her family, Col. John J. Coppinger, who had been married to her deceased daughter Alice.

Amidst all of the above, two aspects of the Harrison-Blaine relationship stand out. From the beginning of the administration, Blaine's health problems interfered with his performance, and Harrison moved in to play a major role in foreign policy. Foster's memoirs plainly described Blaine's second tour of duty at the State Department. According to Foster, the secretary of state obviously was in poor health and frequently was confined to his bed or his room for weeks at a time. As Foster explained it, he himself served unofficially as secretary of state between 1889 and 1892, when the president repeatedly consulted him because of Blaine's recurring attacks of illness and consequent inability to handle the work load of the State Department.[5]

Muzzey was blunt when evaluating the Blaine of the Harrison administration, compared to his previous service as secretary of state:

> It was a different Blaine who accepted the belated invitation of General Harrison to resume charge of the State Department in 1889. . . . The Blaine of 1889–1892 was not the herald of national policies, but the head of a department . . . under the limitations of a due recognition of subordination to a not too sympathetic chief and the handicap of an increasing uncertainty of health.[6]

Why then has Harrison's contribution to the foreign policy of the early 1890s remained fundamentally an afterthought in more than a half-century of historical literature? Julius W. Pratt provided the first hint about Harrison as early as 1936, when he wrote: "Whoever was chiefly responsible, the Harrison administration adopted an expansionist policy which, though barren of results, foreshadowed in its purposes the 'large policy' of 1898." Not until the early 1960s, however, did Walter LaFeber, in his major study of late-nineteenth-century foreign policy, amplify

Harrison's role with this statement: "Many of the administration's ambitious, expansive policies which have been ascribed to Blaine should in fact be more rightly credited to the President. Harrison has never received proper recognition as a creator of the new empire." Another important study in the mid 1960s recognized Harrison as the first president in the post–Civil War era who attempted to coordinate the strategic, diplomatic, and economic factors of United States foreign policy.[7]

Yet the image of a Harrison foreign policy still has to contend with the awesome shadow of James G. Blaine. The literature on Harrison has remained basically unchanged since 1940, when Volwiler published the collection of the correspondence between Harrison and Blaine, including an informative seventeen-page introduction, and a twelve-page article on the significance of the Harrison administration's foreign policy.

Volwiler provided only glimpses of the limitations on Blaine during the early 1890s. The volume of correspondence described, as Volwiler put it, "a transition from the most cordial friendship [with Harrison] to a cold rivalry approaching enmity." Volwiler briefly discussed the contrasting personalities of the two men; the difficulties that developed between them, including Harrison's delay in appointing Blaine as secretary of state; and the most significant aspect of their relationship, Blaine's declining health and his frequent inability to carry out the duties of his office. Volwiler, while tantalizing other historians with these details, revealed two unfortunate developments that would make it even more difficult for those who followed to achieve a real understanding of the role played by either Harrison or Blaine in the administration's foreign policy. Harrison's secretary, Elijah W. Halford, had kept a diary, which he had read to Volwiler and then burned! Furthermore, Volwiler learned that in 1891, Blaine had ordered Louis A. Dent, Blaine's secretary, to burn most of the secretary of state's personal papers.[8]

The literature on Blaine, however, includes two major works that, though they predate Volwiler's publications, have left a permanent impression. Alice Felt Tyler's invaluable book *The Foreign Policy of James G. Blaine* was written almost sixty years ago. The index contains a total of seven references to Harrison; she barely mentions his role in the formulation of policy. This is particularly surprising because Tyler wrote frankly of the situation facing Blaine in the early 1890s: "Mr. Blaine was, in the winter and spring of 1892, a sick man, a doomed man." There may not be much argument about Blaine's condition by 1892, but Tyler also acknowledged the steady deterioration of his health before he became secretary of state in 1889: "Mr. Blaine was not at any time during the next three years a well man." She then admitted that Harrison "was determined to keep a controlling hand on foreign affairs."[9]

Muzzey's biography of Blaine, which is more than a half-century old, similarly ignores the same contradictions. In analyzing the book for the *American Historical Review* in 1936, Volwiler quoted Muzzey: "It was Harrison, not Blaine, who outlined the [foreign] policy of the incoming Administration." Volwiler then claimed that Muzzey had lost sight of that observation. Volwiler added, "Blaine was a broken man by 1891."[10]

Modern scholars have filled in some of the details about the real Blaine in the Harrison administration. Blaine "was careless about attending Cabinet meetings and said they bored him. He was forgetful; the despair of the State Department." H. Wayne Morgan, who emphasized that Blaine suffered from Bright's disease, gout, and nervous headaches, added, "He seldom arrived at the State Department on time, and after the Pan-American Conference, the President and departmental staff increasingly conducted foreign affairs." At the same time, John Grenville and George Berkeley Young have explained the difficulty in trying to fix Harrison's place in the historical record: "We know little about Harrison beyond the bare bones of his career. . . . Success in American politics demanded discretion; Harrison was certainly discreet. He carefully covered the tracks of his path to power."[11]

Clearly, from the day he took office, Blaine leaned heavily on his son Walker. As early as April 1889, Mrs. Blaine acknowledged, "I suppose he [Walker] is about as hard worked a man as there is in Washington, but it pays to stand between his Father and the pressure." Blaine clearly informed the president that Walker was serving as at least acting assistant secretary when he said: "Walker is very much obliged for your kind invitation. But he can't leave the Dep't when I am absent and therefore asks permission to decline."[12] Where was Blaine? Generally, he was not with the president.

To the public, it may have seemed as though Harrison studiously avoided taking Blaine with him on any presidential trips. When Harrison left for New York on 28 April 1889 to attend the one hundredth anniversary of George Washington's inauguration, he took every member of the cabinet except Blaine. The obvious implication that Harrison did not wish to be overshadowed by Blaine does not apply in this case. Blaine was confined to his home with lumbago. When the *New York Times* wondered why Blaine did not even come to see the president off, it quoted Walker, who described his father's lumbago as still too severe to allow him to leave the house.[13] Less than two months in office, Harrison already had to contend with Blaine's incapacity.

Added to the chronic irritation of Blaine's various illnesses was a condescending attitude that the secretary of state occasionally displayed in communications with the president; he lectured the novice. For instance, in the early days of the administration, Blaine advised on the wording of a document that the president had prepared: "I venture always with diffidence to suggest any change in a paper by the president. But since I am asked let me suggest the following: 'gracious' & 'very gracious' & 'gratefully' are peculiarly English phrases of intense loyalty and may offend some American ears." It had to annoy Harrison when such lectures came from a secretary of state who informed him on 2 May 1889, "I . . . still am confined to the house with the most vicious and stubborn attack of lumbago."[14]

Blaine remained ill while the Harrison administration immediately confronted one of the critical issues of the 1890s—the future of the nation's influence in the Pacific. Almost as soon as Harrison took office, he faced a major diplomatic negotiation on the fate of Samoa. The United States, Germany, and Great Britain each had obtained the right to construct a naval base in that collection of islands in the distant Pacific. By the mid 1880s, the Germans had launched a campaign to establish a dominant position on or even exclusive control of the islands. Germany encouraged a native revolt against the king and supported a potential puppet monarch, Tamasese. The three powers tried but failed to work out a solution on the status of Samoa at the Washington Conference between 25 June and 26 July 1887. A crisis then developed, which remained unresolved as of 4 March 1889.

German naval vessels arrived late in 1887 and conducted open warfare against the king; Germany formally recognized Tamasese. However, a new claimant to the throne then led an uprising against Tamasese. The rebel Mataafa seemed to have gained control by late 1888—but in the process, his forces massacred a German detachment, killing twenty and wounding another thirty. The humiliated Germans threatened all-out war, and President Grover Cleveland sent three naval vessels, a clear message to Germany.

The United States had completed the construction of only two modern cruisers. But three vessels of the old navy—the Pacific flagship *Trenton,* along with the *Vandalia* and the *Nipsic*—at least showed the flag and indicated undiminished concern for the future of Samoa. Germany, clearly wanting to avoid a clash with the United States, on 21 January 1889 called for another conference to try to work out a settlement of Samoan affairs. On 5 February the United States agreed to attend the proposed conference, but the naval forces of the two nations continued to confront each other in Samoan waters. Cleveland sent three ships to indicate that the United States had no intention of withdrawing from Samoa; Brig. Gen. Benjamin Harrison was not likely to back down from the implications involved. Then came the devastating storm of 16 March, which eliminated the three American vessels and their German counterparts as factors in Samoa. The United States lost fifty men; and the sobered powers proceeded to another conference, in Berlin, beginning on 29 April.[15]

Harrison selected a distinguished bipartisan three-man delegation to represent the United States: two Republican stalwarts, John A. Kasson and William Walter Phelps, were joined by Democrat George H. Bates. The sixty-seven-year-old Kasson had represented Iowa in the House of Representatives on and off over three decades; he had gained diplomatic experience as minister to Austria-Hungary and to Germany. Phelps, forty-nine, was a Yale graduate and attorney whose career had paralleled Kasson's in that he had represented New Jersey in the House of Representatives and had served as minister to Austria-Hungary. Bates, forty-three, was also an attorney from Delaware and a close political ally of former Secretary of State Thomas Francis Bayard. Bates had investigated the Samoan situation for the Cleveland administration in 1886. The choice of Bates was particularly controversial because in April 1889, as the conference opened, he published an article in the *Century Magazine* in which he vigorously opposed Germany's position in Samoa.[16]

Blaine's instructions to the delegation carefully explained the importance of the American position in Samoa. He asserted that "our interest on the Pacific is steadily increasing; that our commerce with the East is developing largely and rapidly; and that the certainty of an early opening of an Isthmian transit from the Atlantic to the Pacific (under American protection) must create changes in which no power can be so directly or more durably interested than the United States."

It took just nine sessions for the three powers to determine the immediate future of Samoa. In a massive work on relations between the United States and Samoa, which was written more than a half-century ago, George H. Ryden examined blow by blow the details of the conference. But he also made it clear that Harrison had played a key role in deciding the status of the Pacific outpost, by taking a firm stand on almost every aspect of the negotiations. The president resisted Germany's wish to exclude Mataafa as a possible ruler unless the Germans also agreed to exclude Tamasese; he refused to consider any indemnity for Germany; and he opposed possible British control of the chief justice of Samoa, insisting that authority to fill the position be delegated to the neutral king of Sweden and Norway. The conference, which closed on 14 June, restored the king, but the participants also established a three-power protectorate, a first for the United States.[17] Harrison had not turned his back on the path that would lead toward empire in the Pacific.

Acknowledgment of Harrison's pervasive role in the negotiations has come from two important sources in the Blaine camp. Phelps, who would become Harrison's minister to Germany, had to admit to White-law Reid, minister to France, in August 1889: "24 hours before the treaty was signed it looked as if the Commissioners might need to wait there six months or to go home immediately with defeat. Harrison at the last minute made a slight concession—the only one of any kind that he made during the conference—and the result was the immediate birth of the Samoan treaty."[18]

Even Mrs. Blaine commented on Harrison's diligence in the matter, while revealing the inconvenience forced upon the president by Blaine's illness: "I found the President here going over the Samoan despatches with your Father . . . he was examining those despatches with care and great intelligence and though I am not drawn to him I cannot refuse him the homage of respect."[19]

As for Blaine at the time of the Berlin Conference, few contemporaries would have believed this description of the secretary of state: an old man, suffering from lumbago, he "chafed under the close supervision maintained by the President, who suspiciously scrutinized with a legal eye all correspondence, sometimes revising Blaine's instructions and frequently demanding minute changes of agreements reached by the commissioners."[20]

While Blaine remained at home with lumbago, he assured the president on 2 May that "in Samoan affairs we have thus far gained every point." The secretary of state took pride in the "tremendous concessions by the German Govt." and optimistically predicted: "The form of Government will be all we desire."[21] But Blaine had little to do with the outcome of the conference.

The *Washington Post* then advised the nation's capital on 14 July of rumors that Walker Blaine had been de facto secretary of state for two months. On the next day, the *New York Times* informed its readers of a rumor that Blaine had resigned. According to the *Times*, Blaine was having more bad days than good ones; his illnesses included lumbago, which kept him confined to his room for a fortnight. Taking note of the fact that Blaine would be on vacation until September, the *Times* speculated that the rest might enable him to continue in office. Incapacity, then vacation, seems to sum up the record of most of Blaine's first half-year as secretary of state. Harrison proved understanding, however; he even visited Blaine in Maine during August.[22] And the time away from Washington apparently did some good, because Blaine came back late in the year to make his most important contributions to the accomplishments of the Harrison administration. Blaine had enough left within himself for a last hurrah.

Congress had taken the initiative by 1888, authorizing President Cleveland to invite the Latin American nations to a Pan-American conference in Washington. Ironically, beginning in October 1889, Blaine then presided over the first modern Pan-American Conference, which was part of a comprehensive attempt by the Harrison administration to expand the nation's political and economic influence in Latin America. A specific goal was to replace Great Britain as the dominant economic force in Latin America. Blaine hoped to create among the nations of the hemisphere a new relationship, one based on peace and economics. As in the case of the Berlin Conference on Samoa, Harrison appointed an outstanding bipartisan ten-man delegation to represent the United States; he exercised particular care to include every section of the nation. The Republican chairman was sixty-three-year-old John B. Henderson, a distinguished attorney and former judge who had represented Missouri in the Senate while still a young man. Led by Republican steel magnate Andrew Carnegie, all of the other members of the group had impressive credentials.

The remaining Republicans chosen by Harrison were Cornelius N. Bliss of New York and Thomas Jefferson Coolidge of Massachusetts, each of whom was involved in textile interests; Morris M. Estee of California, who had served as chairman of the Republican National Convention of 1888; and fellow Hoosier Clement Studebaker. Harrison selected four Democrats: Henry Gassaway Davis, who was the father-in-law of Stephen Elkins and had represented West Virginia in the Senate for twelve years; Charles R. Flint of New York, who had business interests that included shipping to South America and some ability to understand and converse in Spanish; John F. Hanson of Georgia, who had interests in textiles and owned the *Macon Telegraph*; and William Henry Trescot of South Carolina, who once had served as assistant secretary of state and spoke fluent Spanish.[23]

The conference opened on 2 October, but the next day the delegates departed on a whirlwind tour of the industrial centers of the United States to see what this nation had to offer in modern economic development. They covered six thousand miles in forty-two days and returned to begin deliberations on 18 November. Except for a ten-day break over the Christmas holiday, they remained in session for five months, until 19 April 1890. The Harrison administration quickly realized, however, that the conference might accomplish very little: the first two months were spent on disputes over rules and procedures.

The United States presented an ambitious agenda. Harrison and Blaine hoped to make progress on such issues as arbitration among the nations of the hemisphere, the creation of a customs union and improved customs regulations, steamship communication, a common silver coin, and copyright and extradition laws. But the delegation from traditionally hostile Argentina was primarily responsible for creating an atmosphere of suspicion at every turn.[24]

Blaine's reputation in the development of foreign policy in the late nineteenth century has been built around the new departures that he launched during his first term as secretary of state in 1881, including the attempt to arrange a Pan-American conference at that time. It does not detract from his vision of what the United States could accomplish in the hemisphere to point out that the initial conference must be kept in perspective: the results were disappointing. The United States had accomplished very little. Harrison and Blaine could point only to the precedent for additional conferences in the future and the creation of the Bureau of the American Republics.[25] As it turned out, however, the failure to make any breakthrough in hemispheric relations convinced both Harrison and Blaine to pursue more vigorously another approach toward Latin America—commercial reciprocity.

In a memorandum prepared shortly after he left the White House, Harrison emphasized that the United States did not fail to reach its objectives because of any lack of effort by Secretary of State Blaine, who had died in January 1893. According to the former president, "In the conference of the American Republics Mr. Blaine did a very hard, successful and brilliant work." Indeed, the secretary of state had attended some forty-four of the seventy meetings of the conference.[26] Perhaps Harrison had not been unhappy to keep Blaine preoccupied for the second half year of his tenure at the State Department.

By the time the conference had ended, Blaine's life had been changed dramatically by an unbroken series of tragedies. First came the death of Melville G. Blaine, brother of the secretary of state, at the age of sixty-three. James G. Blaine, who was about to turn sixty, died just before his sixty-third birthday. Two devastating blows then jolted Blaine. Walker Blaine, the eldest child and his father's pride, died of pneumonia on 15 January 1890. The death of thirty-four-year-old Walker, a graduate of Yale (1876) and Columbia Law School (1878), left a grief-stricken father who was thus deprived of his most important assistant at the State Department. Blaine did not even have a chance to recuperate; less than three weeks later, his eldest daughter, Alice Blaine Coppinger, died on 2 February. Unbelievably, the thirty-year-old Alice had become ill at Walker's funeral and had never recovered.[27] Blaine's first two children were gone so quickly. The impact became apparent in the ensuing months.

Within a week of Alice's death, Harrison provided a revealing description of Blaine for Whitelaw Reid: "Mr. Blaine . . . seems to bear up with a fine courage, though at times when he is not engaged, his face is a very sad sight to look upon. Still he has . . . already taken up his work and I do not much fear that he will break down." In fact, Blaine apparently turned to work to forget, even though he reported once again to Harrison on 17 March that he was suffering from a little rheumatic attack.[28] He carried on for another few months; then his health seemed to deteriorate.

Through all the personal tragedy, Blaine went right from the Pan-American Conference to the fight for another important initiative in the hemisphere, the commercial reciprocity amendment to the McKinley Tariff of 1890. For a while, he had to devote what seemed to be his last reserve of energy to both issues; as early as February 1890, he launched a vigorous effort to convince the Ways and Means Committee of the House of Representatives to support reciprocity. The last Republican administration, that of President Arthur, had made a belated and unsuccessful effort to establish reciprocity as a policy in Latin America in 1883/84. Not one of the three treaties that had been negotiated—with Mexico, with Spain for Cuba and Puerto Rico, and with the Dominican Republic—ever went into effect. The House of Representatives stubbornly refused to approve the required enabling legislation in the case of Mexico; the Senate continued its traditional policy of having as little as possible to do with the Dominican Republic by simply ignoring the treaty with that Caribbean nation; and typically, incoming President Cleveland withdrew from the Senate the still-pending agreement covering Cuba and Puerto Rico.[29]

The Harrison administration attempted the most ambitious reciprocity program of the late nineteenth century and secured eight treaties in all—with Spain and the Dominican Republic once again; with Brazil; with Great Britain for its West Indian possessions and British Guiana; with Guatemala; with Nicaragua; with Honduras; and with El Salvador. The Harrison administration, realizing that the Pan-American Conference had not provided any means of increasing exports to Latin America, hoped to accomplish that objective through the reciprocity treaties.[30] Before Harrison and Blaine could implement this program, they had to wage an intensive campaign to persuade Congress of the need for reciprocity.

Walter LaFeber has vividly described the struggle to obtain reciprocity as the final great political effort of Blaine's career. At the same time, LaFeber insisted that the amendment had passed the Senate "principally because the President lobbied intensely for the proviso." LaFeber also emphasized that in the steaming Washington summer of 1890, "Harrison sweated through dinner parties and conferences planned to bring together congressmen chary of the reciprocity issue, while an ailing Blaine enjoyed the sea breezes at Bar Harbor [Maine]." The memoirs of John Foster, who would negotiate the reciprocity treaties, provide the foundation for acknowledging Harrison's crusade for reciprocity. Foster credited Harrison with quietly interfering to bring about a compromise and to ensure the inclusion of reciprocity in the McKinley Tariff. Under pressure, the Senate finally passed the amendment on 10 September. An even more reluctant House of Representatives then went along with the decision on 27 September.[31]

It is clear that more than two months in Maine in the summer of 1890 did not allow Blaine to bounce back as he had in 1889. Blaine, for instance, did not even attempt to undertake the complicated task of negotiating individual reciprocity treaties. According to John Foster, Blaine delegated that responsibility to him in October 1890 because of Blaine's health problems.[32] Foster went right to work with his customary efficiency.

The Harrison administration had a uniquely aggressive form of reciprocity to offer to the Latin Americans. The amendment allowed sugar, molasses, coffee, tea, and hides to be admitted duty-free into the United States. But the nations of the hemisphere were expected to respond with at least equal generosity or to face a reimposition of the duties on the five products. Brazil proved to be a convenient first target, based on the terms of the amendment; the South American giant exported a huge amount of coffee to the United States.

Foster admitted frankly in his memoirs that an agreement with Brazil served two purposes: it would be a test case to prove the viability of such treaties, and it could be used to coerce the Spanish into making a similar agreement for Cuba. Brazil was particularly vulnerable to pressure when a revolution in November 1890 left the future of the nation in doubt. And Foster put the pressure on in November. He warned that Brazil, which had sold 310 million pounds of coffee in the United States in 1890, would see that market jeopardized by a three-cent-a-pound duty under the terms of the amendment. In that case, Foster cautioned, Brazil could face serious competition from Mexico and the Central

American nations. On 5 February 1891, Brazil signed the first treaty, which went into effect on 1 April. The result was a greatly expanded market for agricultural products from the United States.[33]

As expected, Spain followed, signing a two-stage agreement on 31 July 1891. The first stage went into effect on 1 September; the second in July 1892. Andrew Carnegie, who recently had served the Harrison administration as a delegate to the Pan-American Conference, made a remarkable prediction about reciprocity and Cuba's future:

> Cuba was in an uproar in which all classes joined . . . [they wanted] freedom for Cuba to enter into reciprocity with the Republic or a request from Cuba to Washington that she be permitted to enter the Republic. . . . Cuba will hereafter be of as little good to Spain as Canada is to Britain, nay, may and probably will become the source of serious trouble and danger to Spain.[34]

While the Dominican Republic then fell into line on 1 August 1891, with a treaty that was to go into effect on 1 September, the remaining agreements came too late to have any real impact on trade during Harrison's administration. El Salvador approved what was only a provisional treaty on 31 December 1891, a final version of which was not completed until 27 December 1892; Great Britain signed for the West Indies on 1 February 1892, though British Guiana was not covered until 1 April; then Nicaragua, Honduras, and Guatemala all signed between March and May. The time element did not really matter, however; the effort soon turned into an exercise in futility. The Democrats gave the nation the Wilson-Gorman Tariff in mid 1894: they removed sugar from the list of duty-free products, thereby abrogating the Republican reciprocity treaties.[35]

Meanwhile, the correspondence between Harrison and Blaine that began with the summer of 1890 reveals an interesting mixture of Blaine's illnesses and a variety of other issues, all of which tried the patience of a president who frequently had to do double duty. Establishing a pattern, Blaine wrote to Harrison on 21 June, to request a position for a friend, and admitted, "There is nothing more distasteful to me than to solicit official favors from you." He then reported to the president on 30 June: "I had a chill yesterday and a violent fever. I am better today and able to do some work."[36]

While the two stood closer together in the battle for reciprocity than on any other issue facing the administration, Harrison was not the type to react too well when he received this advice from Blaine—resting at Bar

Harbor—in July: "May I hope that you will not consent to the throwing away of a hundred millions of sugar with nothing in return. . . . I want *you* first and last to keep Yourself and the Administration free from mistakes and especially from gigantic blunders." And the secretary of state persisted in a not so subtle questioning of the president's ability to win the struggle in Congress. Just five days later, Blaine advised Harrison: "I think it would be a mistake to make Agricultural products the *sole* basis for reciprocity on the Sugar question. . . . I think we ought to have the privilege of using both [agricultural and manufactured exports]—giving preference to farm products."[37] Their relationship was still amicable, however, and Harrison invited Blaine to join him at Cape May, New Jersey, in late July.[38] Did that visit make the secretary of state aware, however, that in contrast to the vigorous president, he would not be prepared to resume a full schedule in late 1890?

A very revealing exchange of letters between the president and the secretary of state in August provides important insight as to Blaine's state of mind at the time. He seemed all too well aware that the president could take over at any time. Blaine sent a warning to Harrison about a possibly important development in the continuing dispute with Great Britain over the seal herd in the Bering Sea:

> I think it will be found that the Right Honorable Joseph Chamberlain has quietly come to this country as an aid to Sir Julian [Pauncefote, British minister to the United States] in the Behring Sea controversy. . . . It will be an immense piece of presumption for him to do under false colors what even a Minister Plenipotentiary from England cannot do . . . viz: secure a personal interview with you. I write this to place you on your guard. If Mr. Chamberlain desires to converse on Foreign Affairs, I hope you will refer him to your Secretary of State.

Harrison merely answered: "I have not heard anything of Mr. Chamberlain's being in Washington. . . . You may be sure that I will not be entrapped into any reference to foreign affairs except as they proceed through your department." Harrison may not have given very serious thought to this exchange. While the secretary of state tried to protect what he regarded as his prerogative, he also told the president, "For several days after I last wrote you I was under the weather with a cold & a slight tendency to gout."[39]

Several studies of the contributions made by Secretary of the Navy Benjamin Tracy to the foreign policy of the early 1890s have pointed out that the former brevet brigadier general, who had lived at the White House while he was slowly recovering from the devastating house fire of February 1890, clearly replaced Blaine as Brevet Brigadier General Harrison's most influential advisor and confidant. Tracy would play a major role in the dispute with Chile in 1891/92, for instance. But months after the fire, Tracy still required lengthy rest periods at regular intervals, while he struggled to regain his strength.[40] Increasingly, Harrison was completely on his own. He would be very well prepared when the administration faced its most serious series of challenges in foreign affairs in 1891/92. Harrison would respond with an aggressive stance on every one of the situations where he took charge, possibly letting out his frustration over Blaine's condition and over Tracy's, as well as over the very unfavorable political climate that confronted the Republican party after the congressional elections of 1890.

In vain, the president left Washington for a grueling one-week tour of the Midwest early in October 1890. The highlight of the campaign swing came in an emotional reunion with the First Brigade, Third Division, Twentieth Army Corps in Galesburg, Illinois, on 8 October. Harrison had commanded the First Brigade, which included his Seventieth Indiana Regiment. Nevertheless, the Republicans suffered huge losses in those states where Harrison had campaigned—including four seats in the House of Representatives in Missouri, five in Kansas, seven in Illinois, and nine in Ohio—and many considered him a lame duck.[41] Then came Blaine's crippling physical collapse in 1891. Harrison suddenly had the opportunity to assume the uncontested control of foreign affairs. Harrison had recalled the glory days of his leadership when he spoke at Galesburg; he was about to assert that leadership once again.

Writing more than thirty-five years ago, Donald M. Dozer contributed an important speculation about the Harrison foreign policy that unfolded in 1891/92. Dozer wrote: ''There is good reason to believe that the more aggressive foreign policy which the Harrison administration adopted after 1890 was dictated largely by political considerations looking toward the Republican convention and the presidential election of 1892.'' Dozer then cited ''the firm position which Harrison took in the negotiations with Italy and Chile and his vigorous handling of the troublesome Behring Sea controversy with Great Britain during Blaine's illness in 1891 and 1892.''[42] Harrison's motivations may not be as significant as the results: the beginning of a new, more determined foreign policy for the United States. Indeed, in the Western Hemisphere—from the Bering Sea to the Pacific coast of South America—and on the continent of Europe itself, Harrison would establish an American presence that seemed entirely appropriate by the end of the nineteenth century.

8

★ ★ ★ ★ ★

HARRISON'S FOREIGN POLICY

In 1891, with Secretary of State James G. Blaine completely incapacitated, Benjamin Harrison seized the opportunity to put his imprint
on the nation's foreign policy. Just seven years later, the United States
would go to war with Spain and obtain an empire. While Harrison was
not an imperialist, in the sense that he did not seek territorial acquisi-
tions, he contributed an aggressive attitude, which seemed to signify
that the nation no longer would tolerate being taken lightly by any of the
world powers of the time.

Immediately, problems with three of the major European nations—
Great Britain, France, and Germany—and with one of the lesser
powers—Italy—came under the personal direction of the president after
Blaine's collapse. In each of these situations, as part of what represented
the most contact with Europe since the days of Secretary of State
William Henry Seward twenty years before, a tougher line quickly
became evident. At the same time, the president faced the most serious
single diplomatic problem of his administration in the Western Hemisphere, a crisis with Chile, which almost resulted in war. While war talk
with Great Britain remained simply speculation, the United States
actually was preparing for hostilities with Chile, should Harrison not
receive the satisfaction he demanded.

Harrison demonstrated repeatedly that he had little patience for
drawn-out diplomatic negotiations. With the support of an exceptionally
competent group of foreign-policy advisors, the president easily arrived
at his position in each dispute. Once there, Harrison left little room for

compromise. Instead, he relied on the ultimatum to achieve his objective.

The president worked closely with Secretary of the Navy Benjamin Tracy, particularly in the confrontations with Great Britain and Chile. On a day-to-day basis, Harrison could turn in full confidence to First Assistant Secretary of State William Wharton, who, more often than he could have imagined, would be forced to stand in for Blaine. But Wharton, a political appointment, was new to the State Department. For experience, Harrison came to rely on Second Assistant Secretary of State Alvey A. Adee, who had completed the first decade of what was to be almost a half-century at the State Department, and fellow Hoosier John Foster, a former minister to Mexico, Russia, and Spain. Foster did not accept an official position within the administration but left himself free to serve as an advisor to the president and as acting secretary of state before he replaced Blaine in mid 1892. Members of Harrison's team provided a definite direction for the nation's foreign policy during the early 1890s. They did not look back to the era of awkward, adolescent diplomacy. Led by the president, they represented a nation that had come of age.

An evaluation of Harrison's impact on the nation's foreign policy should emphasize the president's style, without overlooking his objectives. While Harrison definitely agreed with those who favored a ''large'' policy, including at least the construction of a Central American canal and the establishment of an increased presence in both Latin America and the Pacific, historians have correctly concentrated on how he pursued those goals. Harrison has been described, without exception, as vigorous, firm, belligerent, militant, and chauvinistic in the conduct of foreign policy. Clearly, the president stimulated the national self-assertion that led the United States inevitably toward the dramatic events of 1898.

In his third annual message on 9 December 1891, Harrison said to the people of the United States: ''The work of the State Department during the last year has been characterized by an unusual number of important negotiations and by diplomatic results of a notable and highly beneficial character.'' He did not, however, spell out his own role in the negotiations, a role that he would continue to develop in the presidential election year of 1892.

Harrison gave the appearance of having gone through a transformation in 1891. On 1 October, after he had failed to obtain the first Caribbean naval base for the United States in Haiti earlier in the year, he said to Blaine: ''You know I am not much of an annexationist; though I do feel that in some directions, as to naval stations and points of influence, we must look forward to a departure from the too conservative opinions which have been held heretofore.'' The same president who earlier in the year had refused to consider the Portuguese offer to establish naval bases in Portugal, in the Azores, and on both coasts of Africa would explain to Whitelaw Reid, minister to France, again in October: "I did not feel that it was very important for us to secure coaling stations for our men of war in either the European or African possessions of Portugal, but have regarded it as very important that in the West Indies, . . . [in the] Pacific islands, [and in] South America, we should have such stations.'' Finally, the same president who would have to face a decision on the annexation of Hawaii before he left office made his boldest statement on the subject, to Blaine, once again in October: "The necessity of maintaining and increasing our hold and influence in the Sandwich Islands is very apparent and very pressing."[1]

One could perhaps argue that the failure in Haiti helped to convince Harrison to take personal charge of foreign affairs. The chronic instability in Haiti produced a revolution in August 1888. A new government lasted only briefly, because two of its leaders—General Hyppolite and General Légitime—were soon fighting each other. President Grover Cleveland had remained neutral in the conflict. While Légitime held the South and the most important city of Port-au-Prince, Hyppolite controlled the North and one particular asset—Le Môle St. Nicolas naval base—which drew increasing attention to his cause once Harrison and Blaine had assumed the direction of foreign policy.

At the very least, the new administration did nothing to hurt Hyppolite. More importantly, the United States clearly helped to bring him victory by refusing to recognize a naval blockade proclaimed by Légitime. Hyppolite soon had the upper hand and took over the government in October 1889. Harrison and Blaine then decided to collect Le Môle St. Nicolas as payment for leaning toward Hyppolite during the short civil war. They moved quickly. The most distinguished black leader in the nation, Frederick Douglass, had taken his post as minister to Haiti by November. A year of preliminary sparring followed, however, until the Harrison administration emphasized the importance of the negotiations by sending Rear Adm. Bancroft Gherardi to join Douglass in January 1891.

The choice proved disastrous. Gherardi immediately expressed serious reservations about Douglass, describing him as too kind to the Haitians and hopelessly weak. Gherardi was blunt: the situation required an ''able, vigorous, aggressive white man'' as minister. Before the end of January, the admiral made it quite clear that he favored a hard line. As Gherardi put it, ''My main problem is the belief the United

States [would] never take the offensive." In April, as the negotiations collapsed, the United States had five naval vessels in Haitian waters and two more on the way, but Haiti called the bluff and did not give in.[2] In early 1891, Harrison could not bring himself to use force against Haiti, but by early 1892, he did not hesitate to consider doing so against Chile.

The failure in Haiti does not adequately explain the change in attitude, however. More important is the return of Blaine to the State Department in that key month of October, after an absence of six months. Harrison may have felt sure that Blaine would not return, yet Blaine had come back to haunt the president. While Blaine failed to acknowledge publicly Harrison's role in the conduct of foreign policy, he remained the favorite of many Republicans for the presidential nomination in 1892. Though reluctant to run for a second term, Harrison would not step aside for Blaine under any circumstances. A close examination of Harrison's stance in the situations that he faced in 1891 suggests that he acted with vigor to separate himself from Blaine, a mere shadow of "Jingo Jim." The diplomatic and personal correspondence reveals the increasing divergence brought on by the more belligerent president, a situation that was compounded by the almost complete incapacity of the secretary of state, as the two men headed for the final break on the eve of the Republican National Convention of 1892.

As early as 17 March 1891, Blaine's secretary informed the president that the secretary of state felt somewhat indisposed and was unable to leave his bed. The next day, the secretary told Harrison that Blaine "is not able to be up . . . his cold makes it difficult to converse." The *New York Times* then reported, on 1 April, that Blaine had been struck by gout and remained at home. A little more than a month later came the devastating attack, which had seemed imminent for several years. Blaine collapsed at Andrew Carnegie's home in New York on 7 May and could not get out of bed the following day. While Bright's disease continued its inexorable progress, Blaine exhibited all the symptoms of a nervous breakdown. This came at a difficult time for Harrison, who was on a month-long trip to the Pacific Coast as of 14 April and would not return from the nine-thousand-mile presidential excursion until 15 May.[3]

Carnegie faithfully kept the president informed. He wrote seven times beginning 10 May, frankly telling Harrison: "Absolute rest and freedom from all work [is] essential for at least six weeks . . . [he] speaks little and with some difficulty." Blaine then personally advised Harrison on 22 May that he could not return to Washington in any "namable time." Harrison, however, had arrived back in Washington, where he had plunged immediately into foreign affairs. The *New York Times* explained on 31 May that the secretary of state remained in New York, while the president had taken charge of the dispute with Great Britain on the fate of the seal herd in the Bering Sea. The *Times* said that Blaine had left Harrison with a situation in disarray, one that would require days of painstaking study to determine exactly where the United States stood in the negotiations.[4]

In mid August the president learned from Secretary of the Navy Benjamin Tracy that Blaine's illness was a sudden and complete attack of nervous exhaustion. Tracy informed Harrison that even Blaine's most intimate friends were not able to see him for weeks. Tracy concluded prophetically: "At his age complete recovery must be counted in years." Finally, in late September, the *New York Times* acknowledged that Harrison had been running the State Department for some time.[5]

What about the Blaine who finally returned to the State Department in late October? The *New York Times* declared that Blaine appeared feeble and far from well. True, Blaine would continue to serve until early June 1892; but Harrison summed up the record best when, at the end of December, he wrote comments on a note sent by Blaine to break a scheduled appointment. As Harrison emphasized, it was the third such incident. Blaine simply had forgotten the two previous appointments![6]

Throughout much of 1892, there was a distinct emphasis on Blaine's health; it had a greater effect than ever on his relationship with Harrison. On 4 January, Harrison told Blaine that he had received no reply to a request for the secretary of state to call at 10 A.M. Blaine now added to the president's frustration. He replied the same day and explained that after "hovering on the borders of the 'grip' for three days," his condition had worsened. Blaine insisted that he had not received Harrison's request. But the next day, he apologized to Harrison: he had found the note hidden under a pile of papers and felt mortified. Two weeks later, even Whitelaw Reid's ever-loyal *New York Tribune* admitted that the secretary of state had been taken ill at a cabinet meeting on 19 January.[7]

Then came yet-another personal crisis for Blaine in February. Blaine's youngest surviving son, James G. Blaine, Jr., went through a highly publicized divorce, which dragged his parents into the news-papers. When the former Mrs. James G. Blaine, Jr., accused her former in-laws of interfering in the marriage, the secretary of state was forced to make a public statement, which was carried in both the New York and the Washington newspapers on 29 February. In what had to be a particularly trying experience for a man in failing health, Blaine explained how his son, who had not quite been eighteen when he had secretly married a woman of twenty-one in 1886, had been separated from his wife for three and one-half years before the divorce.[8]

The strain of dealing with the divorce might have brought on another total collapse. On 6 March, Blaine's secretary advised Harrison that the secretary of state was too sick to sign a communication to the president on the controversy in the Bering Sea. The subsequently destroyed diary of Elijah W. Halford indicated that Blaine was seriously ill on 7 March; he had a temperature of 103 degrees and was visited by a physician four times during the day. Halford remembered Blaine as being in a stupor and behaving abnormally. The president then pointed out, on 22 March, that Blaine, though he remained at home, joined the entire cabinet in approving an especially strong dispatch to Great Britain in the Bering Sea dispute.[9]

David S. Muzzey's biography of Blaine reenacted the scene that then brought the "Plumed Knight" to the end of the line as secretary of state: "One day in May he suddenly rose from his seat at the Cabinet table and left the room. While his colleagues were gazing at one another in embarrassed silence Secretary [of War Stephen] Elkins hastened after Blaine and found him outside bordering on a state of collapse." Muzzey thus described the secretary of state at that time; Blaine "feared that a sudden attack might prove fatal."[10]

It is impossible to determine exactly why Blaine finally resigned during the first week in June, shortly before the Republican National Convention. The combination of his deteriorating health and what had become during 1892 a constant struggle with Harrison over their respective approaches toward foreign policy apparently brought him to the decision. Harrison forced Blaine's hand by dictating policy in the three unresolved disputes with Chile, Great Britain, and Italy. In the wake of Harrison's aggressive approach to all three questions, the relationship of the president and the secretary of state collapsed completely.

The secretary of state made no move to resign, however, until the timing seemed a direct challenge to the president. Blaine played a minimal role as secretary of state after 1890. His health was broken; still he remained a serious threat to Harrison at the Republican National Convention of 1892. The president had sought to create differences of opinion that might have brought about Blaine's earlier departure from the administration. With Blaine out of office, even his most ardent supporters could not claim that he continued to direct foreign policy. But it was not to be that way. Blaine lingered on, as his reputation has for almost a century.

When Harrison and Blaine took office in 1889, pork products from the United States had been excluded from some parts of the European continent for a decade. Eventually, the loss may have reached a quarter of a billion dollars. In 1879, the United States had exported a staggering 1.2 billion pounds of pork products, worth $80 million; and 89 percent of the total went to Europe. The absolute value was important to American farmers and to the economy of the nation. Pork products represented 10 percent of all exports from the United States. While the European nations were claiming that pork products from the United States could cause trichinosis, thereby justifying the prohibition on imports, a prime motivation was the drive to protect domestic producers from competition that easily undersold them. It proved to be more astute politically to appear to be protecting the masses from tainted pork products than to admit that the same people were being denied access to a cheap staple of their diet.

Italy, as early as February 1879, was the first nation to ban the importation of pork products from the United States. Portugal, Greece, and Spain followed within a year. But Spain revoked its decision in a few months, and Greece did so in 1884; furthermore, the four nations that had acted first and much of the rest of the Continent accounted for only 2 percent of all pork exports to Europe. More important to the economic well-being of the United States were the markets in Great Britain, Germany, and France.

In June 1879, Germany launched a protective tariff policy. The German government a year later banned the importation of all pork products from the United States except for ham and bacon. France followed, in February 1881, with a complete prohibition. In London, the *Times* published the report of an acting British consul in Philadelphia, who described widespread hog cholera in the United States. The British themselves, who received 60 percent of all pork exports to Europe, refused to panic and never participated in the ban. The Continental nations chose not to differentiate between hog cholera and trichinosis.

In March 1881 the prohibition spread to Austria-Hungary, followed by Turkey and Rumania. But Germany, which took 10 percent of all pork exports to Europe, and France, which accounted for 8 percent, were the most important nations involved. For instance, Germany had imported 131 million pounds of pork products in 1881, worth $11 million; the amount was cut in half in 1882. Then, by March 1883, Germany had extended its regulations to ban all pork products from the United States. Thus the matter drifted, with Denmark being added to the list of involved nations in 1888.[11]

The Harrison administration quickly began the campaign to end the restrictions against a valuable export and clearly concentrated on France and Germany as the key to the rest of the Continent. What unfolded had important political implications for both the 1890 congressional races and the presidential election of 1892. Harrison, as usual, wanted a quick solution, perhaps with an eye on the farm vote. He used two Republican stalwarts—Whitelaw Reid, as minister to France, and William Walter Phelps, as minister to Germany—to help achieve his goal. Admittedly, both Reid and Phelps might have hoped that Blaine would be the nominee in 1892, but they worked hard for the benefit of the party.

From the beginning, Reid spelled it out for Blaine: Reid had been informed by the French foreign minister that the issue, purely and simply, was protection. In such a situation, the problem was about to be compounded for Reid in 1890, as Congress moved inevitably toward the passage of its own brand of protection—the McKinley Tariff. But Reid took a hard line toward the French. He wrote directly to Harrison in January 1890 with clear advice: "If there should be a strong movement in our Congress toward increasing the duty on wines . . . it might have a good effect. . . . Possibly a higher duty on silk might be judicially proposed at the same time."[12]

The Harrison administration did not forget about Germany. Animosities over Samoa, which were temporarily settled at the Berlin Conference of 1889, could have influenced the decision to go slow with Germany. Yet patience began to wear thin when Blaine learned in March 1890 that Denmark had decided to ban American pork products because of pressure from Germany. In April, Blaine told Phelps to lose no opportunity to impress upon the German government the restiveness of the United States at being excluded from a legitimate market.[13] That, however, was about as far as Blaine would go.

The pace of diplomacy picked up during the summer of 1890. Reid, looking ahead to the congressional election, sent an incredibly blunt communication to the French foreign minister on 3 July. Reid acknowledged that he might be entering into an unwarranted discussion of French domestic affairs; nevertheless, he presented an indictment:

> You have deprived your people, particularly the poor laboring classes, of a cheap and highly prized article of food. . . . Nobody in the United States says that our pork is diseased but your own public men have again and again admitted the adulteration of French wines. . . . Surely it is not wise . . . to drive American statesmen . . . to consider whether if France

still prefers prohibition to duty the United States has not great reason to do the same.[14]

Two major developments increased the determination of the Harrison administration to obtain a favorable settlement as quickly as possible. First, Congress passed the Meat Inspection Act at the end of August—an attempt to remove any grounds for prohibiting American pork products. The law allowed the president to exclude products from any nation that continued to discriminate against exports from the United States.[15] When this was combined with the commercial reciprocity amendment in the McKinley Tariff, Harrison had all the opening he needed, especially in the case of Germany. Then came the disastrous congressional elections of 1890. Any chance of success with France seemed to be shattered. Reid shared the French attitude with Blaine: "The majority against us [in the House of Representatives] was so big that our French friends are misled . . . they do not believe we will after such a popular rebuff, attempt to enforce the retaliatory bill."[16]

But Harrison, spurred by the election results and tiring of the drawn-out negotiations, was about to take charge. He received complete support for a more aggressive policy from Secretary of Agriculture Jeremiah Rusk. In his second annual message, on 1 December 1890, the president pointed to the increase in the export of hogs during the year ending 30 June 1890—forty-five thousand more than in the previous year—but warned that continuing "nonacceptance will quite clearly reveal the real motive of any . . . restriction . . . and . . . the duty of the Executive will be very plain."[17]

The beginning of 1891 brought new attention to Germany. In early January, Rusk shared his feelings with Blaine. Speaking specifically of Germany's prohibition, he said: "It does not comport with the self-respect and dignity of this government to longer tolerate such a policy." Rusk stated that if Germany failed to respond, he would recommend to Harrison a suspension on the importation of certain products in retaliation. Blaine, who resented Rusk's interference, ignored Rusk's advice and instructed Phelps several days later to do no more than use discretion in discussing the matter with the German foreign minister.[18]

A cooperative Congress improved the inspection process in March—microscopic inspection would now be performed at the time of slaughtering the animals—and Rusk immediately advised Harrison to retaliate against continuing prohibition by any nation. The word clearly reached Germany and France. Phelps reflected Blaine's attitude when he complained that Rusk's nasty intervention had set back the effort to get Germany to lift the prohibition.[19]

Reid faced renewed frustration in France. The government had agreed to a duty of twelve francs on one hundred kilograms of pork products, but a report by the Tariff Commission had recommended a duty of at least fifteen francs. Reid asked for instructions: should he stand fast for a twelve-franc duty, or should he intimate that if France refused, the president would retaliate?[20]

Germany, with large exports of beet sugar to the United States, clearly proved vulnerable to pressure from Harrison and Rusk; the president knew he had two weapons to use against German sugar. The inspection law permitted him to retaliate against any product, and the reciprocity amendment of the McKinley Tariff reinforced that power. It allowed five products to be admitted duty-free, including sugar. The amendment threatened, however, to reimpose duties on those products when imported from nations that failed to respond by lowering their tariff barriers.[21]

Germany reacted quickly. The negotiations that followed came after Blaine's collapse and revealed that he was completely out of touch with Harrison's approach. Blaine, still prostrate in New York, wrote to Harrison on 26 May to relay an offer from the German minister in the United States: Germany would admit pork products if the United States would not retaliate against German sugar. The ailing secretary of state advised Harrison to accept the deal because "it is a matter of great consequence that pork be on our list of exports once more."[22]

On the next day, Harrison demonstrated uncharacteristic humor when he replied to Blaine: "General Rusk has been in and he is delighted with the prospect of getting the restrictions upon our meat products removed. He says if we take care of the hog it don't much matter what becomes of the seal." Yet Harrison took the proposed package deal with Germany very seriously. On the following day, he clearly rejected Blaine's advice; Harrison did not favor trading pork for sugar. The president sounded logical when he explained: "Certainly they would not accept our meat unless satisfied of its soundness and if satisfied . . . ought not to ask us to pay a large consideration to be admitted to a privilege given freely to other nations." While Harrison's hard line may have prolonged the negotiations with Germany, he might have been letting off frustrations over the possibility of achieving only a limited victory with France. Early in June, Reid had to report that the Chamber of Deputies had voted overwhelmingly for a twenty-franc duty.[23] Harrison had now reached his limit.

In mid June, First Assistant Secretary of State William Wharton told Phelps that the president would be willing to discuss with Germany some type of reciprocal arrangement that would be separate from the repeal of the prohibition. Wharton then told Reid that Harrison had offered to admit sugar from France, but not from French colonies, duty-free if France would decide on the minimum duty for pork products and would make additional trade concessions to the United States. According to Wharton, the president insisted that ending the prohibition had nothing to do with a trade agreement. In early July, when Phelps had learned that Germany expected additional concessions in any reciprocal arrangement, he admitted that he had not seen the need to consider a policy of retaliation until then.[24]

In the midst of the battle over restrictions on pork, only Blaine, incapacitated and ill-informed, still favored settling with the Germans on their terms. On 30 July he advised Harrison that the United States needed German sugar, particularly in the absence of an agreement with Spain covering exports from Cuba and Puerto Rico. He thought that everything honorable should be done to obtain sugar from Germany.[25]

Harrison answered bluntly, reiterating his opposition to a pork-for-sugar deal. He believed that Germany was not entitled to any considerations upon accepting the federal inspection of pork products from the United States. On the other hand, he thought Germany should grant additional concessions to the United States for importing sugar duty-free. Harrison broke the news to Blaine: "With the arrangement . . . for Cuban sugar we can be pretty independent." The reciprocity agreement with Spain had been signed the day before in Washington. The president then assured Blaine that he remained anxious to secure the German market for pork products; but if Germany would not give in, he was ready to use the retaliatory power that Congress had given to him. Blaine replied humbly: "Now that I understand it I fully appreciate your course in regard to Germany."[26]

Before the end of August, Acting Secretary of State John Foster acknowledged two promises that the German government had made: the prohibition would end when the improved inspection would go into effect on 1 September; there would be tariff reductions on agricultural imports from the United States. In response, the president had agreed not to use his retaliatory power. Finally, on 3 September, Phelps could report that the German government had signed the decree ending the prohibition. The importance of Germany was emphasized within a week, when Denmark immediately ended its prohibition.[27]

The ending of pork prohibition by Germany was a far greater achievement than a somewhat unsatisfactory settlement with France. Reid reported in early November that France's Senate had voted overwhelmingly for a duty of twenty-five francs, against the wishes of the government. He then relayed the disappointing news—the Chamber of Deputies had approved the Senate version of the bill. Finally, however, on 5 December, Reid could report that the prohibition had been repealed.[28]

Reopening both Germany and France and the rest of the Continent to American pork products far outweighed the possible difficulties of competing in the French market. In his third annual message, on 9 December 1891, Harrison could boast that Germany, Denmark, Italy, Austria-Hungary, and France had repealed their prohibitions, in that order. Harrison reminded the nation of successful diplomacy, with the presidential election less than a year away. He said: "An enlarged foreign market for these meats will be felt not only by the farmer, but in our public finances and in every branch of trade." The president felt confident that the end of the prohibitions would help dispose of a large agricultural surplus, thus avoiding lower prices. Harrison spelled it out: "The Secretary of Agriculture estimates that the restrictions upon the importation of our pork products into Europe lost us a market for $20,000,000 worth of these products annually."[29]

In his final annual message, on 6 December 1892, Harrison detailed the dramatic increase in exports of pork products to Europe; the report came a month after the presidential election. In May 1892, the United States exported 82 million pounds to Europe, compared to 46.9 million in May 1891. The figures for June showed even more improvement: 85.7 million pounds, compared to 46.5 million. Exports had been up 41 percent in July and 55 percent in August; for the four-month period, exports were up 62 percent.[30]

Success in Europe, including the somewhat hollow victory in France, proved that Harrison had "taken care of the hog." This accomplishment, after ten years of drift under previous administrations, would seem more significant when the economy of the nation collapsed in the Depression of 1893.

Beginning in the summer of 1886, antagonism over the fate of the seal herd in the Bering Sea added to the already deep hostility between the United States and Great Britain/Canada, which stemmed from at least three causes: old animosities, developed during the Civil War; the continuing refusal of the United States to conclude a commercial reciprocity treaty with Canada; and the century-old dispute over the rights of United States fishing vessels in Canada's Atlantic waters. As soon as the Civil War had ended, the United States chose in 1866 to terminate the reciprocity agreement with Canada that had been in effect since 1854, the first and only one that the United States ever entered into. The inevitable result followed: the Canadians made life increasingly difficult for fishing vessels from the United States. Although the

Treaty of Washington in 1871 had settled the fishing dispute for fifteen years, the provision for compensation to Canada would soon trouble the waters; and the United States continued to avoid reciprocity for the rest of the nineteenth century.

The unhappy relationship failed to improve during the 1880s. In 1877, Canada had been awarded $5.5 million as compensation for fishing rights under the terms of the Treaty of Washington, a sum that many in the United States considered outrageous. The anger mounted until the United States terminated the fishing provisions of the treaty on 1 July 1885. Only a modus vivendi delayed a showdown until 1886. The two sides then engaged in a deliberate policy of alienating each other. The Canadians intercepted fishing vessels in the Atlantic, and at the same time, the United States introduced a new aspect to the mutual hostility by stopping Canadian vessels that were hunting for seals in the Bering Sea off the coast of Alaska.

Democratic President Grover Cleveland attempted to settle the fishing dispute with the Bayard-Chamberlain Treaty of 1888, but the Republican-controlled Senate refused to ratify it in the highly partisan atmosphere of the presidential-election year. As it turned out, however, the two sides had agreed to another modus vivendi, which would be continually renewed and would eliminate the fishing problem until a final settlement a quarter of a century later. President Cleveland also sought a solution to the problems in the Bering Sea. While the United States seized three Canadian vessels that were engaged in pelagic (on the open sea) sealing in 1886 and six more in 1887, none were captured in 1888, as the Cleveland administration tried but failed to negotiate a settlement.[31] The two sides brought a fundamental difference of opinion to the issue: the Canadians insisted that pelagic sealing did not endanger the herd; the United States, which controlled the Pribilof Islands and the right to hunt seals on the islands as part of the Alaska Purchase, argued that pelagic sealing would destroy the herd.

An unsolved problem immediately confronted the new administration. A law that Congress passed on 2 March 1889 instructed the president to issue an annual proclamation against hunting seals and other fur-bearing animals in Alaskan waters. Naval vessels were to cruise the waters and arrest violators; punishment would be fines of $200 to $1,000 or imprisonment for up to six months—or both. President Benjamin Harrison issued the proclamation on 21 March 1889, after less than three weeks in office. As the sealing season approached, Secretary of the Treasury William Windom soon ordered Capt. L. G. Shepard of the *Rush* to cruise the Bering Sea and seize any vessels that were violating the laws of the United States.[32]

The United States captured eight Canadian ships in 1889, a sharp increase, particularly in comparison to no such incidents the year before. Late in August the British Legation in the United States opened the incredibly complicated correspondence that would continue without interruption during the Harrison administration. The British informed Secretary of State Blaine that they had heard repeated rumors about interference with vessels outside the three-mile limit of the Pribilof Islands. Great Britain asked the United States to send stringent instructions to prevent a recurrence of such interference.[33] Blaine replied calmly that the United States had heard "the same rumors, probably based on truth." He also made clear to the British from the start that Harrison had both a very real interest and very definite attitude in the negotiations: "It . . . is the earnest desire of the President . . . to have such an adjustment as shall remove all possible . . . misunderstanding . . . the President believes . . . the responsibility for delay . . . cannot be properly charged to . . . the United States."[34]

Although Harrison had made up his mind, Blaine revealed from the start an ambivalence that would become typical during his tenure as secretary of state. He wrote to Harrison on 25 August and advised against allowing Great Britain to take the initiative on the issue; but he noted in a postscript that the sealing season would soon end anyway, so the United States would not have to make any further seizures of Canadian vessels.[35] That is precisely why the dispute could drag on from one sealing season to another.

Great Britain did indeed seem to have the initiative. Sir Julian Pauncefote, the British minister to the United States, proposed at the end of April 1890 that there be a closed season on all sealing in May and June and from October to December and a permanent ban on pelagic sealing within ten miles of the islands. Meanwhile, a commission representing both sides in the dispute would study the problem and recommend any regulations necessary in order to save the herd.[36] A severe restriction of sealing on the islands, even for five months, had not been contemplated by either Blaine or Harrison. They were not ready to accept such a proposal in 1890, and historians have raised some questions about the administration's motive on this particular point.

In March 1890 the United States granted to the North American Commercial Company a twenty-year lease to hunt seals on the islands. This corporation was controlled by Stephen Elkins, who was to become secretary of war at the end of 1891, and by Darius Ogden Mills, the father-in-law of the United States minister to France, Whitelaw Reid.[37] Harrison and Blaine stood fast against equating sealing on the islands with the pelagic variety. Whatever the motivations of either side in the dispute, the first real crisis had to be dealt with in the summer of 1890. It seemed clear in June that Great Britain did not intend to prevent Canadian vessels from engaging in pelagic sealing. Instead, Blaine learned on 4 June that the British South Pacific Squadron of four ships had been sent to the Bering Sea; "it is rumored that [their] instructions indicate apprehension of a war."[38] By 14 June, Pauncefote delivered his government's formal protest against any possible interference with Canadian vessels in the Bering Sea. He had done so reluctantly, however; and he proceeded within two days to present an unofficial rough draft of his views on a possible settlement of the impasse. Pauncefote, one of the most important diplomatic representatives Great Britain has ever sent to the United States, suggested the following: if the United States would agree to arbitrate the issue of the seizures of Canadian vessels and would cease to interfere with those vessels, then Great Britain would use a proclamation to keep ships out of the Bering Sea during the 1890 season.[39]

The British threat to use force was one of the key factors in the eventual settlement of the Bering Sea dispute. There were no seizures of Canadian vessels in 1890. The emphasis should be placed, however, on the British perception that the Harrison administration would not back down. The British had blinked first, as they would in the repeated crises that followed, and they formally proposed arbitration in August.[40]

But by March 1891, with a greatly augmented Canadian fleet of some fifty ships preparing for the approaching season and with the secretary of state showing the first signs of his impending collapse, Harrison clearly began to seize the initiative for the United States. First, Blaine told Pauncefote that the president wanted a modus vivendi that would protect the seal herd until the completion of arbitration. A bit more than two weeks later, Harrison proposed an end to all hunting of seals during the arbitration, at least for the 1891 season.[41] The last proposal brought on the most serious crisis of the negotiations.

Harrison left on the presidential excursion to the West Coast in mid April. Blaine surprised him in Pasadena, California, on 23 April, when he reported that the British had agreed to end all hunting of seals while the arbitration proceeded. Harrison insisted, two days later from Santa Barbara, that he had never intended to end all sealing. Since the company that held the lease was required to provide for the natives on the islands, it should be allowed to take some seals as compensation. Blaine then sent an extremely aggravating letter to Harrison on 29 April. While the secretary of the Treasury had decided that the company should be allowed to take sixty thousand seals in 1891, the British now insisted on an end to all sealing. Blaine did not give Harrison welcome advice when he suggested that it would be embarrassing to resist the British on the point because of the president's original suggestion.[42]

On the next day, Harrison answered angrily that this difference of opinion might represent a good reason to withdraw from the negotiations, if Blaine thought that would be the best alternative. Instead, one of Blaine's last tasks before his complete collapse was to send a long explanation of the disagreement to Pauncefote on 4 May. Blaine maintained that the British had not replied to Harrison's offer by the time the president had left for the West Coast, and the United States had proceeded to authorize the taking of sixty thousand seals in 1891. Acknowledging that the British had now agreed to end all hunting, Blaine insisted that Harrison felt it necessary to allow the company some quota, both as food for the 303 natives counted in the 1890 census and as compensation. Harrison now proposed that a mere seventy-five hundred be taken, only males, and that all other sealing end until 1 May 1892.[43]

The contract of the North American Commercial Company was the factor that persuaded the Harrison administration to set the original figure of sixty-thousand seals for 1891.[44] There was a genuine feeling on the part of the president that the company was entitled to take some seals, based on its obligations. Moreover, he did not consider that the figure of sixty thousand would in any way be devastating to the herd. Harrison, in making the proposal to end all hunting, had never meant an absolute end to hunting on the islands, and when he compromised on the figure of seventy-five hundred, he did so reluctantly and then drew the line.

Pauncefote quickly provided Blaine with a very positive British response. Yet the end was not in sight. With Blaine now seriously ill, Second Assistant Secretary of State Alvey Adee sent a long memorandum to the president on 22 May, in which he reported that Pauncefote had admitted the cause for further delay—objections from Canada. The Canadians were concerned about vessels that might already be in the Bering Sea when sealing would be halted. If interfered with, such vessels should be entitled to indemnities. Furthermore, the British themselves were not happy with the implications in Blaine's last communication that the arbitration had to be completed by 1 May 1892. Pauncefote had concluded: "If your government will be patient for a very few days, I am sure I shall receive a definite instruction . . . which if it may not close the agreement . . . will certainly show the points on which a friendly agreement can be reached or will at least give good practical reasons for our inability to accept your conditions."[45]

Harrison had no more patience either for the British or for the Canadians. His correspondence clearly reveals the additional burden that Blaine's incapacity had placed on the president as of May 1891. In a separate communication to the president on 22 May, Adee reported about a careful search at the State Department and at Blaine's home, which had failed to turn up the original copy of a note from Pauncefote to Blaine.[46] The enfeebled Blaine did not help matters at all when he advised Harrison on 23 May: "The paper that you inquired for . . . was prepared on the 4th day of May." On 25 May the besieged president wrote to Blaine to explain that the note of 4 May had been found, but what could not be found was a note in which Great Britain had agreed to end all hunting. Harrison was forced to speculate as to whether the message might have been delivered verbally. Then he assured the secretary of state that Adee, despite a serious hearing problem, had proven useful in Blaine's absence.[47]

That same day, another lengthy memorandum from Adee revealed that the British had been given an ultimatum, nothing less. Adee put it thus: "In the judgment of the President further delay was quite impossible. . . . If the agreement to suspend [sealing] were not at once reached the President would be obligated to release our revenue vessels." According to Adee, Pauncefote had asked if Harrison would wait three or four days. The second assistant secretary of state had replied: "In the President's judgment it was now a matter of hours, not days."[48]

Within three days, Pauncefote reported that the House of Commons would be asked to consider a bill giving the government the power to prohibit sealing in the Bering Sea. The United States minister to Great Britain, Robert Lincoln, then confirmed the introduction of a bill that would prohibit sealing by an order in council.[49] The crisis was not over yet, however. With the British seemingly intent on provoking Harrison, a hurdle remained. When Pauncefote forwarded an outline of the final agreement, it included the irritating provision that none of the seventy-five hundred seals to be taken by the company should leave the islands, reportedly an attempt to guarantee that only the natives would benefit. Harrison was indignant, and Wharton immediately relayed the message to Pauncefote: "This new condition . . . is entirely inadmissible." Wharton concluded with what seemed to be Harrison's final word on the subject: "The value of such an agreement is daily lessening and the President . . . feels . . . he must ask that the negotiations be brought to a speedy determination."[50] Thus, on 11 June, Pauncefote told Wharton that Prime Minister Lord Salisbury was not completely satisfied but "in view of the urgency of the case, His Lordship is disposed to authorize me to sign the agreement.'' The agreement was signed on 15 June, and Harrison immediately sent orders to the Departments of the Navy and the Treasury to begin enforcing it.[51]

The two nations had by no means settled all aspects of the problem, however. As early as 6 June 1891, Pauncefote made it quite clear that the modus vivendi could not be renewed in 1892.[52] Such a warning carried particularly serious implications, because the two sides did not even approve the arbitration of their differences until December 1891.

On 29 February 1892, the very date that the two nations formally signed the arbitration treaty, Pauncefote replied to a communication from Blaine that accused Great Britain of once again indulging in delaying tactics. The secretary of state had warned the British: Harrison insisted that the arrangement remain in effect beyond 1 May. The British instead offered a compromise that would prohibit sealing for thirty miles around the islands and would allow the United States to take a maximum of thirty thousand.[53] Harrison was in no mood to compromise or to engage in any more drawn-out negotiations. As usual, Blaine was seriously ill and completely out of step, while Harrison moved rapidly toward a showdown early in March. Blaine, in a communication that he was too sick to sign, sent advice that did not really interest Harrison. Blaine tried in vain to calm the president by downplaying British actions: ''If we get up a war cry and send naval vessels to [the] Behring Sea it will re-elect Lord Salisbury. . . . I think Lord Salisbury has done this on purpose.''[54]

Instead, First Assistant Secretary of State William Wharton relayed to the British the reaction from an angry president: ''President notices with the deepest regret the indisposition of Her Majesty's Government to agree upon an effective *modus* . . . certainly the United States cannot be expected to suspend the defense by such measures as are within its power of the property and jurisdictional rights claimed by it.''[55] Two weeks later, Harrison sent the strongest communication of the lengthy correspondence. Wharton assured the British that Harrison considered the situation extremely urgent and grave. The latest information available to the United States indicated that forty-seven Canadian sealing vessels had sailed for the Bering Sea, a development that the president viewed as a crime against nature. The first assistant secretary of state continued with a warning: if Great Britain forced the United States to defend its jurisdictional and property rights, the president remained ''not willing to be found responsible for [the] results [which] may follow.'' But the British should not be mistaken; Harrison was no longer thinking in terms of loss or gain. The self-respect of the nation was at stake.

Harrison would accept nothing less than a renewal of the modus vivendi. Wharton concluded: "President will hear with regret that Her Majesty's Government continues to assert a right to deal with this subject precisely as if no provision had been made for a settlement of the dispute and in that event this government . . . will be compelled to deal with the subject upon the same basis." Harrison meant business. On the very next day he forwarded to the Senate, which had not yet ratified the arbitration treaty, the correspondence on the Bering Sea dispute.[56]

The Senate quickly formed a united front by responding on 25 March with a resolution declaring that the resumption of sealing would be "inconsistent with [the] dignity and interest of the United States and [the] proposed arbitration." The resolution urged that Harrison use his power to preserve the seals and, if necessary, to refuse to exchange ratifications of the arbitration treaty. Senator John Sherman, chairman of the Foreign Relations Committee, sent a copy of the resolution to the president and personally emphasized that the Senate expected Harrison to protect the seals.[57]

Within a day of the Senate's action, Great Britain yielded once again, rationalizing its decision with the pending ratification of the arbitration treaty. Pauncefote explained that ratification permitted an extension of the modus vivendi, if only the United States would agree that the arbitrators could determine the damages for either side that had been caused by continuing limitations on sealing.[58]

Cooperation between the president and the Senate was shown when ratification followed by a unanimous vote on 29 March. The modus vivendi was then extended on 18 April. The arbitration did not begin until 23 February 1893; the arbitrators reached their decision in August. They ruled against the United States on all points but agreed to the need for regulations so as to preserve the seal herd. The regulations as drawn—which provided for a closed season on sealing from 1 May to 31 July, no sealing within sixty miles of the islands, and no use of firearms or explosives—clearly made the decision more acceptable to the United States. The regulations may have eased the pain when the United States, in June 1898, paid Great Britain $473,151.26 for damages.[59]

Former Secretary of the Navy Tracy helped to establish a mood of resignation as to the outcome of the arbitration with an article entitled "The Behring Sea Question" in the *North American Review* of May 1893. Tracy argued at length that the United States did indeed have a property right in the seals and that it was justified in repelling the assault on that property. But he defended submitting the issue to arbitration by simply admitting that the only other alternative for the Harrison administration was war.[60] Yet Harrison at least flirted with the unthinkable alternative. And against a lesser foe, Chile, he did not hesitate to consider the use of force to obtain satisfaction.

According to Fredrick Pike, "After 1880, the United States came to be regarded, along with Argentina, as Chile's principal adversary in international affairs."[61] And the man who had been most responsible for creating that feeling was James G. Blaine, as secretary of state for President James A. Garfield in 1881. Chile had an enduring distrust of the United States. Blaine had intervened in the War of the Pacific in a manner that had left a permanent legacy with more serious implications than mere distrust—hatred does not seem to be too strong a term to use in this instance.

The War of the Pacific decided who would dominate the west coast of South America, as Chile won an overwhelming victory against the combined forces of Peru and Bolivia, capturing Lima in January 1881. When Blaine took over as secretary of state, he began a frustrating effort to bring the war to an end. He sent the career diplomat William Henry Trescot and Walker Blaine, who was serving as third assistant secretary of state, to South America in December. The Trescot-Blaine mission was designed to prevent territorial acquisition by the victors, even to the extent of rallying the nations of the hemisphere against Chile. Frederick T. Frelinghuysen, the incoming secretary of state for President Chester A. Arthur, had quickly reversed Blaine's approach toward Chile, and the war had come to an end on Chile's terms late in 1883.[62] But the United States could not erase the bitter Chilean memories.

At the beginning of the 1890s, Chile faced internal upheaval. By mid October 1890 the minister to Chile, Patrick Egan, had told Blaine of the worsening struggle between President José Manuel Balmaceda and the political opposition in the Chilean congress. Egan predicted that Balmaceda would win a mandate in the elections scheduled for March 1891. This dispatch provides a good indication of Egan's sentiments during the civil war that soon followed. Egan, an Irish immigrant, had not come to the United States until 1883; he then had served as the militant leader of the Irish National Land League of America. Egan apparently believed that support of Balmaceda would thwart British influence in Chile.[63] His actions would cause Chileans to view him as an enemy in the crisis of 1891/92.

On New Year's Day 1891, Balmaceda delivered his "Manifesto to the Nation," which explained why the president was putting into effect a budget that the congress had refused to approve. He declared that the people of Chile could decide the issue at the upcoming elections. Egan soon reported that six ships of the Chilean navy had joined a rebellion led by the congress. Within another week, Egan called for naval vessels to protect the interests of the United States.[64] Just what were those interests?

As late as January 1891 the minister to Peru had informed Blaine that no merchant or naval vessel from the United States had visited the west coast of South America since August 1889.[65] But the prospect of a Central American canal quickly increased the importance of the neglected Pacific Coast in the early 1890s.

The idea of a possible Nicaraguan canal held the attention of the United States in the 1880s, as the nation reacted to the attempt by the legendary Ferdinand de Lesseps to construct a canal across Panama. Though Lesseps encountered devastating obstacles from the beginning, the United States concentrated on Nicaragua as the most viable alternative. A group of American investors secured a canal concession from Nicaragua in 1879, but they would have no more success than Lesseps. From the start, they sought—but did not obtain—a financial guarantee from Congress. Lacking the guarantee, they could not raise the necessary funds in the United States, and their concession was about to expire in 1884. The rumor that the investors might turn to Europe for money apparently convinced lame-duck Secretary of State Frelinghuysen to make an unprecedented effort to obtain an American canal in Nicaragua through the Frelinghuysen-Zavala Treaty at the end of 1884. While Congress was awaiting the inauguration of Grover Cleveland as the first Democratic president since the Civil War, the Republicans in the Senate could not produce the required two-thirds vote, so the treaty failed in January 1885.

A second attempt to finance a canal across Nicaragua was under way by 1887. Again, the effort was completely dependent on the support of the federal government. Some preliminary work would be done beginning in October 1889, but by 1891 the company was facing bankruptcy. Thus, President Harrison vainly appealed to Congress in his third annual message of December 1891 for a guarantee of the bonds of the Maritime Canal Company of Nicaragua. When Congress did not respond, the project was abandoned before the end of 1892.[66]

Yet the interest aroused by the potential canal, combined with the rapid development of the new navy, meant that the United States would no longer turn its back on any area in the hemisphere. By 1891 the United States possessed seven new cruisers; and many more cruisers and the first three battleships were under construction. This nucleus of a modern fleet would play a very central role in every crucial development in the conflict of 1891/92.

By the end of February 1891, Egan acknowledged the arrival of the *Pensacola* of the old navy. That was only the beginning. The first serious challenge for the United States developed just as Blaine collapsed, while Harrison was touring the western states. The rebels had managed to purchase a large stock of rifles and ammunition in the United States, and on 5 May the Chilean minister advised Blaine that a ship, the *Itata*, would pick up the supplies in San Diego. On the next day, Attorney General W. H. H. Miller informed the president, who was then in Seattle, that he had instructed the district attorney in San Diego to detain the *Itata* and its cargo. Harrison responded immediately, endorsing the action. But on 7 May, Miller reported to Harrison that the *Itata* had fled. Four cabinet members, but not Blaine, who fell ill that day in New York, advised the naval pursuit of the *Itata*.[67]

Secretary of the Navy Benjamin Tracy did not hesitate to use the new navy. On the next day he ordered the *Charleston* to use force, if clearly sufficient, against any war vessel that might be accompanying the *Itata* and to link up with the *San Francisco* in the chase. And on 9 May, Tracy ordered Acting Rear Adm. George Brown, on the *San Francisco*, to join up with both the *Charleston* and the *Baltimore*. In just over a week, Tracy was able to call off the pursuit. He informed the *Charleston* that the *Itata* had been given orders to return to the United States.[68]

The rebels had given in, but they would not forget. The bitterness increased when, in August, they accused Rear Admiral Brown of spying on a troop landing and of informing the Chilean government about the threat to Valparaiso.[69] The attitudes on both sides were hardening for the crisis that was about to develop.

The minister to Chile played a major role in the first element of the crisis, which began to unfold in mid August. As the rebels moved toward victory, Egan reported to the State Department that he had already granted asylum to eighty refugees and that Balmaceda himself had asked for protection. The refugee problem set the stage for a complete breakdown in relations. In early September, Egan made it clear that he had refused to give up the refugees, even with a guarantee for their lives; they would be transported to safety in Peru. The tension eased temporarily when Balmaceda proceeded to take his own life. But on 25 September, Egan still had nineteen people under his protection, including seven former government ministers who were wanted for prosecution. Egan described a stand-off with the authorities: he had asked for safe conduct for the refugees, while security police were arresting any persons trying to enter the legation.[70]

On that same day, Capt. Winfield Scott Schley of the *Baltimore*, then in Valparaiso harbor, assured the secretary of the navy that he would not give the crew shore leave because he hoped to avoid conflict.[71] Unfortunately, Captain Schley later decided to allow his restless crew to go ashore. An inevitable collision then followed in mid October. On 18 October, Egan reported that there had been a fight two days earlier, involving sailors from both nations. He described the casualties from the *Baltimore* as one sailor dead and five wounded. Captain Schley then amplified the details: two of the ship's crew had died. Schley admitted that the fight had started in a saloon but insisted that the men had been sober. He emphasized that some members of the police force had helped the sailors but charged that others had fired on his men. He vividly described the incident for the secretary of the navy: "It is the unanimous opinion of the surgeons of my vessel that some wounds were inflicted by bayonet thrusts, showing clearly the participation of the police."[72]

The United States soon sent a frank communication to Chile's foreign minister, Manuel Antonio Matta. First Assistant Secretary of State Wharton wondered why Chile had not yet expressed regret. He emphasized that if Schley's report was correct, Chile was expected to offer reparations. Matta, who had a long history of animosity toward the United States, responded quickly on 28 October in a tone that clearly provoked the president. Matta said that the United States had formulated demands and had advanced threats that were not acceptable. The actual showdown did not occur until December and January, because Harrison held out hope in November that he could still obtain satisfaction. When President Jorge Montt assumed full powers, Egan anticipated a much more friendly feeling toward the United States. Harrison politely welcomed the new Chilean minister, Pedro Montt, brother of the president.[73]

But any hope for improvement in relations failed to materialize. In his third annual message, on 9 December, Harrison told the people of the United States that

> this Government is now awaiting the result of an investigation . . . by the criminal court at Valparaiso . . . it is expected that the result will soon be communicated . . . together with some adequate and satisfactory response. . . . If these just expectations should be disappointed or further needless delay intervene, I will by special message bring this matter again to the attention of Congress for such action as may be necessary.[74]

Did Harrison mean war? There is no question that the United States immediately began to plan for it. On the same day as Harrison's annual message, Tracy asked Rear Admiral Brown about the ships that would be needed to guarantee victory in case of a collision with Chile.[75] Yet Chile seemed determined to bring Harrison to the boiling point, adding insult to injury.

Egan soon informed Blaine of a communication from Foreign Minister Matta to the Chilean minister in the United States; it was outrageous, and it had been read in the Chilean senate with the sanction of President Montt. The dispatch contained attacks on Harrison, Tracy, and Egan:

> Matta insisted that both Harrison and Tracy had received information on the incident which he labeled "erroneous and deliberately incorrect." The president and the secretary of the navy, therefore, had been "led into error."
>
> Matta denied that Chile had ever threatened refugees, or the Legation, or the minister, "notwithstanding deliberate provocations and indiscretions."
>
> The Chilean government felt "confident of our accuracy and right and final success notwithstanding intrigues from so low and threats from so high."[76]

Four days later, Egan warned the secretary of state about rumors of a possible attempt to burn the legation or a nearby house to drive out the remaining refugees. And on the last day of 1891, Rear Admiral Brown responded to several urgent communications from Tracy, offering the following advice: four or more ships of the new navy easily could take control of six cities on the Chilean coast, and he thought Valparaiso would have to be blockaded by as large a force as could be made available.[77]

In January 1892 the United States and Chile came close to war. The personal papers of Capt. Alfred T. Mahan contain a clipping dated 2 January from the *Army and Navy Journal*. The article described the Chilean situation as extremely grave and declared: "There is not an official in the government who doesn't regard war as imminent and not a few who believe it inevitable." The journal was probably very accurate, with the single outstanding exception of Blaine. On 2 January, Blaine, "hovering on the borders of the 'grip,'" told Harrison that a communication from Chile contained what seemed to be in effect an apology. Harrison replied just two days later in a tone that became typical in 1892: "I do not see how the statements here made, if true, are conclusive; nor do I think that they constitute an apology. I have been giving some pretty careful study to the statements which have emanated from Chile . . . and they seem to me to be quite unsatisfactory."[78]

Harrison's attitude seems clear. And Tracy's personal papers contain two documents that indicate that the United States was actively planning for war: an undated list of seventeen "vessels ready in view of possible service against Chile" and an undated memorandum headed "whether to direct naval force against nitrate port (Iquique) or coal port (Lota)."[79]

Meanwhile, the Chilean minister in the United States informed Blaine on 8 January of his nation's decision to prosecute three Chileans and one of the sailors from the *Baltimore*. Pedro Montt emphasized that an investigation had cleared the police of any involvement in what was described as nothing more than a drunken brawl. The decision to put one of the sailors on trial and to whitewash the police would never have been acceptable to Harrison. But the weary Blaine, who seemed eager to compromise, responded on the same day and asked whether Chile would also agree to do the following: withdraw Matta's offensive note; stop interference at the legation; and grant safe conduct to the remaining refugees.[80]

Within a few days, Egan was able to provide an affirmative reply on two of the points. The legation was not being guarded. And Luis Pereira, the new foreign minister, who had replaced Matta in what seemed to be another positive step by Chile, had granted a verbal safe conduct to the refugees. By 15 January, Egan indicated that Chile had given in on the third point as well. Pereira made it clear that Chile had no objection to withdrawing those parts of Matta's note that the United States considered disagreeable.[81] Why then, did the two nations almost end up at war just ten days later?

Blaine clearly launched the peace initiative on his own, without the support of Harrison or anybody else in the administration. The secretary of state was willing to make two important concessions to Chile: the United States would agree to arbitrate the dispute and to recall Egan as minister. As of mid January, there was no support in the administration for any concession to Chile. On 16 January, Tracy inquired in Callao, Peru, as to whether it would be possible to purchase five thousand to ten thousand tons of coal if the United States were to go to war with Chile. On that same day, Blaine exhibited a marked change of tone. He told Egan that Matta's message had contained palpable insults to the president and to other governmental officials, including Tracy; and the United States wanted every discourteous part of it withdrawn in suitable terms of respect that were freely offered. The secretary of state insisted that such action be taken very promptly.[82]

On the next day, Tracy ordered Rear Admiral Brown to gather men for special duty devoted to the torpedo defense of the Pacific Coast. By that time, Harrison was convinced that he would never achieve an acceptable settlement without using the threat of force. Egan informed Blaine that Pereira had withdrawn the previously given personal assurance for the safety of the refugees.[83] With Matta's note not yet withdrawn and with the situation for the refugees still clearly precarious, the Chileans had run out of time. Chile received a virtual ultimatum on 21 January. The Chileans could no longer misunderstand the attitude of the United States, nor could they count on Blaine to keep the debate under control. In fact, Blaine signed the communication, which made quite clear that the president had carefully studied the facts and had reached the following conclusions: (1) the assault had been an attack on the uniform of the United States Navy, originating in hostility to its government; and (2) the authorities in Valparaiso had failed in their duty, and one of the sailors had been killed by the police or by a soldier. The ultimatum continued: "The note of December 11 . . . [was] in the highest degree offensive to this government . . . I am now . . . directed by the President to say . . . if the offensive parts . . . are not at once withdrawn and a suitable apology offered . . . he will have no other course open to him except to terminate diplomatic relations."[84]

Harrison did not even give the Chileans time to think it over. On 25 January, Tracy warned Acting Rear Adm. John Walker to keep ready, because the president was about to present a special message to Congress; sailing orders would have to wait for action by the House and Senate.[85] That day, Harrison delivered a lengthy statement to Congress and the nation, inviting the Congress to take such action as it should deem appropriate.

According to the president of the United States, there was only one side to the story. He began with a defense of Egan. Harrison vividly described the abuses by Chilean authorities at the legation but insisted that Egan had done nothing unworthy of his position. Harrison then blasted the conclusions of the Chilean investigation. The president made it clear that his view of the incident had not changed at all: "I am still of the opinion that our sailors were assaulted, beaten, stabbed, and killed not for anything they . . . had done, but for what the Government of the United States . . . was charged with having done." After a blow-by-blow account of the attack on the sailors, Harrison emphasized the participation of the police: "The evidence of our sailors shows . . . our men were struck and beaten by police officers before and after arrest."

Finally, the president condemned the government of Chile, saying, "The communications of the Chilean Government in relation to this cruel and disastrous attack upon our men . . . have not in any degree taken the form of a . . . satisfactory expression of regret, much less of apology.'' The president was emphatic in asking for the ''grave and patriotic consideration which the questions involved demand.'' He left no doubt about his attitude: ''If the dignity as well as the prestige and influence of the United States are not to be wholly sacrificed, we must protect those who in foreign ports display the flag or wear the colors.''[86]

Harrison has been accused of delivering his special message even though Chile had already satisfied every demand. On 4 February 1892 the *Nation* attacked the president in either case, whether he had or had not known that a complete apology from Chile had arrived earlier, on 25 January.[87]

Theodore Roosevelt, however, inspired by the president's use of the ''big stick,'' eloquently defended Harrison in a lengthy article written for the presidential campaign in August 1892. Young Roosevelt first boasted that Chile had yielded to Harrison's ultimatum because the United States ''had made ready a [naval] force amply sufficient to insure the destruction of the Chilean Navy, the bombardment of the Chilean forts, and the ruin of Chile's foreign commerce, as well as probably the rending from it of the nitrate ports which had been taken from Peru.'' He then announced dramatically: ''The entry by the telegraph operator on the last sheet of the telegram containing Chile's reply to the ultimatum, the original of which I have before me, shows that it was received at the telegraph station in Washington, at 6 A.M. on the 26th.''[88]

Chile yielded to the United States on every point: a proud nation, but one of only two and one-half million people, had no choice and had almost run out of ways to apologize. Pereira was willing to have the dispute settled by arbitration or by the Supreme Court of the United States. The foreign minister deplored the error of judgment in Matta's infamous dispatch and pledged that any parts that were considered offensive would be withdrawn.[89] There are two major conclusions to be derived from this episode. First, if Blaine expected to direct policy with Chile, he had been completely repudiated by Harrison. But Blaine was not prepared to step down yet; he even endured one more humiliation at the end of January. Harrison's personal papers contain a proposed communication from Blaine to Egan in which the secretary of state congratulated Chile for the frank and ample withdrawal of Matta's note. Blaine told Harrison that he considered the communication expedient but admitted that the president might regard it as too cordial. Blaine was, of course, absolutely correct. He informed Harrison that he preferred the note that had been substituted by the president to his own.[90]

Also, Harrison struck a responsive chord with Roosevelt and others who welcomed the new era in foreign policy. Lt. Jerrold Kelley, who was proud to be serving in the new navy, contributed an article to *Harper's Weekly* on 30 January 1892, which set the mood of those who saw the crisis with Chile as a stimulating challenge. As Lieutenant Kelley put it: "We can be especially proud . . . of the . . . mobilization of our compact but effective fleet . . . now that there are guns and ships fit for our officers and men to handle, we can reasonably expect that the successes of our former memorable sea wars will be repeated even against so gallant a foe as Chili [*sic*]."[91]

Finally, there were two contemporary comments which seem equally appropriate for describing the new mood of the 1890s. The first came from the *Spectator* of London, which reflected the view of a not uninterested Great Britain with this pithy statement at the time of the showdown between the United States and Chile: "Anglo-Saxon bullying is apt to lack grace and finesse, as has been shown 100 times over in our own history."[92]

The second came from Rear Adm. Bancroft Gherardi. In a report to Tracy, Gherardi, while he was on a goodwill mission to Chile, described the low ebb in relations between the two nations: "One point of agreement of all parties in Chile is that the United States stand on [the] Baltimore affair was reprehensible." But the situation did not really upset Rear Admiral Gherardi, who could have spoken for Roosevelt with this simple statement, which most perfectly indicated how far the United States had come by 1892: "Our demonstration brought home to Chile [the] fact that [the] United States as a government is no longer to be trifled with."[93]

The tidal wave of new immigrants to the United States during the late nineteenth century brought an alien element to the major coastal cities. The millions of Italians and Russian Jews faced equally hostile reaction from a nation that was disturbed by the changing pattern of immigration, but the unique conditions that had forced the Russian Jews to abandon the Pale may have helped to ease their particular struggle for acceptance. As a matter of fact, the plight of the Russian Jews and the simultaneous devastating Russian famine at the beginning of the 1890s were as important as any other developments of the period in getting the people of the United States involved in the new foreign policy.

In contrast, however, to sympathies aroused by Russian brutality and hunger, the people of cities such as New Orleans reacted with increasing anger to those Italians in their midst who seemed to have transported elements of organized crime from their native Sicily. The violence of gang warfare became intolerable, and New Orleans decided to do something about it. A courageous young superintendent of police, David C. Hennessy, led a crackdown after continuing gang violence had aroused the city. He was scheduled to testify before a grand jury when assassins gunned him down on 14 October 1890; Hennessy, who was thirty-two years old, died the next day. In the aftermath of the murder, nineteen persons were indicted; but the citizens of New Orleans could not accept the outcome of the trial for the first group of nine. On 13 March 1891, a jury returned a verdict of not guilty for six of the defendants, declaring that it could not reach a verdict on the remaining three. Thus, lynch law prevailed when a mob stormed the jail on 14 March and murdered eleven of the accused.[94]

The diplomatic confrontation developed quickly. The excited Italian consul in New Orleans, Pasquale Corte, told the minister in Washington that he held the authorities responsible and warned that there would be more murders—Corte considered himself to be in great danger. The minister, Baron Francesco Saverio Fava, hurried to the State Department. Blaine, in an immediate communication with Harrison, vividly described the minister as half-crazed.[95]

The Italian government proved to be unwilling to tolerate any delay. Baron Fava protested in the most solemn manner and accused the authorities in New Orleans of remaining passive during the massacre. He appealed to Blaine to have the guilty brought to justice and made it clear that Italy reserved the right to ask for reparations. But complicating factors included the temperament exhibited by Antonio Rudini, marchese di Starabba, the premier and foreign minister, who stipulated the following: "Italy had to have official notice that the guilty parties would be turned over to the authorities. The minister was to present a demand for indemnity; if the United States replied with a mere declaration and no commitment, that would not be sufficient."[96]

Yet the breakdown of Blaine's health became the key factor in a deteriorating situation. With Blaine's health shaky, the constant badgering by the Italian government might have taken him over the edge. Baron Fava reported that he had gone to see Blaine on 26 March. The secretary of state startled Fava by asking: "What do you come to ask for now?" The minister described Blaine as agitated in maintaining that the federal government could not act. When Baron Fava emphasized his impending recall, Blaine replied, "All right . . . and we will recall our legation."[97]

The next day, Baron Fava had an even more amazing conversation with the secretary of state. Blaine was incredibly blunt:

> I do not recognize the right of any government to tell the United States what they must do. . . . [We] can't give assurances on punishment and it is quite indifferent to me what may be thought of in Italy of our institutions. . . . [We] can't give [an] official declaration on [the] spot and you may do as you choose.

Baron Fava then left the United States on 31 March. On the following day, the United States minister to Italy, Albert G. Porter, warned Blaine that Italy might be led toward a "more extreme course."[98]

Instead, Italy did nothing over the next five months. And in this instance, at least, Blaine did not miss any major developments while he was incapacitated, because Harrison indicated that he would not take the initiative to settle the issue. In Harrison's opinion, the Italians had overreacted. One aspect of the tragedy kept in proper perspective the right of the Italian government to be involved at all. As United States Attorney William Grant explained, one of the murdered men had been born in the United States, and only three of the remaining ten had not yet become naturalized citizens.[99]

In September the Italian government made the inevitable overture. Rudini admitted that he had acted hastily under pressure from parliament. The premier, who called Consul Corte tactless and had recalled him, revealed that the consul had wanted a war vessel sent to New Orleans. While acknowledging the complications caused by the federal system of government in the United States, Italy thought that there should be some indemnity. Harrison took a hard line and informed the absent Blaine that he would not open correspondence on the matter while Italy had no minister in the United States.[100]

At this point, Blaine and Harrison seemed to be in perfect harmony in their approach to Italy. Blaine, who had not yet returned to Washington, wrote to Harrison in early October. While requesting that he be allowed to handle the dispute, Blaine completely endorsed the president's stand: "I think it is a case in which we cannot allow a single bit of negotiation, except with the Minister."[101]

Harrison responded two days later; he reiterated his determination not to take the first step: "The return of a minister to Washington would be an essential preliminary to any further discussion of the question. . . . You know I have been very decided in my views about the case from the beginning. They acted hastily and foolish and ought not to have too much help in a necessary retreat."[102]

While Italy made another gesture in October by repealing its prohibition against the importation of pork products from the United

States, Harrison did not budge until his third annual message, on 9 December. He then acted with some apparent reluctance. Harrison called the lynching most deplorable and discreditable but insisted that Italy had presented claims in a manner "not such as to promote a calm discussion of the questions involved." The president made it clear for Italy that the "absence of a minister plenipotentiary at this capital has retarded . . . correspondence, but it is not doubted that a friendly conclusion is attainable." Italy now saw the opening, and before the end of December, the premier and the king of Italy had both expressed their satisfaction with Harrison's statement.[103]

In mid March 1892—almost a year to the day since the attack in New Orleans—the premier offered to have a minister return to Washington so the two sides could proceed to negotiate the amount of indemnity to be paid by the United States. The premier also emphasized that the principle of indemnity was more important than the amount. The Harrison administration quickly accepted and agreed to the return of the minister of Italy.[104] Suddenly, however, the Italian premier insisted that the United States had to provide positive assurances on the principle of indemnity.[105] This development led to a flurry of letters between Harrison and Blaine—all sent and received within one week—which brought their relationship to a point where only one question remained: how much longer would Blaine continue in an impossible situation?

Returning from his most recent bout with illness, on 23 March Blaine asked the president: "Do you think it safe to let the Italy matter drift in view of the fact that the Italian government is to appoint one of the Paris arbitrators [in the Bering Sea dispute]? The matter could be arranged in a few moments if you felt willing." But Harrison quickly deflated the secretary of state with a rather devastating comment: "I am entirely willing to have you deal with the Italian matter as you think best. It seems to be now largely a question of etiquette, and I do not stand much on that."[106] Apparently, both of them then thought about it over the next few days.

On 26 March the president indicated that he did not really intend to have Blaine take complete charge of even this relatively minor problem, explaining: "It was not my understanding that the Italian government expected the affair to be concluded before they returned their Minister. . . . I had not thought that the amount of indemnity was to be settled and the whole affair concluded while the present status exists, and would rather it should be so managed."[107]

One can only imagine what went through Blaine's mind during the three days before he sent his final statement on the dispute with Italy. When he wrote to Harrison on 29 March, his resignation was still a bit

THE PRESIDENCY OF BENJAMIN HARRISON

more than two months away, but the tone clearly set the stage for a dramatic development in their relationship.

Blaine seemed to be getting it off his chest in a lengthy criticism of the president:

> I followed your directions in the Italian matter and suspended negotiations . . . but I think something more should be said. . . . I would have completed the matter in the course of 24 hours. But you seem to think it can be done . . . in Italy . . . it is apparent to me that this is far more embarrassing than to pay the money here and have nothing said. . . . It strikes me that this would be a bad policy. . . . You had the impression that the language in your [annual] message was sufficient to satisfy Italy and have her send a Minister here. But four months have passed by and no minister is here yet. We have waited eleven months during which period our minister . . . has been passing his time in Indianapolis drawing $12,000 a year from the Treasury. I believe he will continue in the same position for months to come on the basis you have adopted.[108]

Such a letter could have ended with, "I therefore submit my resignation as Secretary of State," yet Blaine was to stay on until practically forced out of office by subsequent events. But Blaine's 29 March communication had to be doubly disturbing to Harrison, because the minister in Indianapolis was Albert G. Porter—former congressman, governor of Indiana, and law partner of Benjamin Harrison—the man who had nominated Harrison for president at the 1888 Republican National Convention.[109]

9

★ ★ ★ ★ ★

PRESIDENTIAL TRAVELS

Every president receives countless invitations to visit parts of the country and to speak to American audiences. Most requests have to be turned down, but some have such urgency that they must be fitted into the busy presidential schedule. Leadership in the nation was in the hands of persons who had fought in the Civil War, and many dedications, memorials, and civic functions were devoted to this remembrance of an aging generation. President Benjamin Harrison received his most favorable public response when he spoke to large audiences and almost his poorest when he dealt with individuals. He knew that his speaking ability was one of his top assets, that it could assist him politically, and he responded positively to many invitations to travel. He also regarded it as a patriotic duty, since many of his visits evoked speeches on a patriotic theme. Thus, by the end of his four years in the presidency, Benjamin Harrison had become one of the most-traveled presidents to that time. Moreover, his rail journey to the West Coast in 1891 was the longest journey undertaken by any president while in office.

Transportation facilities, primarily improved railroads, had greatly expanded by 1889, and the rail network throughout the country had reached almost its maximum mileage. A limited portion of Harrison's presidential travels also took place on the water—on the East, the Gulf, and the West coasts. In Washington, D.C., and its environs, he could be seen on almost any fine day walking or riding in one of the coaches or buggies he had purchased from the Studebaker Brothers Manufacturing Company of South Bend, Indiana. An examination of Harrison's presidential travels also shows how the press and the public responded to the Chief Executive outside the national capital during this era. The make-up of the presidential party varied from time to time, and security arrangements were minimal during Harrison's presidency.

Public response to Harrison's travels was generally positive. The press devoted as much space to his journeys as it did to any of his other presidential activities. Harrison's general willingness to travel away from Washington and the interest of citizens in seeing their president combined to make his travels an important asset to his administration.

Even before his inauguration, plans were under way for Harrison's first journey as president. He was the centennial president, and he had extensive correspondence with New York City's Centennial Celebration Committee, for the commemoration of Washington's inauguration on 30 April 1789.[1] Harrison was delighted to go, but he refused to make an extended address in New York City. Nevertheless, he was a central figure in the three days of celebration, 29 April through 1 May 1889; in a sense he was Washington's diminutive stand-in for the pomp and ceremony of the inaugural centennial. Harrison usually detested playing to the galleries; nevertheless, he thoroughly enjoyed his role in the New York City celebration, even though he found the three days extraordinarily fatiguing.[2] Protocol, far more than was usual in the republican United States, filled these days. There was much rejoicing for the nation's first hundred years under the Constitution.

The presidential party included the cabinet—except for Blaine, who canceled at the last moment because of lumbago—plus cabinet spouses, members of the secretary of state's family, several Supreme Court justices, and members of Congress. They departed in private coaches on the Pennsylvania Railroad shortly after midnight on Monday 29 April and passed through Baltimore, Wilmington, and Philadelphia, reaching Elizabethport, New Jersey, before 7:30 A.M. In 1789, George Washington's horse-drawn coach had taken a week to go almost the same distance. The travelers of 1889 marveled at the speed, almost thirty miles an hour, and their accommodations, for they arrived at their destination clean and rested, compared to those of a century earlier. The governor of New Jersey provided breakfast and a reception, then President Harrison boarded a barge which carried him to the USS *Despatch*, from which he reviewed approximately six hundred vessels of all kinds in New York's harbor.[3]

Later, Harrison was delivered to the foot of Wall Street to receive formal greetings from former Secretary of State Hamilton Fish and other officials. A reception, held in the fashionable Lawyer's Club on Broadway, included former Presidents Hayes and Cleveland and governors from most of the states. This was followed by another reception in City Hall, where everyone in a large crowd sought to shake the president's hand. Commerce had adjourned for a time; businesses, offices, and stores in New York City were closed for the festivities; and all commercial signs as well as show windows were draped with bunting and American flags. So many visitors filled Manhattan Island that the claim was made that it was "the largest assemblage of people ever witnessed on this continent."[4] After a fine dinner, a gala Centennial Ball was held in the Metropolitan Opera House. Unlike Washington, Harrison watched the festivities but did not dance. President and Mrs. Harrison retired after midnight to the Fifth Avenue mansion of Vice-President Levi Morton.

The most important day was 30 April, the centennial day and a national holiday in 1889. Artillery salutes, echoing across New York City at sunrise, aroused the city early and made it a memorable and lengthy day. Formal activities on Centennial Day began at St. Paul's Chapel, where President Harrison was escorted to George Washington's pew, with former Presidents Hayes and Cleveland being seated nearby. Following the pattern used in 1789, music, scripture, and prayers at this service were highlighted by a sermon by the Episcopal bishop of New York, Henry Codman Potter. Potter's sermon became the most controversial aspect of the entire centennial celebration; some commentators took it as a direct condemnation of Harrison's brief term, and others regarded it as a general criticism of the era. The bishop's sermon contrasted the simplicity and integrity of George Washington with the selfish self-seeking of later government officials. Potter, a professed Republican all his life and not interested in the reform of Mugwump factions of the party, lashed out at

> the conception of the national government as a huge machine existing mainly for the purpose of rewarding partisan service—this is a conception so alien to the character and conduct of Washington and his associates that it seems grotesque even to speak of it. It would be interesting to imagine the first President of the United States confronted with someone who ventured to approach him upon the basis of what are now commonly known as "practical politics."

A watchful New York City newspaper reported that

> when Bishop Potter read that part of the address relative to the tactics and character of the modern "practical politicians" and

contrasted the difference in the treatment of him by President Washington and the President of later days, there was a marked movement indicative of surprise among the gentlemen who sat directly in front of the pulpit. . . . President Harrison, who heretofore had permitted his eyes to wander about the church, fixed his eyes steadily upon the Bishop's face and never removed them until the address was ended. It was evident that that part of the Bishop's short talk had created a sensation of no mean proportions.[5]

There was no doubt in contemporary views that Bishop Potter's sermon was the most remarkable address of the many given during the centennial celebration. Interpretations of the bishop's remarks varied widely and often possessed political overtones. One journal found Bishop Potter's address remarkable for its moral lessons. The bishop told a reporter that he was not needed in order to make "taffy and platitudes" and that he detested the scramble for office and the lack of statesmanship that had been evident in recent presidents.[6]

The *New York Sun*, a Democratic newspaper, was critical about Potter's knowledge of American history. If he had been knowledgeable, he would have found "abundant reason, not for praising the past at the expense of the present, but rather for thankfulness that the past is past, never to return." An Independent daily, the *Washington Post*, spread assurances that the president was meeting every responsibility "with a high and conscientious and statesmanlike sense of obligation." The national capital's Republican paper, the *Washington Press*, labeled the sermon as pessimistic. Potter had "overpraised the past and libeled the present." Perhaps President Harrison inwardly agreed with the bishop, because the president's own extemporaneous remarks a short while later at the Federal Sub-Treasury Building, the site of Washington's inauguration, included a statement that "we have come into the serious, but always inspiring, presence of Washington. He was the incarnation of duty, and he teaches us to-day this great lesson: That those who would associate their names with events that shall outlive a century can only do so by high consecration to duty. Self-seeking has no public observance or anniversary." Years later, Harrison's private secretary, E. W. Halford, made a point in his personal reminiscences that while Harrison had the "ability to grasp questions of administration . . . he was not a 'practical politician.'"[7]

After the morning's activities on Centennial Day, there was no respite for President Harrison, as he reviewed some fifty thousand troops from a stand set up in Madison Square on Fifth Avenue. The parade took six hours and included units from all of the armed forces and auxiliary services. That evening the general public was regaled with open-air concerts and fireworks, while Harrison and about eight hundred invited guests were entertained with a banquet at the opera house. For a second time, President Harrison was on the program to speak; the excitement of the celebration was helping him to prepare. Well after midnight, the president responded in a final toast of the evening. His closing remarks in a patriotic vein implored:

> Here may I not ask you to carry those inscriptions that now hang on the walls into your homes, into the schools of your city, into all of your great institutions where children are gathered, and teach them that the eye of the young and the old should look upon that flag as one of the familiar glories of every American? . . . It is a spiritual thought that is in our minds—it is the flag and what it stands for; it is the fireside and the home; it is the thoughts that are in our hearts, born of the inspiration which comes with the story of the flag, of martyrs to liberty.[8]

Thus began Harrison's familiar crusade, which he used throughout his years in office and frequently included in later speeches. Five years later, when asked about his attitude towards flying the flag over all public and educational institutions, he responded:

> I gave orders that the Flag should be displayed over the Executive departments and over the White House while I was in Washington; and during the Washington Centennial Exercises in 1889 in New York, I suggested that the Flag, which during the parade hung over the business houses of the city, should be sent to the school houses. A love of the Flag and an understanding of what it stands for should be sedulously promoted in all our educational institutions.[9]

Artillery salutes at dawn opened the final Centennial Day, and again there was a parade on Fifth Avenue, with local institutions, businesses, and ethnic groups providing the marchers and the floats. After reviewing the activities for five hours, Harrison departed for Jersey City to board his car for Washington. Mrs. Harrison and other family members remained in New York City for another week, while Harrison, with his cabinet, took the five-and-one-half-hour train ride back to the nation's capital.[10]

President Harrison enjoyed walking, and whenever the weather was favorable, he took late afternoon walks around the District of

Columbia. He preferred walking out Connecticut or Massachusetts Avenue or north on Sixteenth Street. An occasional White House visitor might accompany him on these jaunts, but more frequently, Elijah Halford was his companion. Usually, passers-by ignored the simply dressed Harrison, but he was willing to chat briefly if recognized. When there were few people on the streets, Harrison would vary his walking by examining goods in shop windows. On returning to the White House with Halford, Harrison once commented, "There is my jail." Harrison, like most of the presidents, disliked the White House's circus atmosphere, and even his daily walks at times could be burdensome.[11]

On other occasions, President Harrison would get fresh air by riding in his dark green Studebaker landau or another vehicle across the District of Columbia line into Maryland or Virginia, or he would handle the reins himself in a buggy. After the election in 1888, among the plans that he made for moving to Washington was the purchase of five vehicles made by Studebaker Brothers of South Bend, Indiana, from Clem Studebaker, a close friend. Clem and his brother were invited to Indianapolis early in January to show Harrison pictures of carriages. Eventually, Harrison bought a landau, for use in the inaugural parade and other special occasions, and four other vehicles. The catalog price for them, including harnesses, robes, and a coachman's livery, totaled $7,075. These vehicles were finished simply, with no insignia or gilt; ebony and silver were used instead. The assignment of a Studebaker relative as postmaster in Dallas, Texas, was credited by some newspaper stories to the gifts provided by the Studebaker company. A Studebaker letter to the offending newspaper maintained that Harrison's carriages were sold to him. "We have made him a present of none, either in whole or in part, directly or indirectly." Harrison was also looking in Indiana for horses that were sixteen hands high and bay in color. Eventually, four Kentucky thoroughbreds—Abdullah, Billy, Lexington, and John—were shipped to Washington. Albert Hawkins, the veteran black coachman, considered them "the finest horses in the presidential stables since he had been at the White House." Later, Harrison acquired two Morgan horses from Vermont.[12]

Harrison was back in New York City on 30 May 1889 to review the Decoration Day parade, just as Cleveland had done in 1888. On his longer trips, Harrison, as an avowed Sabbatarian, opposed unnecessary labor on Sunday. Official correspondence to the White House, for instance, was never opened on Sunday during the Harrison years. Generally, Harrison's views on Sunday work permitted regular chores but required no extra duty from others on his behalf. Thus, daily newspapers began to report Harrison's Sunday activities, and in light of the president's views that one should not work on Sunday, they were especially critical of travels that the president took on that day, whether for business or for pleasure. Thus, Harrison's Sunday pleasure excursions down the Potomac in May and June 1889 were fully reported, whether they were on the U.S. naval ship *Despatch* or on the postmaster general's yacht, the *Restless*. Generally, church services were held on these craft, but one critical comment was: "The President appears to have come to the conclusion that it is not inconsistent with the Presbyterian idea of keeping holy the Sabbath day to go on an excursion of pleasure every other Sunday." Sometimes a presidential trip on a railroad coach would begin in the early morning hours of Monday. Waiting to start a journey until after midnight was also criticized, because the train crew was obligated to use part of Sunday in readying the train.[13] When engaged in extensive presidential travels, Harrison sought to use Sunday as a layover day in certain locations, and usually he attended a Presbyterian church in the vicinity.

On the fourth weekend of June 1889, the president's family accepted an invitation from John Wanamaker to visit Cape May Point, New Jersey. There the Wanamakers had a large cottage, not considered pretentious, which could be reached easily by rail from Philadelphia. Caroline Harrison, especially, enjoyed her trip to Cape May, and happiness associated with this vacation spot caused it to be a special place in later years.[14]

In the summer of 1889, when humid, sultry Washington weather settled over the capital city, Harrison decided that he must have a vacation from the heat. So, for July and August he moved with his wife, daughter, grandchildren, and father-in-law to Deer Park, in western Maryland, not far from the main track of the Baltimore and Ohio Railroad. There he occupied a cottage owned by former Senator Henry Davis of West Virginia and Davis's son-in-law Stephen Elkins. Two years earlier, Benjamin and Caroline Harrison had spent part of the summer at Deer Park, after he had lost his reelection bid for the United States Senate. Another Studebaker carriage was delivered to Deer Park in 1889, for a total cost of $460.80. Presidential business, while he was at Deer Park, was confined to morning hours; afternoons and evenings were reserved for outdoor exercise, such as fishing and hunting, and for leisure.[15] Usually, Harrison would spend half of each week in Washington, with long weekends reserved for Deer Park.

From the Deer Park vacation site, Harrison went on three more presidential trips on which his wife, Caroline, did not go. The first was to the Roseland Park estate, in Woodstock, Connecticut, of Henry Bowen, publisher of the *Independent*. Bowen, a leading Republican, planned a gala Fourth of July celebration every year. In 1889, President Harrison reluctantly spoke at the Fourth of July festivities. Accompanying Harrison were Secretary Tracy and a naval aide, Secretary and Mrs. Noble, Associate Justice Miller, Senator Joseph Hawley, and Congressman Tom Reed. From Roseland Park, Harrison's party took a special train to New London, boarded the *Despatch,* and sailed to Newport, Rhode Island, where he had dinner with the governor of Rhode Island. Secretary Tracy then guided Harrison through neighboring naval installations. The *Despatch* took Harrison back to Jersey City and a train bound for Washington; eventually, he returned to Deer Park.[16]

Harrison's second trip out of Deer Park was a ten-day excursion in August to Maine to visit Secretary of State James G. Blaine at Bar Harbor. Walker Blaine arranged this tour for the presidential party, which included Secretaries Redfield Proctor and William Windom and private secretary Elijah W. Halford. After going by rail to Jersey City, the party boarded the *Pilgrim* for a smooth overnight voyage to Boston, where members of Harrison's party were treated as guests of the Commonwealth of Massachusetts. From there they departed on a three-car Boston and Maine train, the rear coach of which was reserved for the presidential party, on a roundabout journey of several hundred miles through New Hampshire and Maine to Bar Harbor. Except on the rail trip to and from Bar Harbor, the press and the public saw little of the president on this journey. Secretary Tracy arrived at Bar Harbor later, and another naval-yard inspection was included on the return trip. Harrison's time at Stanwood, Blaine's house, was filled with serious political discussion, mixed with rounds of buckboard rides, lawn parties, formal dinners, and visits with a variety of guests.[17]

The third trip for Harrison from Deer Park that summer was a journey back home to Indianapolis, to participate in the cornerstone ceremonies of the Soldiers and Sailors' Monument, followed a day later by the annual reunion of the Indiana Seventieth Volunteers, his old regiment. This trip was also politically motivated in an effort to heal some of the injury to the Republican party that had resulted from the difficulties produced by James Tanner as comissioner of the Bureau of Pensions. Traveling with the president this time were Secretaries Miller and Rusk, Halford, and a large number of political friends. Harrison went to sleep in his private car near Deer Park on the night of 20 August, his fifty-sixth birthday, and it was attached to a Baltimore and Ohio train at 6:00 A.M. the next morning. A brief stop was made at Cincinnati, and arrival in Indianapolis was at 9:00 P.M., where Harrison was greeted by a large contingent of friends.[18]

The cornerstone of the Soldiers and Sailors' Monument was laid with great ceremony; the event attracted national attention. An enormous crowd gathered in the center of Indianapolis to watch the parade going to the area that later became known as Monument Circle. Fifteen thousand veterans escorted President Harrison to the dedication site. Harrison had proposed such a monument to all veterans in 1884, not expecting that he would be the featured speaker when the 250-foot monument made of Indiana limestone was completed. Harrison spoke extemporaneously to a responsive crowd. Drawing avid cheers was the reminder of his hope that "there might be builded a noble shaft, not to any man, not to bear on any of its majestic faces the name of a man, but a monument about which the sons of veterans, the mothers of our dead, the widows that are yet with us, might gather and, pointing to the stately shaft, say: 'There is his monument.' The hope expressed that day is realized now." Harrison's other comments appealed to loyalty to the nation, even though the monument was erected in memory of Indiana soldiers.[19]

The fifteenth annual reunion of Harrison's old regiment, the Seventieth Indiana, came the next day in Tomlinson Hall. Again he spoke extemporaneously in a patriotic vein. For the moment, some of the agitation prompted by the Tanner affair was quieted.[20] The president, in spite of the unprepared nature of his statements, was impressive to most audiences.

On their return from Deer Park to the White House, the Harrisons had been in Washington for only an hour or so early in September before they were on the road again to take part in the Old Log College celebration, located a few miles outside of Philadelphia. Created in 1726 as a Presbyterian seminary, Old Log College was regarded as the cradle of Presbyterianism in America. After traveling on the Baltimore and Ohio to Philadelphia, the president and his wife were hosted at the Wanamaker's country home, Lindenhurst. On the next day, the president, with a large party in carriages, drove another nine miles to Old Log College, where Harrison made a speech and was acclaimed as a Christian president.[21]

Harrison responded willingly to invitations of this nature during his first two years in the White House. Thus, on 14 September 1889, he attended only the first day of Baltimore's six-day celebration of the seventy-fifth anniversary at Fort McHenry of the writing of the "Star Spangled Banner" by Francis Scott Key in 1814. Harrison, accompanied by Secretaries Windom and Tracy, stood as he reviewed a four-hour parade containing a thousand floats and fifteen thousand marchers. A reception and a dinner followed, and Harrison's party boarded a train for Washington that evening.[22]

While President Harrison was getting ready for his first session of Congress, Caroline went on shopping trips to Philadelphia with Mrs. Wanamaker. Mrs. Harrison also made regular trips to New York to visit her ailing sister. At another time she took a trip to Florida with Mrs. Wanamaker. Harrison complained about her absences—he missed her, and the White House seemed so empty without her. Also, Elijah Halford collapsed from heavy work on 4 October 1889, and he was off duty for several weeks, creating heavier burdens for the president.[23]

At times, Harrison had to get away from the confinement of Washington. At least twice that fall, Harrison went duck hunting. In mid November, he was a guest of Baltimore members of the Benjies Point Ducking Club, which he reached by private railroad car. In late December he went duck hunting in Cypress Swamp, on the James River below Richmond, an area that had formerly been owned by his ancestors, the Virginia Harrisons. His companions this time were Senators Hawley and Edmunds, Justice Gray, Judge Albert Clifton Thompson, and Commodore Bateman. Bateman provided the yacht to get to the swamp from Richmond, which was the depot used by Harrison for his rail trip from Washington. Harrison's duck hunting there was a failure, but the national news reported that he had killed Gilbert Wooten's hog, thus making Wooten a famous man. Harrison lacked experience in coon hunting; he usually required dogs to be successful; and when he shot the hog, he thought he was shooting a coon.[24]

Between these two hunting trips, Harrison went to Chicago to take part in the dedication on Monday 9 December of the Auditorium, which was then the nation's best-known building outside the capital. The Republican National Nominating Convention was held in this un-finished building in 1888, and President Cleveland had participated in the cornerstone laying on 9 June 1887. Harrison left Washington on Friday and stopped in Indianapolis, where he stayed with his daughter, Mary McKee, and her husband. He attended Sunday church services at the First Presbyterian, his old church, and visited with many friends that afternoon. With many members of his family he boarded an overnight sleeper for Chicago. The dedication ceremonies were in the evening, but the president's day was filled by visits to the Board of Trade, the Union League Club, and the Marquette Club. Harrison, Vice-President and Mrs. Levi Morton, and governors from midwestern states were the honored guests. An overflow crowd, reputed to number fifteen thou-sand, packed the Auditorium. Again, Harrison's brief speech was extemporaneous. His final paragraph so aptly fit the purpose of the building that it was later inscribed on a bronze tablet and placed on a wall of the building:

> It is my wish, and may it be the wish of all, that this great building may continue to be to all your population that which it should be—an edifice opening its doors from night to night, calling your people here away from the care of business to those enjoyments, and pursuits, and entertainments which develop the souls of men, which will have power to inspire those whose lives are heavy with daily toil, and in its magnificent and enchanting presence lift them for a time out of these dull things into those higher things where men should live.[25]

Harrison felt that he was tied more closely to his desk in 1890 because of the lengthy first session of the Fifty-first Congress. Nevertheless, he found many opportunities to travel away from Washington. In February he journeyed to Pittsburgh, to take part in the dedication of the first of many Carnegie free libraries, this one located in nearby Allegheny. The next month he had a very successful three-day duck hunt at the Benjies Point Ducking Club.[26]

Decoration Day (also known as Memorial Day) was one of the biggest American holidays during the late nineteenth century. In 1890, President Harrison agreed to go to Cleveland to participate in the dedication on 30 May of the Garfield Memorial, located in Lake View Cemetery. Accompanying him on this journey were the vice-president, four cabinet members—Windom, Wanamaker, Miller, and Rusk—and Congressmen McKinley and Charles Champlin Townsend. The absence of Blaine in the presidential party was again noted in the press; the old gossip persisted that Blaine and the president had had a falling out. Former President Hayes headed the reception party, which greeted the president and his retinue. Sizable crowds watched the parade and the dedicatory ceremonies, Harrison's brief remarks again echoed his strong advocacy of the flag as a universal emblem for the country. He said, in part, ''The selection of this day for these exercises—a day consecrated to the memory of those who died that there might be one flag of honor and authority in this republic—is most fitting. That one flag encircles us with its folds to-day, the unrivaled object of our loyal love.''[27]

Most of Harrison's official presidential journeys were scheduled so that there was relatively little slack time. When the itinerary for this trip was published, he was presented with an invitation to visit the Scotch-Irish Congress, which was assembled at Pittsburgh at the time he was going through the city. At first, Harrison said no, that there was no time in his schedule. Inadvisedly, he changed his mind, so that he arrived in Pittsburgh at 7:00 A.M. on Saturday 31 May. Plans for receiving him were incomplete and in turmoil. Harrison was in a hurry and was frustrated by each delay. Obviously irritated, he departed for Washington three hours later. The Scotch-Irish Congress presented Harrison with a massive floral piece, depicting the coat of arms of Pittsburgh, which was placed on the presidential train. In Washington it was taken to the White House and "given a prominent place in the Blue Room."[28]

In 1890, Mrs. Harrison left early for a summer vacation, so that extensive repairs, including new electrical wiring, could be started in the White House. She went to Cape May Point, on the south tip of New Jersey, with most members of the family on 19 June, to a sizable new cottage, built especially for her.[29] Her excitement with the area during the previous summer had led John Wanamaker and other Philadelphia friends to acquire a lot on 3 March and to construct a summer residence with broad porches and twenty airy rooms. This gift became the object of national discussion in which Mrs. Harrison and the president were vigorously criticized. It became an issue that provoked partisan attack and defense.

Even when Harrison wrote a private business letter to John Wanamaker on 2 July, enclosing a personal check for $10,000 and requesting him to "be good enough to see to the right disposition of the check inclosed," the issue was not settled. The *New York Times* interpreted Harrison's payment for the house as having been forced by the attacks on him, while the more friendly *Washington Star* came to his defense. President Harrison headed for Cape May Point on 3 July, and he used the Summer White House as a point of departure for trips that he took in August. In September, because the remodeling at the White House was not yet completed, the Harrison family resided in a Queen Anne cottage at Cresson Springs, Pennsylvania, in the mountains west of Altoona. Occasionally, Harrison made trips to Washington, but not often enough to satisfy Republican kickers, who were complaining about the long session and were critical of the president for spending time in the mountains when the party was deeply involved in the tariff bill.[30]

The issue of the Cape May cottage inspired an anti-Harrison opera singer to add this extra verse to a song in a Gilbert and Sullivan show in Chicago, which he sang when Russell B. Harrison was in the audience:

The President said a vacation he'd take;
Said he to himself, said he,

Down by the blue sea, where the high breakers break,
Said he to himself, said he;
For the place needs the boom that my presence will bring,
And my friends who belong to the real-estate ring
Have promised a cottage, to which I shall cling;
Said he to himself, said he.[31]

While his family was at Cape May, President Harrison traveled to the annual national encampment of the Grand Army of the Republic in Boston. Other dignitaries there included Vice-President Morton; Secretaries Noble, Rusk, and Tracy; General Sherman; Admiral Gherardi; Speaker of the House Reed; and governors from the area. The president's route to Boston was by rail from Cape May to New York City, where he, along with Noble, Rusk, and Halford, boarded the admiral's flagship, the USS *Baltimore*, on Saturday afternoon 9 August. There was a layover for part of Sunday morning off Nantucket Island; then the *Baltimore* got under way and arrived in Boston Sunday evening. In two days the president reviewed a lengthy parade and made three rousing speeches, emphasizing loyalty to the flag as a symbol of the nation.[32]

In September, while the Harrison family was vacationing in Cresson Springs, Pennsylvania, the president made four public appearances where he made speeches. The first was at the hotel in Cresson on Saturday 13 September; this was followed a week later by an excursion through a mining district, which included Osceola, Houtzdale, and Philipsburg. The longest speech was after a parade and demonstration at Houtzdale, where he addressed a crowd estimated at ten thousand. Again he emphasized loyalty to the nation.[33]

Polls that were taken in the fall of 1890 indicated that the Republicans were slipping badly and that they would lose many races in the November elections. The first session of the Fifty-first Congress had just adjourned, after having been in session for more than three hundred days. So Harrison took a week-long circuit around the states of Ohio, Indiana, Illinois, Iowa, Kansas, and Missouri then back to Washington, in an effort to prop up midwestern candidates. This journey, of 2,851 miles, was the second-longest trip taken by Harrison during his four years in the presidency. A nonpolitical purpose for this trip was to attend the reunion of the First Brigade, Twentieth Army Corps, of which Harrison was president, in Galesburg, Illinois; but elections were near, and the president was given a chance to communicate to crowds in a genuinely friendly way. Departure for this trip was just before noon on Monday 6 October, with Secretary of the Navy Tracy and private secretary Halford in the official party.[34]

This trip had a set schedule, so Harrison's remarks frequently included allusions to the short time he had to talk with the people at each stop. Otherwise, he would comment on the local area and make a personal connection to the region. Almost none of his speeches were bona-fide political ones; his most unifying themes again were interest in the flag, loyalty to the nation, the value of education, and the prosperity enjoyed by all American citizens. Thirty-seven speeches by Harrison were recorded by stenographer E. F. Tibbott and were disseminated to the news media.[35]

Five of these speeches were made in Galesburg, Illinois, which was reached on 8 October, as Harrison and Tracy rode in the cab of the locomotive with its engineer, Frank Hilton, who had served in the army under Harrison. The first speech to the general public, at Court House Park, was lengthy but was presented without notes. There he spoke to the First Brigade Association, which included his dearly beloved Seventieth Indiana Regiment; and he made many personal comments about this organization and the conditions it had faced during the Civil War. He made brief remarks at the cornerstone laying of a building at Knox College, at a banquet of Phi Delta Theta—the fraternity that Harrison had helped to found in his student days at Miami University—and at the First Brigade's banquet. It was truly an action-filled day among other busy days on this tour.

On Thursday 9 October, Harrison reached Ottumwa, Iowa, where he was met by his older brother, John Scott Harrison, of Kansas City, Missouri, and was escorted to the residence of an older sister, Sally (Mrs. T. J. Devin). Nearby he reviewed a parade and a demonstration; these were followed by a public reception at the Coal Palace Exhibition, where he was introduced to the audience by the governor of Iowa. St. Joseph, Missouri, was reached on the following morning, and there Harrison addressed a crowd, although it was barely light at 6:30 A.M. Additional speeches that day were made at Atchison, Topeka, Nortonville, Valley Falls, and Lawrence—all in Kansas—and two were made in Kansas City, Missouri. St. Louis was reached at 9:30 A.M. on Saturday morning 11 October, in time to review a lengthy parade. Later, Harrison addressed the businessmen of the Merchants' Exchange and another group that was attending festive activities at the Music Hall.

Indianapolis, Indiana, was reached in time to spend a quiet Sunday, 12 October, at home. Then it was on to Anderson, Muncie, Winchester, Union City, and the Ohio communities of Degraff, Bellefontaine, Crestline, Mansfield, Wooster, Orrville, Massillon, Canton, and Alliance. In his final recorded speech of the tour, at Alliance, he gave what was probably his most political and uplifting account of his trip:

Let us not doubt that we are now—as I have seen the evidence of it in a very extended trip through the West—entering upon an up grade in all departments of business. Everywhere I went, in the great city of St. Louis and the smaller manufacturing towns through which we passed, there was one story to tell—and I have no doubt it is true in your midst—every wheel is running and every hand is busy. I believe the future is bright before us for increasingly better times for all, and as it comes I hope it may be so generally diffused that its kindly touch may be felt by every one who hears me, and that its beneficent help may come into every home.[36]

Pittsburgh was passed at 7:30 P.M., and Harrison's western political journey of 1890 ended the next morning in Washington. Unfortunately for Harrison and the Republicans, the polls were correct; Republicans took a drubbing in 1890. His optimistic speeches failed to turn the election around, and he faced a hostile Fifty-second Congress in 1891.

However, the year 1891 found Harrison taking the longest journey for any president up to that time—a five-week trip on a special palatial railroad train to the West Coast in April and May. Harrison's first trip that year was to New York City, to attend the funeral of Gen. William Tecumseh Sherman, who died on 14 February. A four-car special train from Washington, carrying the presidential party, all of his cabinet, Mrs. Blaine, and Elijah Halford, plus delegations from the House of Representatives and from the army, arrived at Jersey City on the evening of 18 February. Harrison was one of the speakers to eulogize Sherman. After the funeral, most of the president's party returned directly to Washington.[37]

Later, in mid March, Harrison was able to get away from Washington to shoot ducks at Benjies Point, Maryland. The first story concerning Harrison's western tour hit the press on 3 April; more detailed plans were provided a week later.[38] The 9,232-mile trip, which lasted for one month and three days, began just after midnight on Tuesday 14 April. It passed through Virginia, Tennessee, Georgia, Alabama, Arkansas, Texas, the territories of New Mexico and Arizona, California, Oregon, and Washington and returned to the nation's capital by way of Idaho, Utah Territory, Colorado, Nebraska, Iowa, Missouri, Illinois, Indiana, Ohio, Pennsylvania, and Maryland. Postmaster General Wanamaker had the itinerary privately printed in a small book for use by the president's party. A tight daily schedule was maintained throughout, and the return to Washington was proclaimed as having been exactly on time.[39]

The travelers who accompanied Harrison were members of his family for the most part. Included were Mrs. Harrison; Mrs. Dimmick, Caroline Harrison's niece; son Russell B. Harrison and Russell's wife; daughter Mary McKee; Postmaster General Wanamaker; Secretary of Agriculture Rusk; Marshal Dan Ransdell; stenographer Tibbott; the president's military aide, Maj. J. P. Sanger; George W. Boyd, the manager of the train, and his wife; and three newsmen from major press associations. Harrison's youngest brother, Carter B. Harrison, and Carter's wife became part of the tour two days out of Washington; and a relative of Mrs. Russell Harrison's came aboard at Los Angeles for the rest of the trip.

The five-car passenger train was described as exceeding "in beauty, convenience, opportunities for luxurious ease while traveling, and cheapness—to him—[of] any train ever used by any President of the United States." Each car was named; the president's car was the New Zealand. Its double drawing room was furnished in blue plush and was set apart from the sleeping chamber. There were rumors that the entire trip was being financed by Senator Leland Stanford of California, and there was speculation about the cost of the trip, which was made "in a style that no Czar of the Russians could travel in, if he were so disposed." Estimates for the total cost ranged from $6,000 upwards to $50,000. The latter figure happened to be the annual salary for the president.[40]

Because the trip was well publicized and because presidents were seldom seen along the selected route, the president was greeted by large, enthusiastic crowds at each stop. Harrison sought to shake hands with those who could get near him, but usually he ended by speaking briefly to all. Most of the president's remarks were made from the back of the observation car. Several speeches were lengthy major efforts on a central topic, presented to large groups. On occasion, Wanamaker and Rusk also spoke. Wanamaker visited post offices whenever he could. The president's extemporaneous speeches were copied by stenographer Tibbott. When produced in small print, they made two hundred pages of text.[41]

There is no doubt that this trip produced demanding, hard work for President Harrison. He was involved from early morning until late at night, shaking hands and making speeches. Sometimes he would barely have started a meal when he would have to make another appearance before a crowd. Occasionally the irritation of being always available came through in his speeches, but generally he was good humored, and it was obvious that he enjoyed his experiences with responsive crowds. In addition, matters of state had to be decided—this was the time when the crisis over the *Itata* with Chile erupted, and there were other issues of concern in foreign affairs.

On this western tour, a general effort was made to avoid travel on Sundays. The Sunday stops included Galveston, on 19 April; San Francisco, on 26 April and 3 May; and Glenwood Springs, Colorado, on 10 May. The final departure from the three layover cities was, in each case, shortly after midnight on Monday morning. At Galveston, San Francisco, and Seattle, Harrison and his party traveled part of the way on water; otherwise the trip was taken by train, or side trips in local areas were made by carriage.[42]

The first part of Harrison's western tour was through the Old South, where he failed to use this opportunity to speak for the Lodge election bill and the Blair education bill. Instead, he made general statements, such as, "While exacting all our own rights let us bravely and generously accord to every other man his equal rights before the law." He usually remarked about the prosperity he saw all around. Sometimes he referred to his Civil War experiences.[43] Most often, his speeches in the Old South emphasized the value of economic changes that no longer put sole reliance on agriculture as a source of income and stressed that industry, mining, and commerce were important adjuncts of a successful southern economy. Consequently, support of the new tariff law made sense in the New South.

Harrison's advisors listed his speech at Galveston as the most important of the entire trip, while *Harper's Weekly* rated the San Francisco message as Harrison's biggest stump speech. His extemporaneous remarks contained polished phrases and complete paragraphs; his skill as an orator was evident. At Galveston he responded at length to a formal address of welcome by pointing out the advantages that could come to Galveston, and to the United States as a whole, by fully endorsing the reciprocal trading features of the McKinley Tariff Act. Finally, in his comments that attracted the greatest attention nationwide, he described the necessity of providing subsidies for the American merchant marine so that in distant "ports, so long unfamiliar with the American flag, there shall again be found our steamship and our sailing vessels flying the flag that we all love, and carrying from our shores the products that these men of toil have brought to them to exchange for the products of other climes."[44]

At both El Paso, Texas, and San Diego, California, Harrison used his proximity to Mexico to repeat the friendly feelings he had voiced in 1889 at the Pan-American Congress. President Porfirio Díaz was not able to meet Harrison at either El Paso or Juarez. At both border cities, Harrison acknowledged friendly greetings that had been sent by Mexico's president. In very diplomatic language, Harrison said Americans no longer coveted Mexican territory but now coveted their friendship and trade.

Flowers and bedecked triumphal arches were used throughout the tour to greet the president and his party. The most impressive and massive floral piece was displayed at Santa Paula, California. Activities that were planned for President Harrison and his party varied from place to place. In California the pace of the trip was decreased to some extent; a whole week was spent in the San Francisco vicinity. Side trips were taken also in southern California. Several trips were made on San Francisco Bay, one to a nearby shipyard, where Mrs. Harrison christened the armored coast-defense vessel *Monterey*, the first of its kind to be built on the West Coast. Some time was spent at Senator Stanford's ranch in Palo Alto and at his mansion on Nob Hill. A San Francisco newspaper asserted that never since the visits of General Grant and President Hayes ''has there been such an outpouring of people to welcome one man.''[45]

Harrison made many speeches in San Francisco, the longest of which was presented at a banquet at the Palace Hotel on 1 May. The message this time, as shown in this single paragraph, which was interrupted six times by applause and cheers, was a belief

> that we have come to a new epoch as a Nation. There are opening portals before us inviting us to enter—opening portals to trade and influence and prestige such as we have never seen before. We will pursue the paths of peace; we are not a warlike Nation; all our instincts, all our history is in the lines of peace. Only intolerable aggression, only the peril of our institutions— of the flag—can thoroughly arouse us. With capability for war on land and on sea unexcelled by any nation in the world, we are smitten with the love of peace. We promote the peace of this hemisphere by placing judiciously some large guns about the Golden Gate—simply for saluting purposes, and yet they should be of the best modern type.

One of the primary points from the Galveston speech—subsidies for American shipping—was again mentioned, to which the stenographer who recorded the president's words added, ''Enthusiastic and continuous cheering.''[46]

Perhaps typical of the Harrison tour of Oregon and Washington, and elsewhere, was a tight-set routine: the arrival of the presidential party in the special train, a brief pause to exchange pleasantries with selected citizens, and a short speech to the local crowd that had gathered. Harrison had seen the Pacific Northwest ten years earlier as a United States senator, but this time Washington had become a state, and he had signed the proclamation of statehood. Harrison's entrance to Seattle was atypical, as he came in by water.

At 1:15 in the afternoon of May 6, 1891, the steamer *City of Seattle* enroute from Tacoma and accompanied by the *Greyhound, Bailey Gatzert, T. J. Potter,* and *City of Kingston* were met off Alki Point by 30 more steamers, all of them blowing their whistles, strung with patriotic bunting, and packed with passengers in their best attire. This was the proper way for the 23rd president of the United States to enter Seattle: on board its namesake steamer and surrounded by its "mosquito fleet."[47]

The departure for members of the presidential party came three and one-half hours later. As they boarded their train, they were beginning the last third of the trip and were heading back to their homes. Stops in other locations in Washington, Oregon, and Idaho were less frequent, and most of Harrison's speeches were short, but still appropriate for each area visited. At Pocatello, Idaho, Harrison reminded his audience of his first visit to the area in 1881. He also said:

My sympathy and interest have always gone out to those who, leaving the settled and populous parts of our country, have pushed the frontiers of civilization farther and farther to the westward until they have met the Pacific Ocean and the setting sun. Pioneers have always been an enterprising people. If they had not been they would have remained at home; they endured great hardships and perils in opening these great mines . . . and in bringing into subjection these wild plains and making them blossom like gardens.

In Utah the president's train followed a line of closely placed towns, and his speeches were frequent.[48]

The Sunday layover in Glenwood Springs, Colorado, had more activities than had been anticipated in the established schedule. The city was reached early Sunday morning, so as to enable the president and the postmaster general to attend services in the local Presbyterian church. Later they were greeted by a local reception committee and by as many as ten thousand miners from nearby camps. At Glenwood Springs, Leadville, Denver, and other Colorado cities, Harrison remembered the children in the audience with remarks about the importance of children in the home and about the strong efforts that were being made everywhere to develop a well-ordered school system.[49]

At Omaha, Nebraska, Harrison responded to an imposing parade with the third-longest speech of the tour. Perhaps because he was aware of the Populist strength in Nebraska and of their opposition to certain laws that the previous Congress had passed, he met two issues head on in a wide discussion. So he said in support of the McKinley Tariff that the administration had secured "larger foreign markets for our farm products . . . [and] this has brought better prices to the stock-raisers of these great western valleys. I believe, under the provision looking to reciprocal trade . . . that we shall open yet larger and nearer markets for the products of Nebraska farmers." He also acknowledged that one of the functions of our government is to "provide a currency for the use of our people, . . . that whatever money the Government issues, paper or coin, must be good money."[50]

The pace of the journey and the demands on the president were evident in northern Missouri, where he spoke briefly "to an unusually large crowd" at Maryville at 11:00 P.M. on 13 May and at 5:30 the next morning to five thousand people who had gathered in the station at Hannibal. From there to Springfield, Illinois, stops were so short that there was no speech making. In the Illinois capital, Harrison spoke at Lincoln's tomb in Oak Ridge Cemetery and then to a large crowd that had gathered at the Statehouse. At Montezuma, Indiana, the return to his home state and the eloquent greeting so overcame Harrison that "he was unable to respond to the demand for a speech at any length." Those near enough in the huge crowd of fifty thousand in Indianapolis heard him provide a general description of the trip. He ended his speech by saying:

> I left you a little more than two years ago to take up the work of the most responsible office in the world. I went to those untried duties sustained by your helpful friendliness. I come to you again after these two years of public office to confess many errors, but to say to you that I have had but one thought in my mind. It was to use whatever influence had been confided to me for the general good of all our people.[51]

On 14 May, Harrison made eleven speeches at locations in Illinois, Indiana, and Ohio. The western tour was almost over for the tired travelers, with only the last day remaining. Between Baltimore and Washington, Harrison "gathered all the members of his party about him in the observation car, including the train employees and servants, and made a short speech," thanking everyone for "their courtesy and attention." Each employee then on the train, including the conductor and the engineer, received individual thanks. That was speech number 140, according to one counting, and 142, by another. Waiting for them in the Washington depot were three members of the cabinet, but the first to greet Harrison on alighting from his coach were his grandchildren. Several days later, the approximately four hundred gifts to the president and Mrs. Harrison, many of silver and gold, were sorted out and displayed at the White House. The western tour of 1891 had become a memory.[52]

While the presidential western tour was in San Francisco, Harrison's sister Mrs. Betsy Eaton had sustained a serious injury in Cincinnati when she was thrown from her carriage. Later, Harrison invited Betsy to vacation at the Cape May Point cottage. Mrs. Harrison was not happy with the prospect of such a visit. She wrote to her daughter that Betsy "is not helpful, and will require attention."[53]

The president's Decoration Day trip in 1891 was to Philadelphia, where his primary speech was given at the grave of the Civil War hero Gen. George Gordon Meade, in Laurel Hill Cemetery. Accompanying Harrison this time were Wanamaker, Proctor, Tracy, and Halford. Again, after he had made a reference to gruesome memories from the Civil War, his main remarks dealt with the flag as a symbol. He recalled having seen it "waved over every school-house" on his recent tour of the states and in other places in his travels. When his private car was attached to a regular train for the return to Washington, rather than necessitating a special train, his Philadelphia trip was shortened by forty-five minutes, causing the *New York Times* to call it an abrupt departure.[54]

The summer move to Cape May in 1891 came on 3 July, with arrival in time to review a Fourth of July parade. Plans were made to stay at least a month, which was later extended to two and one-half months. Harrison also had an extended absence from Cape May, this time a ten-day tour to Vermont to provide an official dedication for the Bennington Battle Monument. Harrison's travel companions were his son Russell; Halford; Howard Cale, who had been a law apprentice in Harrison's office years earlier; and George W. Boyd of the Pennsylvania Railroad. In crossing New Jersey on 18 August, there were stops but no speeches, since it was raining. In New York, Harrison spoke to crowds at Newburgh, Kingston, Albany, and Troy. At Bennington, Vermont, the president spoke extemporaneously, with his usual apologetic comment, "I come to you under circumstances that altogether forbid preparation." Later, to thirty-five hundred invited guests, seated in a banquet tent, he spoke again, after eating on a "dinner service of rare Sevres and old Delft ware." Included in his remarks was the belief that

> we have come to a time when we may look out to greater things. Secure in our own institutions, enriched almost beyond calculations, I believe we have reached a time when we may take a large part in the great transactions of the world. I believe our people are prepared now to insist that the American flag shall again be seen upon the sea, and that our merchants and manufacturers are ready to seize the golden opportunity that is now offered for extending our commerce into the States of Central and South America.[55]

From Bennington, the Harrison party went to Saratoga, New York, then to nearby Mount McGregor, where they were entertained by former Senator W. J. Arkell. One hundred twenty guests helped the president celebrate his fifty-eighth birthday. Harrison went fishing with Arkell in a private lake the next day; then for four days he rested at Saratoga Springs. On 25 August he began another tour through Vermont, accompanied by Secretary of War Redfield Proctor. In three days he made twenty-three speeches, all but two of which were in Vermont. Then it was back to Cape May, by way of New York City, for additional vacation time. In New York City the president met Caroline, and together, on 31 August, they welcomed their daughter and daughter-in-law, who were returning from Europe on the steamship *Majestic*.[56]

The year 1892 was not kind to the president and his family. Out-of-town journeys were of a very different nature than earlier; they were dominated by the serious decline in Caroline Harrison's health. Thus, in late February, the president and his family, "solely for rest and quiet," took an eight-hour rail trip for a week's visit to Virginia Beach, Virginia, where they stayed in the Princess Anne Hotel. Two grandchildren, Mrs. Dimmick, two servants, and Halford accompanied President and Mrs. Harrison. On Monday 29 February the president went out about twelve miles for a shooting expedition in the marshes on the coast, which had been leased by the Ragged Island Hunting Club. Plans were made for another hunting trip, but bad weather and an urgent message from Washington forced its cancellation, and the Harrison party returned to the White House. Harrison went on another hunting trip to the Chesapeake Bay area near New Church, Virginia, from 7 to 9 April, where he had success in shooting snipe and golden plover. His companions this time were George W. Boyd and Harrison's nephew, Lieutenant Parker of the navy.[57]

Later in April, Harrison went to New York City to lay the twelve-ton cornerstone for Grant's Tomb and to make a speech. The president and Mrs. Harrison, along with cabinet members Wanamaker, Rusk, and Noble, went by private car on this trip. Also with them were General and Mrs. Schofield, private secretary Halford, stenographer Tibbott, and Lieutenant Parker, who was in charge of the arrangements. Cabinet members Elkins, Tracy, and Charles Foster were also present at the Grant memorial, where the president applied the mortar for the cornerstone with a gold trowel. Nearby, a "great fleet of steam and sailing vessels, all with flags flying, were anchored . . . with the warship Miantonomoh in the centre. While the ceremonies of laying the stone were being performed the warship fired salutes."[58]

Two weeks later the President and Mrs. Harrison, accompanied by Mrs. Dimmick and Lieutenant Parker, took a weekend cruise on Chesapeake Bay on the lighthouse tender *Jessamine*. A stop was made at Fortress Monroe on this trip.[59] This and the February trip to Virginia Beach are indications of the president's early concern for Caroline's health.

The last Decoration Day trip for President Harrison was to Rochester, New York, to dedicate the Soldiers and Sailors' Monument. He was accompanied by Noble and Halford, along with eight members of Congress and General and Mrs. Schofield. They left Washington early on Thursday 28 May and arrived in Rochester that night. After the dedication on Saturday, the presidential party rested on Sunday and returned to Washington on Monday 1 June 1892.[60]

Instead of vacationing at Cape May in 1892, the Harrisons leased a cottage in the Adirondacks, near Loon Lake. Unbeknownst to the general public, Mrs. Harrison was suffering from tuberculosis. She had had "coughing spasms and a lung hemorrhage" and had become bedfast by early May. The quiet, the high elevation, and the clear air of Loon Lake were considered essential for her recovery. The five-hundred-mile trip, by special train, started on the afternoon of Tuesday 5 July; arrival at the Loon Lake station, several miles from the rented cottage, was after dark on Thursday. Mrs. Harrison was described as being in a "pitiable condition." Accompanying the presidential couple were Mrs. Dimmick, Lieutenant and Mrs. Parker, and Caroline's personal physician, a Dr. Gardiner. The new environment seemed to help; Caroline improved slowly at first. The president headed back to Washington on Monday 11 July, after responding to an invitation by Senator Leland Stanford to address the annual conference of the

National Education Association, which was meeting in nearby Saratoga. The president spoke on a law-and-order theme, probably in response to labor-management violence in Idaho and elsewhere.[61]

Other members of the presidential family had gone to Cape May, and after a few days in Washington, Harrison, accompanied by Halford, went there for four days.[62] For the next ten weeks Harrison divided his attention between Washington and Loon Lake. It was a busy schedule, for Congress was in session until early August. Harrison had been renominated for the presidency; therefore, healing wounds in various Republican political factions was essential, though Caroline's health remained uppermost in his mind. For two days in late August, Harrison was at Whitelaw Reid's Ophir Farm, visiting with Republican leaders from New York State. Harrison then went north again to Loon Lake and made side trips to Plattsburg and to Saranac Lake to make political speeches. A potential outbreak of cholera in early September caused Harrison to cut short one visit to Loon Lake and to return to Washington for consultation with government officials about plans for a quarantine.

Caroline Harrison's health was deteriorating rapidly, so most of the family hurried to Loon Lake. Not until 14 September did the public learn that Mrs. Harrison had pulmonary tuberculosis. A decision was made in mid September to take her back to the White House. Elaborate plans were made for the trip, which began at 11:00 A.M. on bright, cold 20 September. Harrison's speaking schedule in upstate New York was abandoned. The three-mile carriage ride from the cottage to the railroad took forty-five minutes. The special train, which had a car containing a hospital bed, departed about noon on the twenty-and-one-half-hour run to Washington. In the presidential party this time were Mr. and Mrs. Russell Harrison; Mr. and Mrs. J. R. McKee and their children, Benjamin and Mary; Mrs. Dimmick; Lieutenant and Mrs. Parker; Halford; Dr. Gardiner; a Miss Davis, the nurse; Marie Kempe, the children's governess; Josephine Kneip, Caroline's maid; and Charlie, the president's valet. George Boyd handled all arrangements to expedite the trip to Washington. A reporter described the president, on this return to Washington, as "much afflicted, and his eyes, red from weeping, and with dark rings under them, told the tale of his deep distress and sleepless nights at the bedside of his wife."[63]

Harrison nevertheless made a hurried trip to New York City for the Columbian Celebration Banquet on 13 October 1892, which was sponsored by the Lenox Lyceum. With his thoughts on Caroline, the president was still able to respond to a toast at this event.[64]

Caroline Harrison's health declined quickly, and she died on Tuesday 25 October. A simple funeral was held in the East Room of the

White House on 27 October. The departure of the special funeral train came shortly thereafter, bound for Indianapolis; it carried Benjamin Harrison on the last extended trip of his presidency. With the president on this brief return to Indianapolis, where Maj. Dan Ransdell had organized the funeral arrangements, were family members and all of his cabinet. All along the line of the funeral train, people were standing silently, bareheaded, as a demonstration of respect. The presidential party, with Caroline Harrison's body, arrived in Indianapolis at 9:30 A.M. on Saturday 28 October. A crowd of five thousand was standing around the First Presbyterian Church, the Harrison family's church. Inside, the front of the church was covered with flowers. After a brief service, a cortege of more than one hundred carriages followed the hearse to Crown Hill Cemetery and the newly acquired Harrison family plot.[65] The presidential party returned to the train after the funeral and departed for Washington. There were no further out-of-town expeditions for Harrison during the remaining five months of his administration. His defeat in November by Cleveland was not important to him—the grief over the loss of Caroline dominated his thinking throughout those final months in the White House.

An examination of Harrison's traveling companions during his four years as president shows that he did not play favorites with members of his cabinet. There was much newspaper comment about the absence of Blaine on these trips. It is true that Blaine made only one trip with Harrison—to the funeral in New York City of General Sherman in February 1891. If it had not been for "lumbago," Blaine would have been in the presidential party attending the centennial celebration of Washington's inauguration in New York City on 30 April 1889. Blaine's repeated illnesses made it impossible for him to take part in these travels, even if he had wanted to do so. Wanamaker and Rusk made the long western tour with Harrison, and each of them was with Harrison on six other trips. Noble was on six presidential trips, and Windom was on four. Vice-President Morton was present at the destination of six of these trips. Harrison's former law partner Attorney General Miller, a Harrison companion four times, went on fewer presidential trips than anyone else but Proctor, who went on two, and Blaine. Tracy was on eight of the presidential trips; he was an especially close confidant after the tragic fire at his house, in which he lost his wife and other members of his family. Elkins and other late additions to the cabinet were rarely presidential traveling companions, as his major travels came during his first two to three years in office.

Either private secretary Halford or stenographer Tibbott, sometimes both of them, were on every presidential public or private trip away from Washington. They helped the president stay in communication with his office in Washington, or they could help him telegraph a cabinet officer who might also be out of Washington. For instance, while Harrison was vacationing in Cresson Springs, Pennsylvania, in September 1890, he telegraphed to Secretary of the Treasury Windom, who was vacationing in Massachusetts, and asked him to go to New York City to take the necessary action for promptly augmenting the money supply.[66] Close communication with Washington was maintained throughout the lengthy western trip in 1891.

Members of the United States Supreme Court or of Congress were included in some presidential trips; usually their names appear only once in the compilation of those who were traveling with the president. However, Marshal Dan Ransdell, probably in the role of a security guard, frequently accompanied the president. The press reports make no mention of agents of the United States Secret Service serving as guards on presidential trips, though this was part of that agency's responsibility. Infrequent press comments show that local police served in a security role for any area where the president visited: for instance, mounted policemen surrounded the president's carriage when he was traveling from Grant's Tomb in New York City to the ferry station for his return to Washington. Police in other settings were described as holding back a crowd when the president was moved from his observation car to a platform where he could more easily address all who were there. Harrison, like most of his predecessors, received threatening letters; but there was only one news report of an attempt to assassinate him. Later that story was doubted and discredited as having come from suspicious sources that were seeking unduly to build up the United States Secret Service.[67]

George W. Boyd, general assistant passenger agent for the Pennsylvania Railroad, who managed the western tour in April and May 1891, became a family friend. On a number of other occasions he personally handled arrangements for presidential travels. At least twice, navy Lieutenant Parker, a nephew of the president's, managed the travel arrangements for a presidential train. Caroline Harrison traveled with her husband on many public and private trips during his presidency. Other members of the family, including children and grandchildren, were frequent participants in presidential excursions. Caroline Harrison's aged father, the Rev. John W. Scott, lived at the White House and went on vacation trips with the presidential family. Mary Scott Lord Dimmick, a widowed niece of Caroline Harrison's, came to live at the White House to help her aunt with her duties as the White House hostess. From that time she was always included on family vacations or weekend excursions.[68]

President Benjamin Harrison, like most of his predecessors, was besieged from all over the country by invitations that he could not accept to address conventions and special ceremonies. Once or twice each winter the president got away from official duties to go hunting. Harrison responded every year to invitations to attend Decoration Day observances, and he usually traveled away from the family vacation spot during mid and late August. He was frequently away from his family on 20 August, his birthday. When Harrison gave a public address, he almost always began in an apologetic fashion, saying in his opening remarks that there had been no time for preparation. Usually his listeners would respond favorably to his remarks—he was an excellent platform orator even when he did not make adequate preparation for his speech. Harrison, like his presidential predecessors, did not have many persons on his office staff, and none of them were given the responsibility for writing his speeches. Yet even in the heat of a political campaign or in a pause on a railroad journey or to a veterans' group or at the dedication of a building or a monument, President Harrison's extemporaneous speeches were models of superior statesmanship: they were forceful and concise, the elegant expression of a patriot. Moreover, his speeches, whether eight, nine, or only one on a given day, were adapted uniquely to the place and the audience. Harrison was presented to the public in a most favorable role when he addressed a sizable audience. His extensive travels, throughout the country during his four years as president, enhanced his political image and provided American citizens with an acquaintance of one of his most important assets, his ability as an orator and as a public speaker.

10

★ ★ ★ ★ ★

THE PASSING OF THE
CIVIL WAR GENERATION

Death struck Harrison's official family all too often. The mourning was continual in January and February 1890. First, Secretary of State James G. Blaine lost a son and a daughter in rapid succession; then, within days, Secretary of the Navy Benjamin Tracy suffered through the tragic house fire that cost the lives of his wife and a daughter.

One year later, the administration had to deal with the sudden demise of Secretary of the Treasury William Windom in January 1891. The sixty-three-year-old Windom collapsed immediately after giving a speech to the New York Board of Trade and Transportation, an audience of about two hundred at the fabled Delmonico's restaurant.[1] He was replaced by Charles Foster of Ohio, who had served eight years in the House of Representatives and four years as governor. The president himself was not immune, enduring the loss of his wife in the midst of his bid for a second term in 1892. But the nation reserved a special sympathy for Blaine. Shortly after his resignation in mid 1892, the unfortunate Blaine lost a second son. Then the "Plumed Knight" began his own last battle.

Blaine's death in January 1893 seemed to end an era in the history of the United States. Contemporaries surely were aware that with the passing of President of the Confederacy Jefferson Davis, Adm. David Dixon Porter, Gen. William Tecumseh Sherman, former Vice-President Hannibal Hamlin, former President Rutherford B. Hayes, and four justices of the Supreme Court, the nation had lost its most prominent links to the time of the Civil War and Reconstruction. The *New York*

185

Times proclaimed, when Jefferson Davis died at the age of eighty-one in December 1889, that the Civil War finally had been taken out of politics. The *Times* emphasized that a southern policy was not relevant as the nation entered the 1890s and warned that the Republican party had to stand on its current policies—not on memories of the past.[2] Indeed, the Republicans would not survive that reality in either the congressional election of 1890 or the presidential contest of 1892.

Harrison almost had the opportunity to choose a chief justice and a majority of the Supreme Court in just four years. But Chief Justice Morrison R. Waite had passed away at the age of seventy-two in March 1888, and President Grover Cleveland had selected a political unknown, Melville W. Fuller of Illinois, to replace him. The fifty-five-year-old Fuller, then the president of the Illinois Bar Association, was not unknown to Cleveland, who had offered him various posts: the opportunity to be chairman of the Civil Service Commission or solicitor general or a member of a commission to investigate the questionable financial structure of western railroads. Fuller became the eighth chief justice of the Supreme Court in October 1888.[3]

A sensational development—an alleged attempt to assassinate veteran Associate Justice Stephen J. Field—added to the Supreme Court's burden and to the concern of President Harrison in the summer of 1889. The unbelievable background to the outrageous incident belonged to the legends of the West—specifically California—as the frontier was about to disappear.

Both Field and his assailant, David S. Terry, had been on the California Supreme Court during the late 1850s. In fact, Terry had been chief justice, until he had resigned in 1859 to meet United States Senator David C. Broderick in a duel in which Terry killed Broderick! Field, who replaced Terry as chief justice, was elevated to the United States Supreme Court by President Abraham Lincoln in 1863. Field and Terry would cross paths again a quarter of a century later.

In 1886, Terry married one Sarah Hill, who was in the midst of a long legal battle to obtain her share of the estate of former United States Senator William Sharon of Nevada. She claimed they had been married secretly; Sharon had vigorously denied the claim until his death in 1885. Field had become involved in the case when Sharon's executor had sued in 1888 to force Mrs. Terry to give up what had been declared a forged marriage certificate.

From the early days of the Republic, the justices of the Supreme Court had performed strenuous circuit duties as well; for most Americans scattered across the rapidly growing nation, the circuit courts represented the only contact with the federal judiciary. Field was in

California fulfilling his obligations on a circuit, reading a decision against Mrs. Terry, when the Terrys began to shout and threaten. It was apparent that Mrs. Terry was carrying a pistol, while Terry was armed with a knife. Field held both in contempt of court: Terry was given a six-months prison sentence, and Mrs. Terry was sentenced to thirty days in jail. They both swore to get revenge against Field.

When Field returned to the California circuit in 1889, Harrison and Attorney General W. H. H. Miller believed that there was convincing evidence of threatened violence against the justice, so he was assigned a guard, Deputy Marshal David Neagle. After Field had completed his court duty in Los Angeles, he boarded an overnight train for San Francisco. At a restaurant stop near Fresno, on 14 August, the seventy-two-year-old Field suddenly was attacked by Terry, a giant of a man who stood six-foot-three and weighed two hundred and fifty pounds. Neagle, after identifying himself, warned Terry to stop. Then thinking that the attacker was reaching for a knife, Neagle fired twice, killing Terry.

There were no federal laws protecting a United States marshal while performing his duty; therefore, both Neagle and Field were charged with murder. Field was released on his own recognizance by providing a bond of five thousand dollars; within two weeks, the charge was dismissed. Neagle filed a writ of habeas corpus, and a decision in the United States Circuit Court brought his release. But the state of California claimed jurisdiction in the case and appealed the action to the nation's Supreme Court. In April 1890 the Supreme Court, by a vote of six to two, with Field abstaining, sustained the president's decision to protect Field. Harrison had acted, ''as the principal conservator of 'the peace of the United States,' '' and Neagle was freed without a trial. This decision was interpreted as the broadest extension up to that time of the implied powers of the federal government under the Constitution.[4]

When President Harrison was faced with the responsibility of appointing judges to federal courts, he approached the job with great deliberateness; he could not be hurried; this was the kind of service for which he was best qualified. With his typical lack of concern for political considerations, he believed in promoting federal judges, presumably the best qualified candidates, to the Supreme Court. Harrison appointed more judges to the higher courts of the nation than had any previous one-term president.

Harrison made four appointments to the Supreme Court—Associate Justices David Josiah Brewer, Henry Billings Brown, George Shiras, Jr., and Howell Edmunds Jackson. For the first vacancy, Harrison chose David J. Brewer of Kansas, Justice Field's nephew; since 1884, Brewer had been a judge of the Eighth United States Circuit. The fifty-two-year-old Brewer, who had graduated from Yale with honors in 1856, had served on the Kansas Supreme Court for fourteen years before moving up to the federal judiciary. Apparently, he was on Harrison's list of potential cabinet officers until the president-elect was informed that Brewer could not "afford a Cabinet place & should feel constrained to decline if the place were offered him."[5]

Shortly after Harrison's inauguration, Chief Justice Fuller sent the president a formal note, informing him of the death of Associate Justice Stanley Matthews. Since the Senate would not convene to ratify an appointment until December, Harrison slowly assembled information. From his summer retreat at Deer Park, he wrote to a friend in Indiana, "I am now having the first opportunity to turn my thoughts towards the vacancy on the Supreme Bench." He insisted that he wanted "to get the best man and shall not be very much concerned by geography." He mentioned three choices—Henry Hitchcock of St. Louis, president of the American Bar Association; Brewer; and Judge Henry Brown of Detroit.[6]

The president had no difficulty in finding the right candidate for the next seat on the Supreme Court. When he chose Brewer to fill the first vacancy, the most serious rival was Henry Billings Brown. Actually, the two were close friends and had much in common; the fifty-four-year-old Brown had also graduated from Yale in 1856. Brown had been judge of the United States District Court for eastern Michigan, which was within the Sixth United States Circuit, since 1875. Perhaps the nation's foremost authority on admiralty law, he was one of the best-prepared nominees in the history of the Supreme Court—"the complete master of the federal specialties." Brown took Associate Justice Samuel Freeman Miller's position on 29 December 1890. While Brewer became an important vote in determining the extremely conservative trend of the court during the 1890s, Brown would stand out as a moderate.[7]

The appointment of Shiras came late in Harrison's presidency, on 26 July 1892; Jackson did not take his place on the Supreme Court until the inauguration of President Grover Cleveland on 4 March 1893. Shiras, another Yale man, class of 1853, was a highly successful attorney from western Pennsylvania—with an estimated annual income of seventy-five thousand dollars—but he had had no judicial experience. Two other factors added controversy to his appointment. Supreme Court justices could retire at full pay at the age of seventy with ten years of service; thus, there was an unwritten rule that no nominee could be more than sixty years of age. Shiras had turned sixty in January 1892. Furthermore, Shiras was a member of the Pennsylvania Republican faction that was aligned against United States Senator Matthew Quay.

Boss Quay sought to organize opposition to Shiras, which caused a six-months delay in the Senate. But Shiras carried Andrew Carnegie's strong endorsement, and Quay gave up that fight, though not his opposition to Harrison. Shiras, who replaced Associate Justice Joseph P. Bradley, occupied an ideological position between Brewer and Brown as a moderate conservative.[8]

With the death of Associate Justice Lucius Quintus Cincinnatus Lamar on 23 January 1893, Harrison had his last opportunity to make an appointment to the Supreme Court. In the aftermath of his loss to Cleveland in the presidential election, Harrison faced a difficult decision, as he sought to deprive the Democrat of the opportunity to fill the vacancy, perhaps with a prominent former Confederate. Harrison knew that the incoming Senate would be under Democratic control and would reject a typical Republican nominee. The solution: find an acceptable southerner—one who was not closely identified with the Confederacy.

Though almost sixty-one years of age, Howell E. Jackson of Tennessee was a most acceptable candidate. He had served with Harrison in the Senate, and the two men had in fact become very good friends. An expert in patent law, Jackson had been appointed a judge in the Sixth United States Circuit in 1887, and since 1891 had been presiding judge in the new Circuit Court of Appeals in Cincinnati. Apparently, Jackson proved himself to Harrison with a decision that upheld the prosecution of three Tennessee men who had been indicted for conspiring to interfere with the civil rights of five federal marshals. While searching for an illegal still, three of the five had been killed. Harrison later praised Jackson: "You were a believer in the nation and did not sympathize with the opinion that a United States marshal was an alien officer, or that election frauds or any other infraction of the federal statutes were deserving of aught but indignant condemnation and punishment."

While serving in the Sixth Circuit, Jackson had developed a close relationship with Henry Billings Brown and had recommended Brown for the Supreme Court; Associate Justice Brown now returned the favor, endorsing Jackson. On the Supreme Court, Jackson was another moderate conservative. Jackson also was the first Democrat appointed by a Republican president since Lincoln's selection of Stephen Field. Even to the end of his administration, Harrison kept his own counsel and ignored criticism from the leaders of his party.[9]

A historic breakthrough in the federal court system came early in 1891, with the creation of the nine Circuit Courts of Appeal. In his first annual message of 3 December 1889, Harrison called for the creation of "intermediate courts having final appellate jurisdiction of certain classes of questions and cases." Congress responded, motivated by the backlog of more than eighteen hundred cases pending in the Supreme Court in 1890, an increase of six hundred new cases in a single year. The Supreme Court was unable to handle more than four hundred and fifty cases a year; therefore something had to be done. The impact of the new courts was immediate. Less than four hundred new cases came to the Supreme Court in 1891; the figure was below three hundred in 1892.[10]

While Howell Jackson was an active participant in the Supreme Court for not much more than one year—he died from tuberculosis and its complications in August 1895—all four justices that Harrison appointed were involved in what has been described as a revolutionary era for the nation's highest court. In a period of social tension that began with the Haymarket Square Riot in Chicago in 1886 and featured increased militancy from both labor and farmers, the judiciary became the "principal bulwark of socio-economic conservatism," particularly after the United States plunged into the Depression of 1893. In this era of the "new judicialism," the Supreme Court clearly took a stand. In a series of dramatic decisions over a four-month period in 1895—representing perhaps the high point of judicial supremacy in all of American history—the Supreme Court upheld the use of the injunction against strikes, seriously weakened the Sherman Anti-Trust Act, and declared invalid the income tax, which was part of the Wilson-Gorman Tariff of 1894.

On 21 January 1895 the court ruled in the case of *United States* v. *E. C. Knight Company* that the American Sugar Refining Company had not violated the Sherman Anti-Trust Act even though it controlled more than 90 percent of the nation's sugar-refining capacity. The vote was 7 to 1, as David Brewer, Henry Brown, and George Shiras voted with the majority. Jackson, who was already very ill, did not participate. Jackson then reluctantly returned to Washington, however, believing that he might represent the decisive vote in the case of *Pollock* v. *Farmers' Loan and Trust Company*, which determined the fate of the income tax. On 20 May the Supreme Court, in one of its most controversial decisions, struck down the income tax by a 5 to 4 vote. As it turned out, both Jackson and Brown were with the minority. But Brewer and Shiras cast critical votes against the tax.

Just one week later, the very conservative Brewer then wrote the decision in the case of *In re Debs*. The court unanimously upheld the injunction that the federal government had used to break the Pullman Strike of 1894 and to send the leader of the strike, Eugene Debs, to prison. Again, Jackson did not participate; but Brewer, Brown, and Shiras did not waver. In fact, the relatively moderate Brown then left his mark on the nation's history when he wrote the decision in the case of

Plessy v. *Ferguson,* which in 1896 established the validity of segregation in the United States.[11]

As the Civil War faded into history, every aging veteran had to feel the loss when Adm. David Dixon Porter and Gen. William Tecumseh Sherman died on successive days in mid February 1891. Sherman held a special position in the mythology of the Civil War. The *New York Times* reported in great detail about his death; alongside that story, the *Times* carried a brief item on Porter's funeral.[12] But Porter also had made unique contributions to the military history of the United States.

Porter's career tells almost everything about the nation's navy during much of the nineteenth century. He entered the navy in 1829, when not yet sixteen years old. He died while still on active duty as the only admiral in the navy, a few months before his seventy-eighth birthday. Porter had not become a lieutenant until 1841; then he had served in the Mexican War. But soon after, he had left the service—as did many officers in both the navy and the army who realized the impossibility of obtaining promotions during peacetime. He had returned to the navy in the mid 1850s and was still, at forty-eight years of age, a lieutenant in 1861, twenty years after attaining that rank, until the Civil War presented unlimited opportunity. Late in 1861, Porter finally had been promoted to commander. He then had played a decisive role in the successful campaign that brought New Orleans under Union control early in 1862. Before the end of the year, Porter had been designated acting rear admiral. After he had helped Gen. Ulysses S. Grant capture Vicksburg, completing the conquest of the Mississippi River in mid 1863, Porter had become a rear admiral—officially bypassing the ranks of captain and commodore. This had all happened in less than two years.

After the war, Porter had administered Annapolis and had served as the navy's only vice-admiral. When Adm. David G. Farragut died in 1870, Porter had taken over as the navy's ranking officer for the next twenty years, until his death on 13 February 1891. Vice-Adm. Stephen C. Rowan had not been replaced when he had retired at the age of eighty in 1889. Now Porter was not replaced, thus, for all intents and purposes, abolishing the top two positions in the navy.[13]

William Tecumseh Sherman graduated from West Point in 1840; he was in California during the Mexican War but saw no action. Though he had been promoted to captain in the early 1850s, he had chosen to leave the army. With the coming of the Civil War, Sherman had returned as a colonel in June 1861 and almost immediately had moved up to brigadier general. Wounded twice while leading a division at Shiloh early in 1862, Sherman had soon become a major general. He then had advanced rapidly in the command structure in 1863: Sherman led a corps in the great victory at Vicksburg; he commanded the Army of the Tennessee in the decisive battle at Chattanooga. Early in 1864, Sherman had been put in command of the western theater.

Leading three armies, he was about to launch a total war—a grueling campaign involving the active participation of Col. Benjamin Harrison—which would capture the imagination of a weary North. In May, Sherman had moved out toward Atlanta. The city was taken at the beginning of September, raising the possibility that the war might at last come to an end. His forces then had destroyed Atlanta, and sixty thousand men had begun the march to the sea in mid November, devastating much of Georgia in the process. A month later, Savannah had fallen, and Sherman's troops had marched north into the Carolinas. He accepted the surrender of the last Confederate army at the end of April 1865.

The forty-six-year-old Sherman had received the third star of lieutenant general in 1866 and had succeeded Grant as General of the Army in 1869. He held that post for fourteen years, until his retirement in 1883. A legend in his own time who absolutely refused to be a candidate for the presidential nomination at the Republican National Convention of 1884, Sherman died in New York on 14 February 1891. As president, Harrison announced the death of Sherman in a brief message to Congress. But Harrison had special memories of Sherman. The president had distinguished himself in the Atlanta campaign and had formed a close relationship with his commander. Harrison spoke from the heart when he said of Sherman: ''No living American was so loved and venerated as he.''[14]

Less than five months later, the passing of Hannibal Hamlin had special meaning for every living citizen who could remember the Civil War and the time of Abraham Lincoln. Hamlin was part of the Maine political dynasty, including James G. Blaine, which had developed along with the Republican party in the mid nineteenth century. In fact, Hamlin had served twelve years in the House of Representatives and Senate as a Democrat, before he had dramatically announced his conversion to the new party in 1856 as part of the struggle against slavery. Hamlin had remained in the Senate and had emerged as the perfect New England candidate for vice-president, balancing the ticket headed by Lincoln in the 1860 presidential election. Hamlin was a one-term vice-president; political considerations, and fate, had dictated that he be replaced by the loyal southerner Andrew Johnson when Lincoln ran for a second term in

1864. Hamlin had returned to the Senate in 1869 for two more terms, then had ended his career with a brief stint as minister to Spain in the early 1880s.[15] He died at the age of eighty-one on 4 July 1891—a symbolic date which had become the anniversary of the Civil War victories at Vicksburg and Gettysburg.

Rutherford B. Hayes, whose presidency brought the United States beyond Reconstruction, had earned his place as one of the most genuinely decent men of mid-nineteenth-century politics. A graduate of Harvard Law School, Hayes had entered the Civil War as a major and had risen to the rank of brevet major general—he was wounded on three occasions. Hayes had been elected to the House of Representatives before the end of the war, and he soon had become governor of Ohio for two terms. When he won a separate third term as governor in 1875, Hayes had emerged as a legitimate candidate for the Republican presidential nomination in 1876.

Hayes had won the nomination on the seventh ballot—with 384 votes to 351 for James G. Blaine—then had defeated Governor Samuel J. Tilden of New York in the most unique presidential election in the nation's history. The decision of the Electoral Commission was not accepted by Congress until 2 March 1877—with the inauguration scheduled for 5 March, a Monday. Hayes had then served with dignity, for only one term by choice, attempting to "dispel dissension and to restore harmony . . . as the bitterness of Reconstruction steadily subsided." Hayes, who had attended the funerals of former Presidents Ulysses S. Grant and Chester A. Arthur in the mid 1880s, passed away on 17 January 1893, at the age of seventy. Harrison may have been thinking about his own place in the history of the nation when he said about Hayes: "He has steadily grown in the public esteem."[16]

For James G. Blaine, the final agony ended on 27 January 1893. The issues of the Civil War and Reconstruction seemed to die with the man who had been a candidate for the presidential nomination at five consecutive Republican National Conventions between 1876 and 1892. Just ahead lay a devastating depression—then foreign war, an empire, and a new century. These were challenges for the generation of William Jennings Bryan, Theodore Roosevelt, and their contemporaries, who could not remember the Civil War.

11

★ ★ ★ ★ ★

THE END OF
AN ADMINISTRATION

It had seemed apparent in 1888 that the "Blaine Legion" would not abandon the quest for one more opportunity to nominate the "Plumed Knight" as the Republican candidate for president. Whatever the variety of motives that inspired all who rallied behind Blaine for the *fifth* time, they chose to disregard his obvious physical deterioration. Walker Blaine had predicted that his father would be nominated in 1892 "if he keeps alive." Speculation that Blaine might be available for the nomination in 1892 played right into the hands of boss Thomas C. Platt of New York and other powerful figures in the party who had been excluded from the administration; they would use Blaine as a symbol of their dissatisfaction with Harrison. Louis T. Michener, who directed Harrison's political fortunes, acknowledged the importance of Platt: "I have not the slightest doubt that if Platt had been appointed [as secretary of the Treasury] Harrison would have been renominated by acclamation and elected triumphantly."[1] After the devastating losses in the congressional elections of 1890, an increasing number of Republicans became convinced that Blaine alone could save the party from a disastrous defeat in the next presidential contest. Late in 1891, the railroad magnate Chauncey M. Depew shared the mood of the moment with his fellow New Yorker Whitelaw Reid: "The Blaine movement is more than a sentiment, it is a craze. Will he take it? is the one question."[2] At that point, Blaine had been ill for almost four months.

Meanwhile, boss Matthew Quay of Pennsylvania had joined Platt as a leader of the anti-Harrison forces in the party. For at least a year,

Senator Quay had ignored a series of articles in the *New York World* that contained a long list of allegations about his political activities in Pennsylvania. But the Republican reverses in the congressional elections of 1890 weakened Quay, the national chairman of the party. Quay finally resigned that position on 29 July 1891. He believed, however, that Harrison had too readily accepted his resignation.[3] Quay had the excuse that he needed in order to make a complete break with the president. Platt, Quay, and those who collaborated with them planned to use Blaine to stop Harrison. It became clear at the beginning of 1892 that Blaine wanted no part of the scheme. In a letter to James S. Clarkson, who had succeeded Quay as national chairman, Blaine formally withdrew on 6 February. Yet Clarkson paid no attention to such a letter. As determined as Platt and Quay that Harrison should not receive a second nomination, Clarkson was prepared to use the resources of the national committee against the incumbent president of the United States.[4]

There is every indication that Harrison might have turned his back on renomination; but his political enemies forced him to become a candidate, if only to prevent the possible nomination of Blaine. Suddenly, between March and May, Blaine seemed once again to be available. Elijah W. Halford, Harrison's secretary, recalled more than a quarter of a century later that the president had described Blaine on 20 March as "a disturber and an unfriendly critic."[5] Within days of that statement, the president and the secretary of state began an unfriendly exchange of letters about the problems with the Italian government.

If any single person led Blaine into opposition to the president, it was Mrs. James G. Blaine. Never more than tolerant of the man who had snubbed her son Walker, Mrs. Blaine lost patience with Harrison in April, when he refused a personal favor. Mrs. Blaine requested in vain that the president promote Col. John J. Coppinger, the husband of her recently deceased daughter Alice, to brigadier general. The widower had just been promoted to colonel in January 1891; he ranked fifty-sixth in seniority on a list of seventy. Halford's diary detailed Mrs. Blaine's anger when the president said no. Harrison told Halford that Mrs. Blaine spoke "fierce words . . . [and] went out of the room with a harsh look on her face." She bitterly reminded the president, "You had a chance to please us once." Michener believed that Mrs. Blaine then urged her husband to try for the nomination. John Foster, who would replace Blaine as secretary of state, also emphasized the importance of the clash: "It was Mrs. Blaine, not Mr. Blaine, who encouraged his partisan friends to openly push him for the nomination."[6]

Less than a month before the Republican National Convention of 1892, Blaine wrote to Harrison on 9 May and set the stage for a departure from the administration. It is, in fact, difficult to understand how Blaine could have remained in office. Yet he did not resign immediately—perhaps the best indication of his own indecision as late as May. Blaine enclosed a clipping that had appeared in the *New York World* two days before. According to the *World*, the president's son Russell had said that it was out of the question to consider the nomination of Blaine. He had described the secretary of state as "broken down mentally and physically . . . almost as helpless as a child" and had maintained that the president had done all of Blaine's work for the past two years.[7]

On the next day the president snapped at Blaine: he thought that the secretary's extensive experience should have led him to disregard statements that were second- or thirdhand. Harrison emphasized that he was available at any time for an open and frank talk. Blaine sent a reply that for all intents and purposes brought to an end his official relationship with the president. On 11 May, Blaine bluntly described the extremely awkward situation from which he would not extricate Harrison for more than three weeks: "Permit me to suggest that talk on so unpleasant a subject would be painful if not impossible."[8]

The president did not decide until 23 May to seek a second nomination. Writing twenty years later, Halford explained that Harrison was forced into the decision, "when it was plain that his enemies had determined to rally upon Mr. Blaine, and the secretary had agreed to such use of his name." Michener was more specific, pointing to the machinations of Platt, Quay, Clarkson, and two other members of the national committee—Henry Payne of Wisconsin and Samuel Fessenden of Connecticut. Michener said that in September 1891, Clarkson had told him that Clarkson, Quay, Platt, Payne, and Fessenden "were forming an organization to stop Harrison in 1892 but would stop if Harrison consulted and conferred with them on party matters and policies." Michener told Clarkson that they might drive Harrison "to allow his name to go before the Convention . . . for he was not a man to run up a white flag."[9]

As the national convention approached, the organization kept the pressure on Blaine, who seemed powerless to prevent the final sad act in the drama of his political career. Whitelaw Reid, who would be the Republican candidate for vice-president in 1892, received regular reports on cabal activities from Lemuel E. Quigg, a staff member of the *New York Tribune*. On 31 May, Quigg included a perceptive description of the manipulative Platt and of a passive, rather pathetic Blaine: "Platt seems to be confident that Blaine will take the nomination. He said that when he saw Blaine . . . they went over every point. . . . Right in the midst of the talk, Platt says, Blaine looked up and said 'But if I am elected I shall have to stay . . . in Washington during the summer months of the long term of each Congress and that will kill me.' ''[10]

Blaine deserved better than the shabby treatment that was inflicted upon him by the bosses. Nevertheless, the secretary of state submitted his resignation at last on 4 June, just three days before the convention was to open in Minneapolis. He sent a very brief, formal letter to the president: ''I respectfully beg leave to submit my resignation of the office of Secretary of State of the United States, to which I was appointed by you on the 5th of March 1889— The condition of the public business in the Department of State justifies me in requesting that my resignation may be accepted immediately.''[11]

The convention proved to be anticlimactic. While some may have doubted the ability of an incumbent president to win renomination, there was no real contest. Every incumbent Republican president in the late nineteenth century who sought a second nomination could count on a bloc of votes from the shadow delegations that represented the party in the South. Tied to the president by federal patronage, southern delegates would not bring any electoral votes to Harrison's column in the upcoming election. Furthermore, Michener realized that even those delegates might drift away if the president did not win the nomination on the first ballot. At the convention, therefore, he organized a secret caucus of delegates who were pledged to Harrison. For all intents and purposes, a roll-call vote at the caucus would assure the president's renomination before the balloting took place on the convention floor.

Only Harrison and Blaine received formal nominations, and the president won easily on the first ballot with 535 votes. Blaine's last hurrah consisted of 182 votes. But an additional 182 votes for Governor William McKinley of Ohio clearly indicated the depth of the opposition to Harrison within his own party. Many of the delegates from the crucial states of New York, Pennsylvania, and Ohio cast their votes for either Blaine or McKinley.[12] The president was vulnerable and less than enthusiastic as he faced a rematch with Grover Cleveland, the discontent in the South and the West which was leading an increasing number of farmers to turn to the Populist party, and the distractions of personal tragedy—the death of Mrs. Harrison on 25 October.

For all intents and purposes, Harrison did not campaign at all, while any chance that he might win a second term was slipping away in the summer of 1892. Labor unrest brought strikes and violence in July, simultaneously in the West—at the silver mines in Coeur d'Alene, Idaho—and in the East—at Andrew Carnegie's steel mill in Homestead, Pennsylvania. The bloody clashes at both strike sites resulted in numerous deaths; then, as the Homestead walkout in particular dragged on to a typically unsuccessful conclusion, Carnegie's close relationship with the Republican party had a negative impact on the candidate.[13]

The campaign has been described as unspectacular, an understatement. For the first time in the history of the United States, the candidates of both major parties had been president, and they were determined to maintain the dignity of that office. Cleveland, who did not believe in campaigning for the presidency, ruled out any possibility of an extensive personal campaign when he learned of Mrs. Harrison's condition. The former president limited himself to a few appearances in New York and New Jersey—two of the swing states, considered crucial to the outcome of the election.

A low-key campaign fit perfectly with the prevailing strategy of both parties toward the Populists—to ignore the upstart third party, which was demanding the free and unlimited coinage of silver, a graduated income tax, the direct election of United States senators, and more. There was an exception to the strategy in each of the major parties, however. Republicans in the South and Democrats in the West pursued fusion with the Populists in an effort to deprive the real opposition of electoral votes that could determine the victor. With or without fusion, the election proved that the South remained overwhelmingly Democratic, while the West continued as a Republican stronghold.

Meanwhile, Harrison's political fortunes sagged under the weight of a very embarrassing setback. The Populist party was eager to nominate Harrison's least favorite Hoosier, Walter Q. Gresham, for president. Gresham was a maverick Republican who had built a national reputation on a crusade for tariff reform and against the spoils system. In the early 1880s he had waged an unsuccessful battle against Harrison for control of the party in Indiana. He then had served a short term as postmaster general and very briefly as secretary of the Treasury in President Chester A. Arthur's cabinet in 1883/84. A judge of the Seventh United States Circuit Court since 1884, Gresham again had challenged Harrison as a candidate for the presidential nomination at the Republican National Convention of 1888. Gresham chose not to lead the Populist crusade in 1892, but he took a step that may have had even more impact on the outcome of the election. In mid October he dramatically bolted the Republican party and endorsed Cleveland.

In any case, the voters presented Cleveland with the most decisive victory in twenty years—he led Harrison by just under 400,000 votes (Cleveland—5,556,918; Harrison—5,176,108) and an electoral count of 277 to 145. The Populists, who nominated James B. Weaver of Iowa for president, drew the support of about one million voters. Weaver, a brevet brigadier general in the Civil War who had served three terms in the House of Representatives, received 22 electoral votes. The returns proved that in the South particularly, despite the desperate economic situation, the Populists had no chance against the entrenched Democrats. In fact, Weaver endured verbal abuse, as well as threats of physical abuse, at various locations on a campaign swing through Georgia.

The Democrats, who won the first round in the battle over the tariff in the congressional election of 1890, won the second round as well in the presidential election of 1892. The McKinley Tariff remained the major issue, but Democrats found, as the campaign unfolded, that voters also responded to attacks against the so-called Force Bill. The combination of issues carried Cleveland to victory. He swept the Solid South and all four swing states—New York, New Jersey, Connecticut, and Indiana. His momentum led to Democratic victories in Illinois and Wisconsin for the first time since the pre–Civil War era. But it was not a real landslide. While the Democrats took control of the Senate for only the second time since the Civil War, their margin in the House of Representatives—though substantial—was much smaller than it had been in the last Congress.[14] And the Republicans would rebound quickly in the next congressional election, which would be a step toward a decisive victory in the presidential contest of 1896.

Harrison, meanwhile, had four more months in office and one last opportunity—perhaps the most significant since the purchase of Alaska—to determine the future of the United States as a world power. Harrison had agreed with Blaine on the importance of Hawaii, an outpost in the Pacific that was viewed as indispensable from a strategic standpoint. But Blaine died almost at the same time as the dramatic developments that presented Harrison with the opportunity to annex Hawaii in January 1893. As Blaine's death symbolized the passing of the Gilded Age, Harrison's attempted annexation of Hawaii first focused attention on the potential of an important new factor in world affairs—an American empire. The lame-duck Harrison failed to acquire Hawaii, but he lived to see the United States establish a formidable presence in the Pacific—extending from Hawaii to the Philippines—just five years later.

The relationship between the United States and Hawaii began to change significantly with the signing of a commercial reciprocity treaty in January 1875. The treaty clearly indicated a growing awareness of the importance of Hawaii; it was only the second such agreement the United States ever entered into, having been preceded by reciprocity with Canada from 1854 to 1866. And the Senate Foreign Relations

Committee, which repeatedly played a prominent role in tightening the ties with Hawaii, revealed at the time a developing interest in more than trade. Strategic considerations led the committee to add to the treaty a provision that prohibited Hawaii from leasing any of its territory to any other nation.

Reciprocity with Hawaii faced serious opposition, both from domestic sugar producers and from those who were philosophically opposed to the concept of reciprocity; therefore the House of Representatives did not pass enabling legislation until May 1876. The treaty then went into effect in September, to last for seven years. It stipulated that neither side could give the required one-year notice of termination until the end of the seven years, so reciprocity would continue at least until late 1884.

When James G. Blaine was secretary of state for the first time in 1881, he had indicated the nation's steadily increasing interest in Hawaii. By the 1880s, as Blaine put it, the United States regarded Hawaii "as essentially a part of the American system." There would be no turning back, though the opposition to reciprocity with Hawaii intensified its efforts and concentrated on persuading Congress to terminate the treaty. Instead, the Senate Foreign Relations Committee once again took the initiative in June 1884 by supporting the renewal of reciprocity and an additional major step: the committee favored the acquisition of a naval base in Hawaii. While the United States and Hawaii agreed in December to renew the treaty for another seven years and provided that it would go on indefinitely unless either should decide to give a one-year notice, the opposition would not yield. Only the original treaty remained in effect as the debate continued in the Senate.

In April 1886, however, the Foreign Relations Committee added to the stakes by amending the pending treaty to include the acquisition of the harbor of the Pearl River. The Senate approved the new treaty as of January 1887, but not without some interesting manipulations. The amendment covering "Pearl Harbor" passed by a narrow 28 to 21 vote; it apparently received support from some who felt confident that the provision would force Hawaii to reject the treaty. That plan backfired. The powerful element in Hawaii that favored a binding relationship with the United States launched a coup in June and convinced King David Kalakaua to grant a new constitution, which included a parliamentary system of government. Hawaii then ratified the treaty in November.

Many in Hawaii quickly had legitimate reason to question the sincerity of the United States. In 1888, Congress began to discuss a possible change in the tariff, which seemed to be deliberately designed to alienate Hawaii: a reduction of the duty on all imported sugar, to be coupled with a bounty for domestic sugar producers. Both moves appeared to undermine the value of the reciprocity treaty. The Harrison administration immediately faced some hard questions on the future direction of relations between the United States and Hawaii. In fact, the Hawaiian minister to the United States, Henry Alpheus Peirce Carter, wrote to Secretary of State Blaine before the end of March 1889 and informed him of the "surprise and apprehension" in Hawaii over the proposed reduction in the duty on sugar. He enclosed extracts of letters from the Hawaiian foreign minister, who bluntly described the situation: if Hawaii had to seek other markets for its sugar, that could create sentiment against a move by the United States to establish a protectorate or to annex Hawaii in the future.

Less than two weeks later, Carter proposed a comprehensive treaty, which clearly invited the United States to establish a protectorate in Hawaii. The terms included: there would be complete free trade; the United States would guarantee Hawaiian independence; Hawaii would not sign treaties without the approval of the United States; the United States would have the right to land troops in Hawaii to deal with internal or external threats.[15]

Yet such a treaty reflected only the ambitions of the dominant Reform party, composed of the white ruling class. The treaty provided ammunition for those who rallied around King Kalakaua—natives and some antiestablishment whites who turned their National Reform party into a potent political force. In the summer of 1889 the internal situation suddenly seemed to get out of hand. While the two parties began a bitter rivalry before the upcoming elections, a third force—the half-castes—shocked both with an attempted coup at the end of July, apparently in favor of replacing the king with Princess Lydia Kamekeha Liliuokalani. The Harrison administration then set a precedent for intervention by landing seventy marines from the *Adams* to restore order. From that time on, President Harrison permanently stationed a naval vessel in Hawaiian waters.

More important than the naval vessel, perhaps, was the arrival in late September of the new minister to Hawaii. John Leavitt Stevens, who had known Blaine since the 1850s, had gained extensive diplomatic experience as minister to Uruguay and Paraguay during the early 1870s and as minister to Norway and Sweden between 1877 and 1883. About to turn seventy years of age, he seemed to have one last ambition to fulfill—the annexation of Hawaii.

Elections in February 1890 produced what amounted to a stand-off between the two parties. There was no chance in the months ahead to obtain any treaty along the lines proposed by Carter. Yet Congress then brought the relationship with Hawaii to a crossroads. Before the end of 1890, the McKinley Tariff had placed imported sugar on the duty-free list and had offered a two-cent-a-pound bounty to domestic producers. As of 1890, Hawaii relied almost exclusively on the United States as a market—for $13,073,477 of total exports valued at $13,142,829. The new tariff had a devastating effect on the Hawaiian economy. Many of the white leaders realized that an American protectorate—or annexation—represented the only solution to their economic problems. Their ambitions received a serious setback, however, when King Kalakaua died in January 1891 and his sister Liliuokalani took the throne as queen of Hawaii. The Harrison administration then clearly increased its involvement in Hawaiian affairs, perceiving the queen and her supporters as an element hostile to the interests of the United States.[16]

Late in 1891, all of the concerned parties began to make their moves. The new Hawaiian minister to the United States, a Boston-born dentist named John Mott Smith, worked with Blaine to complete a treaty that had three provisions which required very careful consideration by the president: there would be complete free trade; the United States would begin the development of Pearl Harbor within five years or Hawaii could terminate the rights to the naval base; and a cable should be constructed between Hawaii and the United States. Historians have concluded that the president did not submit the treaty to the Senate because of his fundamental opposition to the principle of free trade.[17] That does not say enough about Harrison as of late 1891. It is clear that the president reacted negatively to the attempt to apply pressure on the issues of Pearl Harbor and the cable. The president made his own foreign policy in 1891/92; Blaine did not speak for him, and neither could some white Hawaiians.

Harrison clearly had become more interested in Hawaii by the end of 1891, but he was determined to keep his every move above reproach. Somehow, he hoped that any step by Hawaii toward closer ties with the United States would represent the will of the Hawaiian people—at least of the majority of them. In any case, the president said to Blaine in mid October: "The necessity of maintaining and increasing our hold and influence in the Sandwich Islands is very apparent and very pressing." And in his third annual message, of December 1891, Harrison demonstrated his awareness of Pearl Harbor's potential, without concluding a new agreement on the subject. The president said, "I strongly recommend that provision be made for improving the harbor of Pearl River and equipping it as a naval station."[18]

Before the February 1892 elections, the half-castes—who attracted their share of antiestablishment whites—formed the Liberal party. With three parties in the contest, the results differed little from the deadlock created in 1890. Stevens soon alerted the Harrison administration to the rapidly changing conditions in Hawaii. He asked for instructions in case the government were to be surprised by an orderly and peaceful revolution designed to establish a republic. Stevens admitted that the revolutionaries had confided in him; some of those in the movement favored annexation by the United States.[19] A representative of a secret new organization, the Annexation Club, then came to Washington in May, hoping to persuade the United States to look favorably on a coup. Lorrin Andrews Thurston, a lawyer and former minister of the interior who had been elected to the Hawaiian legislature in February, met with Blaine and Secretary of the Navy Benjamin Tracy, but he was not granted an interview with the president.[20] The entire procedure seemed to be calculated to keep the white Hawaiians at arm's length from the president of the United States.

Hawaii had begun to move toward an internal crisis before the end of 1892. At the very least, Harrison did not discourage any potential move by the revolutionaries when he dealt with Hawaii in his final annual message, in December 1892. The president again urged Congress to take steps to begin the improvement of Pearl Harbor, and he also endorsed the cable project: "I deem it of great importance that the projected submarine cable . . . should be promoted. . . . We should before this have availed ourselves of the concession . . . for a harbor and naval station at Pearl River."[21]

The existing Hawaiian cabinet then resigned on 12 January 1893. The queen saw an opportunity to reassert some of the lost prerogatives of the monarch; on 14 January she proclaimed a new constitution. On that same day the Annexation Club created the thirteen-member Committee of Safety—the first step in the formation of a provisional government. On 16 January, Capt. G. C. Wiltse of the *Boston* landed about 165 men and officers, ostensibly to protect the legation and the consulate. The rebels knew that there would be nothing to fear when on 17 January they then proclaimed a new government, headed by Judge Sanford Ballard Dole.[22]

"Within one month from the outbreak of the Hawaiian Revolution, two weeks of which were spent by the [Hawaiian] commissioners journeying to Washington, a treaty of annexation had been negotiated, signed and submitted to the upper house."[23] Indeed, Stevens began to move so rapidly that he practically presented Harrison with a *fait accompli*. Stevens sent three dispatches on 1 February, including this classic statement: "The Hawaiian pear is now fully ripe and this is the golden hour to pluck it." In a separate communication, Stevens informed Secretary of State John Foster that he had responded to the new government's request and had placed it under the protection of the United States.[24]

At the same time, Foster alerted the nation's diplomats in the major capitals of the world. The president asked that the following facts be called to their attention: recent events had fortified the position and made more evident the paramount concern of the United States in Hawaii; Hawaii constituted an essential and important element in the commercial system of the United States; because of Hawaii's proximity and situation, the United States could never see it transferred without showing the gravest concern.

The immediate replies proved encouraging. The legation in France reported a lack of interest in Hawaiian developments. It seemed unlikely that the French would disapprove of any action or attitude of the United States in Hawaii. Even more important was the response from Robert Lincoln, minister to Great Britain. He relayed an apparent "green light" to the Harrison administration. The British undersecretary of state for foreign affairs had assured Lincoln that Great Britain would not send a naval vessel to Hawaii because British subjects would be secure under the protection of the United States. Lincoln denied reports of any pending protest from Great Britain. Soon, Foster received another important message of encouragement—from Russia. The foreign minister said he spoke only for himself, but he felt certain that the government would look favorably upon the effort by the United States to restore order and to protect its interests in Hawaii. The Russians believed that Hawaii could become an important link in commerce between themselves and the United States.[25]

A treaty was signed on 14 February; on the next day, Harrison forwarded the agreement to the Senate. He vigorously supported annexation, and he attempted to deal with all objections in advance, explaining, "The overthrow of the monarchy was not in any way promoted by this Government, but had its origin in what seems to have been a reactionary . . . policy on the part of Queen Liliuokalani, which put in serious peril not only the large and preponderating interests of the United States . . . but all foreign interests." Harrison termed the monarchy "effete," "weak," and "inadequate." He insisted that "the influence and interest of the United States in the islands must be increased and not diminished."

The president went on to spell out how Hawaii fit into the relationship of the United States with the other great powers of the world—a relationship that seemed more important than ever by the end of the Harrison administration. Harrison was blunt, for if the United States did not act, Hawaii might fall into potentially unfriendly hands: "It is essential that none of the other great powers shall secure these islands. Such a possession would not consist with our safety and with the peace of the world. This view of the situation is so apparent and conclusive that no protest has been heard from any government against proceedings looking to annexation."[26]

It was not to be, even though the Foreign Relations Committee rushed the treaty to the full Senate in only two days. There were only forty-seven Republicans in the Senate, far short of the fifty-nine out of eighty-eight needed for a two-thirds vote of ratification. And the Democrats had captured the control of the incoming Senate, almost certainly ending any chance of ratification. Cleveland simply withdrew the treaty on 9 March. Two days later, he appointed James Henderson Blount, former chairman of the House Foreign Affairs Committee, to investigate the developments that had preceded the treaty between the United States and Hawaii.[27]

The United States would not obtain Hawaii until 1898, but Harrison had stirred the influential leaders of the nation who believed the time had come to look beyond the continent. As the Harrison administration faded into history, Alfred T. Mahan asked rhetorically, in the lead article in the *Forum*, if the United States had to be limited by the Pacific Coast. He maintained that the nation had the strongest right to assert a presence in the northern Pacific. Hawaii would be "a first-fruit and a token that the nation in its *evolution* has aroused itself to the necessity of carrying its life . . . beyond the borders."[28] That dream would be fulfilled, after the devastating depression that had begun to develop even before Harrison left office.

Perhaps the failure to annex Hawaii was the final blow for Harrison's image in the history of the nation. It has been easy to forget the man who served as chief executive between the two terms of Grover Cleveland. Along with every other president in the post-Reconstruction era of the late nineteenth century, Harrison has been relegated to the great middle ground of American presidents: historians have decided that he was "average." Harrison was not among the best presidents—nor was he among the worst—yet the consensus places him near the low end of the "average" group.

Since the 1960s, various studies have asserted Harrison's importance in late-nineteenth-century foreign policy—placing Blaine in proper perspective—and have acknowledged these accomplishments among others: his major contribution to the development of the new navy, the establishment of the first American protectorate in Samoa, participation in the first Pan-American Conference, and a most successful commercial reciprocity policy. At least as important for the "large" policy of expansion and the creation of an empire was the attempt to obtain a first naval base in the Caribbean, the encouragement of the construction of a Central American canal, and, of course, the effort to annex Hawaii—not so much a failure as a final step toward the events of 1898.

The same president who has received only belated recognition for his foreign policy has been condemned for the lack of leadership that allowed the Billion Dollar Congress of 1890 to enact legislation—the McKinley Tariff and the Sherman Silver Purchase Act—that may have contributed to economic collapse in 1893. Subsequent events have overshadowed such achievements as the passage of the Sherman Anti-Trust Act and the most courageous stand by any president of his era in favor of black Americans.

The incredible development of industry and the rapid growth of cities during the late nineteenth century dramatically changed the United States. If Harrison did not really comprehend what had taken place, he was not alone. The increasing number of strikes proved the depth of labor unrest, but the plight of the farmer was the most immediate problem of the 1890s. By 1890, as Jacob August Riis published his classic study *How the Other Half Lives*, which made Americans aware of the horrors of life in the tenements of New York, farmers in the South had hit bottom. And farmers on the plains, who had been suffering through an almost continual drought since 1887, were no better off. Suddenly, in 1893, it was as though the weak agricultural sector of the economy took its toll on the rest of the nation.

The Philadelphia and Reading Railroad declared bankruptcy just ten days before the inauguration of Grover Cleveland. Like dominoes, railroads all across the nation began to topple in rapid succession in 1893. The stock market—and the price of silver—collapsed as well. Ironically, as the Cleveland administration devoted all of its energies to the repeal of the Sherman Silver Purchase Act and tariff reform in 1893/94, the bitterly divided Democrats self-destructed. With no sign of economic revival in 1894, the Democrats endured the same kind of overwhelming defeat in the congressional elections as the Republicans had experienced in 1890. The next House of Representatives would have 244 Republicans and only 105 Democrats. If Harrison had ignored the problems that had led inevitably to the Depression of 1893, the administration that had to deal with those problems failed miserably, according to Donald M. Dozer: "Developments of the next four years were to show that Cleveland was no more skillful than Harrison had been at reading the signs of the times."[29]

Harrison remained active to the end. As the depression brought voters back to the Republican party, Harrison in fact gained the stature of a distinguished elder statesman. In 1894 he delivered a series of lectures at Stanford University; at the end of the decade, he devoted an incredible amount of time and energy to his duties as chief counsel for Venezuela in its boundary dispute with British Guiana. To participate in the subsequent arbitration, he went to Europe for the first time in 1899. In a somewhat surprising move, which estranged his children, the former president married Mary Lord Dimmick, the widowed niece of the first Mrs. Harrison, early in 1896. A daughter, Elizabeth, was born in February 1897. Four years later, after a bout with pneumonia, Harrison died, on 13 March 1901.[30]

The last Civil War general to serve as president had lived to see the United States survive the Depression of 1893, create an empire in 1898, and triumphantly enter a new century. His policies seemed vindicated. The uninterrupted string of Republican victories since 1894 had long ago erased any lingering memories of his failure to win a second term as president.

NOTES

CHAPTER 1
TAKING OFFICE

1. *Kansas Farmer* (Topeka), 4 Apr. 1889; Harry J. Sievers, *Benjamin Harrison, Hoosier President: The White House and After* (Indianapolis, Ind.: Bobbs-Merrill Co., Inc., 1968); William A. DeGregorio, *The Complete Book of U.S. Presidents* (New York: Dembner Books, 1984), p. 331.

2. Sievers, *Benjamin Harrison, Hoosier President*, p. 35; H. Wayne Morgan, *From Hayes to McKinley: National Party Politics, 1877–1896* (Syracuse, N.Y.: Syracuse University Press, 1969), p. 326; the *New York Tribune*, 2 Mar. 1889, and other newspapers advertised through coaches to the inauguration for a round trip fare of $6.50. Similar low rates could be found in transportation to Washington from other cities.

3. William Starr Myers, *The Republican Party: A History* (New York: Century Co., 1928), p. 304; James Ford Rhodes, *History of the United States from Hayes to McKinley, 1877–1896*, 8 vols. (New York: Macmillan Co., 1919), 8:328.

4. Benjamin Harrison, *Speeches of Benjamin Harrison*, comp. Charles Hedges (Port Washington, N.Y.: Kennikat Press, 1892, 1971), pp. 194–203.

5. Sievers, *Benjamin Harrison, Hoosier President*, pp. 35–36; Hayes to Harrison, 5 Mar. 1889, Harrison Papers (hereafter cited as HP), Library of Congress (hereafter cited as LC), ser. 1, reel 18.

6. Letters from Woodrow Wilson to his wife, 28 Feb. and 4 Mar., and from Joseph Ruggles Wilson to Woodrow Wilson, 5 Mar. 1889, in *The Papers of Woodrow Wilson*, vol. 6: *1888–1890*, ed. Arthur S. Link (Princeton, N.J.: Princeton University Press, 1969), pp. 117, 127–28, 138.

7. *Public Opinion*, 9 Mar. 1889, pp. 479–82.

8. Ibid.

9. Sievers, *Benjamin Harrison, Hoosier President*, pp. 33-36.

10. Copy of letter from Harrison to Halstead, 14 Mar. 1889, ser. 1, reel 18, HP.

11. Francis Curtis, *The Republican Party: A History of Its Fifty Years' Existence and a Record of Its Measures and Leaders, 1854-1904* (New York: G. P. Putnam's Sons, 1904; reprint, New York: AMS Press, 1978), p. 206.

12. Sievers, *Benjamin Harrison, Hoosier President*, pp. 37-38; *New York Tribune*, 5 Mar. 1889; H. W. Morgan, *From Hayes to McKinley*, p. 326. No wine was served at the Harrison Inaugural Ball, so it was described as a Temperance Ball.

13. Michael J. Doucet and John C. Weaver, "Material Culture and the North American House: The Era of the Common Man, 1870-1920," *Journal of American History* 72 (Dec. 1985): 563-72.

14. Harrison, *Speeches*, p. 195.

15. Henry L. Stoddard, *It Costs to Be President* (New York: Harper & Brothers Publishers, 1938), p. 246; James Morgan, *Our Presidents* (New York: Macmillan Co., 1952), p. 228.

16. See Harry J. Sievers, *Benjamin Harrison, Hoosier Warrior, 1833-1865* (Chicago: Henry Regnery Co., 1952).

17. Harry J. Sievers, *Benjamin Harrison, Hoosier Statesman: From the Civil War to the White House, 1865-1888* (New York: University Publishers, Inc., 1959).

18. Ibid., pp. 131-43, 164-94.

19. Ibid., pp. 232-34; Albert T. Volwiler, ed., *The Correspondence between Benjamin Harrison and James G. Blaine, 1882-1893* (Philadelphia: American Philosophical Society, 1940), p. 128n.

20. David Saville Muzzey, *James G. Blaine: A Political Idol of Other Days* (Port Washington, N.Y.: Kennikat Press, 1934, 1963), pp. 39, 62, 66-68, 83-99, 108-13, 184, 225; Arthur Wallace Dunn, *From Harrison to Harding: A Personal Narrative, Covering a Third of a Century, 1888-1921*, 2 vols. (Port Washington, N.Y.: Kennikat Press, 1922, 1971), 1: 4-7.

21. James G. Blaine to Stephen Elkins, 1 Mar. 1888, Stephen Elkins Papers, West Virginia University Library, Morgantown, box 2. Ruled out by Blaine were Senator John Sherman of Ohio, Judge Walter Q. Gresham of Indiana and Illinois, Senator William B. Allison of Iowa, senator and former Secretary of State William M. Evarts of New York, Senator Joseph R. Hawley of Connecticut, William Walter Phelps of New Jersey, former Governor Russell A. Alger of Michigan, Senator Shelby M. Cullom of Illinois, and Governor Jeremiah McLain Rusk of Wisconsin.

22. Stoddard, *It Costs*, p. 248; Margaret Leech, *In the Days of McKinley* (New York: Harper & Brothers, 1959), p. 42; Oscar Doane Lambert, *Stephen Benton Elkins: American Foursquare* (Pittsburgh, Pa.: University of Pittsburgh Press, 1955), pp. 115-22; George H. Mayer, *The Republican Party, 1854-1964* (New York: Oxford University Press, 1967), p. 218. There were rumors that Blaine told Carnegie "Phelps and Harrison" and that Carnegie reversed the names in the cablegram.

23. Tom E. Terrill, *The Tariff, Politics, and American Foreign Policy, 1874–1901* (Westport, Conn.: Greenwood Press, 1973), pp. 6–7; Eugene H. Roseboom and Alfred E. Eckes, Jr., *A History of Presidential Elections* (New York: Macmillan Publishing Co., Inc., 1979), p. 108; Stoddard, *It Costs*, p. 191.

24. Sean Dennis Cashman, *America in the Gilded Age: From the Death of Lincoln to the Rise of Theodore Roosevelt* (New York: New York University Press, 1984), p. 214; W. Dean Burnham, *Presidential Ballots, 1836–1892* (Baltimore, Md.: Johns Hopkins Press, 1955), p. 140; Edward Stanwood, *A History of the Presidency from 1788 to 1897* (Boston, Mass.: Houghton Mifflin Co., 1912), pp. 481–82; Carl N. Degler, *The Age of the Economic Revolution, 1876–1900* (Glenview, Ill.: Scott, Foresman & Co., 1967), pp. 98–99.

25. John Spencer Bassett, *Expansion and Reform, 1889–1926* (New York: Longmans, Green & Co., 1926), p. 6.

26. Albert C. E. Parker, "Beating the Spread: Analyzing American Election Outcomes," *Journal of American History* 67 (June 1980): 75; Arthur M. Schlesinger, Jr., and Fred L. Israel, eds., *History of U.S. Political Parties*, vol. 2: *1860–1910: The Gilded Age in Politics* (New York: Chelsea House Publishers, 1973), p. 1428; Franklin L. Burdette, *The Republican Party: A Short History* (Princeton, N.J.: D. Van Nostrand Co., Inc., 1968), p. 52; Blaine to Harrison, 19 July 1888, HP, ser. 1, reel 10.

27. H. Wayne Morgan, ed., *The Gilded Age: A Reappraisal* (Syracuse, N.Y.: Syracuse University Press, 1970), p. 179; A. H. Colquitt, "The Harrison Administration," *North American Review* 154 (June 1892): 650.

28. Mayer, *Republican Party*, pp. 13–14; James A. Kehl, *Boss Rule in the Gilded Age: Matt Quay of Pennsylvania* (Pittsburgh, Pa.: University of Pittsburgh Press, 1981), p. 97; Horace Samuel Merrill, *Bourbon Leader: Grover Cleveland and the Democratic Party* (Boston, Mass.: Little, Brown & Co., 1957), pp. 129–30; Rhodes, *History of the United States*, p. 321.

29. Harrison, *Speeches*, pp. 25–187.

30. H. W. Morgan, *From Hayes to McKinley*, p. 288.

31. Allan Nevins, *Grover Cleveland: A Study in Courage* (New York: Dodd, Mead & Co., 1933), pp. 435–36; Roseboom and Eckes, *History of Presidential Elections*, p. 110.

32. H. W. Morgan, *From Hayes to McKinley*, pp. 311–12. Morgan cites evidence that this was standard fare for handling floaters in Indiana. While the letter was on stationery of the national committee, words were misspelled, and Dudley's signature was not considered authentic. Still, Louis Michener remembered having received such a letter.

33. Ibid., pp. 314–16.

34. Harrison, *Speeches*, p. 109; Davis Rich Dewey, *National Problems, 1885–1897* (New York: Harper & Brothers Publishers, 1907), p. 72.

35. E. Benjamin Andrews, *The History of the Last Quarter-Century in the United States, 1870–1895*, 2 vols. (New York: Charles Scribner's Sons, 1896), 2:159–60; R. Hal Williams, *Years of Decision: American Politics in the 1890s* (New York: John Wiley & Sons, 1978), p. 4.

36. H. W. Morgan, *From Hayes to McKinley*, p. 316.

37. Kehl, *Boss Rule*, pp. 112–13; Burnham, *Presidential Ballots*, p. 140; John A. Garraty, *The New Commonwealth, 1877–1890* (New York: Harper & Row, 1968), p. 304.

38. Kehl, *Boss Rule*, pp. 112–13; Stanwood, *History of the Presidency*, pp. 483–84; Rhodes, *History of the United States*, p. 326.

39. E. W. Halford, "General Harrison's Attitude toward the Presidency," *Century Magazine* 84 (June 1912): 306, 309.

40. Schlesinger, *History of U.S. Political Parties*, p. 1635; J. Morgan, *Our Presidents*, p. 229.

41. Sievers, *Benjamin Harrison, Hoosier President*, pp. 30–31; Harrison, *Speeches*, pp. 189–91.

42. Sievers, *Benjamin Harrison, Hoosier President*, pp. 31–32.

43. Letter from Grover Cleveland to Harrison, 15 Feb. 1889, and copy of letter from Harrison to Cleveland, 18 Feb. 1889, HP, ser. 1, reel 18; Sievers, *Benjamin Harrison, Hoosier President*, p. 33. Some outgoing presidents had not followed these usual formal courtesies. For instance, in 1829, Andrew Jackson did not visit retiring John Quincy Adams. In 1885, Cleveland did not make a call on outgoing President Chester A. Arthur. There was no personal rancor between Harrison and Cleveland, either in 1889 or in 1893.

44. One of Harrison's first requests of his father-in-law, after the inauguration, was that the latter resign as clerk in the mail division of the Pension Office, a position that Harrison had helped Scott obtain when Harrison went to Washington as senator from Indiana. Secretary of the Interior John W. Noble queried both the president and his wife about this resignation before he approved it (see letter from Noble to E. W. Halford, 13 Mar. 1889, HP, ser. 1, reel 18). In his eighties, Scott earned more in this clerkship than he had ever received in his professional positions as a pastor, a professor, or a college president. Scott told his friend Harvey W. Wiley that "my son-in-law has discharged me from my position . . . and I shall go to live at the White House now and do nothing. This is a very hard condition to be in" (see Harvey W. Wiley, *An Autobiography* [Indianapolis, Ind.: Bobbs-Merrill Co., 1930], p. 79).

CHAPTER 2

THE FORMATION OF A CABINET

1. James G. Blaine to Benjamin Harrison, 7 Nov. 1888, HP, vol. 45.

2. Blaine to Stephen Elkins, 8 Nov. 1888, Elkins Papers, box 2.

3. Blaine to Harrison, 9 Nov. 1888, HP, vol. 46.

4. Walker Blaine to Mrs. James G. Blaine, 5 July 1888, James G. Blaine and Family Papers, LC, box 5.

5. E. W. Halford, "How Harrison Chose His Cabinet," *Leslie's Illustrated Weekly* 127 (19 Apr. 1919): 574.

6. John W. Foster, *Diplomatic Memoirs*, 2 vols. (Boston, Mass.: Houghton Mifflin, 1909), 2:250.

7. Blaine to Whitelaw Reid, 27 Nov. 1888, Reid Papers, LC, box 104.

8. Blaine to Reid, 28 Nov. 1888, ibid.

9. William Walter Phelps to Blaine, 6 Dec. 1888, Blaine Papers, vol. 3.

10. Blaine to Reid, 20 Dec. 1888, Reid Papers, box 104.

11. Harrison to Blaine, 17 Jan. 1889, HP, vol. 59.

12. Blaine to Harrison, 21 Jan. 1889, HP, vol. 61.

13. Murat Halstead to Harrison, 7 Dec. 1888, HP, vol. 50.

14. John Hay to Reid, 26 Jan. 1889, Reid Papers, box 105.

15. Mrs. James G. Blaine, *Letters of Mrs. James G. Blaine*, ed. Harriet S. Blaine Beale, 2 vols. (New York: Duffield & Co., 1908), 2:244–45.

16. Reid to Phelps, 23 Feb. 1889, Reid Papers, box 51.

17. Phelps to Reid, 28 Feb. 1889, ibid.

18. Reid to George Smalley, 8 Apr. 1889, ibid., box 141 outgoing.

19. Robert D. Marcus, *Grand Old Party: Political Structure in the Gilded Age, 1880–1896* (New York: Oxford University Press, 1971), p. 157.

20. Thomas Collier Platt, *The Autobiography of Thomas Collier Platt*, comp. and ed. Louis J. Lang (New York: B. W. Dodge & Co., 1910), pp. 164, 192, 206–7; Justus D. Doenecke, *The Presidencies of James A. Garfield and Chester A. Arthur* (Lawrence: Regents Press of Kansas, 1981), p. 45; Marcus, *Grand Old Party*, pp. 145, 148; Donald Marquand Dozer, "Benjamin Harrison and the Presidential Campaign of 1892," *American Historical Review* 54 (Oct. 1948): 51; Benjamin Franklin Cooling, *Benjamin Franklin Tracy: Father of the Modern American Fighting Navy* (Hamden, Conn.: Archon Books, 1973), p. 44.

21. Wharton Barker to Harrison, 28 Jan. 1889, Barker Papers, LC, box 5.

22. Barker to Harrison, 8 Feb. 1889, ibid.

23. Harrison to Barker, 12 Feb. 1889, ibid.

24. James A. Kehl, *Boss Rule in the Gilded Age: Matt Quay of Pennsylvania* (Pittsburgh, Pa.: University of Pittsburgh Press, 1981), pp. 69, 95, 118–19.

25. H. Wayne Morgan, *From Hayes to McKinley: National Party Politics, 1877–1896* (Syracuse, N.Y.: Syracuse University Press, 1969), p. 286; Leland L. Sage, *William Boyd Allison: A Study in Practical Politics* (Iowa City: State Historical Society of Iowa, 1956), pp. 106, 172, 239; Richard Jensen, *The Winning of the Midwest: Social and Political Conflict, 1888–1896* (Chicago: University of Chicago Press, 1971), pp. 100–101; Dozer, "Benjamin Harrison," pp. 50–51; Stanley P. Hirshson, "James S. Clarkson versus Benjamin Harrison, 1891–1893: A Political Saga," *Iowa Journal of History* 58 (July 1960): 219.

26. *New York Times*, 30 Jan. 1891, p. 2; Allan Peskin, *Garfield* (Kent, Ohio: Kent State University Press, 1978), pp. 524–25.

27. Kehl, *Boss Rule*, pp. 39, 49, 57, 116, 118–20.

28. Dorothy Ganfield Fowler, *John Coit Spooner: Defender of Presidents* (New York: University Publishers, 1961), pp. 107, 116; Harry J. Sievers, *Benjamin Harrison, Hoosier President: The White House and After* (Indianapolis, Ind.: The Bobbs-Merrill Co., 1968), p. 20; Dozer, "Benjamin Harrison," p. 51.

29. Sievers, *Benjamin Harrison, Hoosier President*, p. 19.

30. Walter R. Herrick, Jr., *The American Naval Revolution* (Baton Rouge: Louisiana State University Press, 1966), pp. 39–42; Cooling, *Benjamin Franklin Tracy*, pp. 5–9, 22, 29, 36–38, 41–42.

31. Sievers, *Benjamin Harrison, Hoosier President*, pp. 18–19.

32. Oscar Doane Lambert, *Stephen Benton Elkins: American Foursquare* (Pittsburgh, Pa.: University of Pittsburgh Press, 1955), pp. 128, 134–35, 138, 185.

33. Sievers, *Benjamin Harrison, Hoosier President*, pp. 19–20; Harry J. Sievers, *Benjamin Harrison, Hoosier Statesman: From the Civil War to the White House, 1865–1888* (New York: University Publishers, 1959), pp. 65, 201; *New York Times,* 11 Nov. 1888, p. 1.

CHAPTER 3

PATRONAGE BACK IN REPUBLICAN HANDS

1. Davis Rich Dewey, *National Problems, 1885–1897* (New York: Harper & Brothers, Publishers, 1907), p. 150.

2. Copy of a letter from Harrison to Henry C. Greiner, Somerset, Ohio, 9 Oct. 1888, HP, ser. 1, reel 12; Harrison to Mrs. Anna Louisa Ingalls, 31 Jan. 1889, ibid., reel 17; E. W. Halford, "General Harrison's Attitude toward the Presidency," *Century Magazine* 84 (June 1912): 305.

3. Letter from R. B. Harrison, 2 Apr. 1889, HP, ser. 1, reel 18.

4. W. B. Allison to Harrison, 2 Apr. 1889, ibid.

5. Norman E. Tutorow, *Leland Stanford: Man of Many Careers* (Menlo Park, Calif.: Pacific Coast Publishers, 1971), p. 258; Dorothy Ganfield Fowler, *John Coit Spooner: Defender of Presidents* (New York: University Publishers, 1961), p. 118; William E. Connelley, *The Life of Preston B. Plumb, 1837–1891* (Chicago: Browne & Howell Co., 1913), p. 322; James A. Kehl, *Boss Rule in the Gilded Age: Matt Quay of Pennsylvania* (Pittsburgh, Pa.: University of Pittsburgh Press, 1981), p. 117; S. M. Cullom to Harrison, 1 Mar. 1889, HP, ser. 1, reel 18; Shelby M. Cullom, *Fifty Years of Public Service* (Chicago: A. C. McClurg & Co., 1911), p. 249; Harry J. Sievers, *Benjamin Harrison, Hoosier President: The White House and After* (Indianapolis, Ind.: Bobbs-Merrill Co., Inc., 1968), pp. 42–43.

6. William R. Thayer, *The Life and Letters of John Hay,* 2 vols. (Boston, Mass.: Houghton Mifflin Co., 1915), 2:132.

7. *New York Times,* 18 Apr. 1889.

8. Arthur Wallace Dunn, *From Harrison to Harding: A Personal Narrative, Covering a Third of a Century, 1888–1921,* 2 vols. (Port Washington, N.Y.: Kennikat Press, 1922, 1971), 1:100–101.

9. Oscar Doane Lambert, *Stephen Benton Elkins: American Foursquare* (Pittsburgh, Pa.: University of Pittsburgh Press, 1955), p. 126; Arthur Bernon Tourtellot, *The Presidents on the Presidency* (Garden City, N.Y.: Doubleday & Co., Inc., 1964), p. 360.

10. Donald L. McMurry, "The Political Significance of the Pension Question, 1885-1897," *Mississippi Valley Historical Review* 9 (June 1922): 19-22.

11. Donald L. McMurry, "The Bureau of Pensions during the Administration of President Harrison," *Mississippi Valley Historical Review* 13 (Dec. 1926): 347; Mary R. Dearing, *Veterans in Politics: The Story of the G.A.R.* (Baton Rouge: Louisiana State University Press, 1952), p. 393.

12. Dearing, *Veterans in Politics*, pp. 393-94; copy of letter from Noble to Tanner, 24 July 1889, and cover letter from Noble to Harrison, 24 July 1889, HP, ser. 1, reel 21.

13. E.g., J. B. Foraker, Cincinnati, Ohio, to Harrison, 3 Aug. 1889, L. T. Michener to E. W. Halford, 19 Aug. and 10 Sept. 1889, Melville D. Landon to Harrison, 11 Sept. 1889, and John W. Noble to Harrison, 5 Aug. 1889, HP, ser. 1, reel 22; Sievers, *Benjamin Harrison, Hoosier President*, p. 124; Harrison to Tanner, 12 Sept. 1889, HP, ser. 1, reel 22. Tanner reentered a career as a pension agent in Washington, D.C., and in 1904 he was appointed register of wills in the District of Columbia by President Theodore Roosevelt.

14. Michener to Halford, 9 Nov. 1889, HP, ser. 1, reel 23; McMurry, "Bureau of Pensions," pp. 357-58; William G. Glasson, *Federal Military Pensions in the United States* (New York: Oxford University Press, 1918), p. 233.

15. Leland L. Sage, *William Boyd Allison: A Study in Practical Politics* (Iowa City: State Historical Society of Iowa, 1956), pp. 233-38; Clarkson to L. T. Michener, 16 Feb. 1889, and copy of letter from Harrison to Quay, 21 Feb. 1889, HP, ser. 1, reel 18.

16. Stanley P. Hirshson, "James S. Clarkson and the Civil Service Reformers, 1889-1893," *Iowa Journal of History* 57 (July 1959): 269; Sievers, *Benjamin Harrison, Hoosier President*, p. 74. After the election of 1890 Clarkson became president of a company that was planning a new bridge over the Hudson at New York City. In 1902 he was appointed as the surveyor of customs for the port of New York by President Theodore Roosevelt.

17. House of Representatives, 51st Cong., 2d sess., Executive Document no. 1, pt. 4, *Report of the Postmaster-General* . . . (Washington, D.C.: Government Printing Office, 1890), p. 32; House of Representatives, 52d Cong., 2d sess., Executive Document no. 1, pt. 4, *Report of the Postmaster-General* . . . (Washington, D.C.: Government Printing Office, 1892), pp. 80-85. Establishing proportions with these figures shows that they are approximately correct if they properly reflect the number of changes in postmasters over these eight years.

18. Benjamin Harrison, *Speeches of Benjamin Harrison*, comp. Charles Hedges (Port Washington, N.Y.: Kennikat Press, 1892, 1971), pp. 200-201; E. Benjamin Andrews, *The History of the Last Quarter-Century in the United States, 1870-1895*, vol. 2 (New York: Charles Scribner's Sons, 1896), p. 169; *New York Tribune*, 4 June 1889.

19. Ari Hoogenboom, *Outlawing the Spoils: A History of the Civil Service Reform Movement, 1865-1883* (Urbana: University of Illinois Press, 1961), p. 263; Herbert Adams Gibbons, *John Wanamaker*, 2 vols. (New York: Harper & Brothers Publishers, 1926), 1:301; A. Bower Sageser, *The First Two Decades of the Pendleton*

Act: A Study of Civil Service Reform (Lincoln: University of Nebraska Studies, 1935), pp. 128–31; John G. Sproat, *"The Best Men": Liberal Reformers in the Gilded Age* (New York: Oxford University Press, 1968), p. 199; Paul P. Van Riper, *History of the United States Civil Service* (Evanston, Ill.: Row, Peterson & Co., 1958), p. 124; Tourtellot, *Presidents*, p. 174.

20. Sageser, *First Two Decades*, p. 139; Frank Mann Stewart, *The National Civil Service Reform League: History, Activities, and Problems* (Austin: University of Texas Press, 1929), pp. 53–56; Claude Julien, *America's Empire* (New York: Pantheon Books, 1971), p. 54; Van Riper, *History of the U.S. Civil Service*, p. 125; John A. Garraty, *Henry Cabot Lodge: A Biography* (New York: Alfred A. Knopf, 1953), p. 105; a letter from Will Cumback, of Greensburg, Ind., to Harrison, 8 May 1889, which complimented Harrison on his selection of Roosevelt, HP, ser. 1, reel 20. Roosevelt was anti-Blaine in 1884, and Blaine did not want him in the State Department.

21. George H. Mayer, *The Republican Party, 1854–1964* (New York: Oxford University Press, 1967), p. 222; Leonard D. White, *The Republican Era: A Study in Administrative History, 1869–1901* (New York: Macmillan Co., 1958), pp. 307–8; Stephen Skowronek, *Building a New American State: The Expansion of National Administrative Capacities, 1877–1920* (New York: Cambridge University Press, 1982), pp. 75–78.

22. Matthew Josephson, *The President Makers: The Culture of Politics and Leadership in the Age of Enlightenment, 1896–1919* (New York: Harcourt, Brace & Co., 1940), p. 48; Sageser, *First Two Decades*, p. 158; Theodore Roosevelt and Hugh S. Thompson to Harrison, 24 June 1889, and Roosevelt to Halford, 24, 28, and 30 July 1889—all in HP, ser. 1, reels 21 and 22. In the last letter in this group, Roosevelt wrote that he felt "that the honest administration of the Civil Service law is at stake."

23. Michener to Halford, 19 Aug. 1889, HP, ser. 1, reel 22; H. Wayne Morgan, *From Hayes to McKinley: National Party Politics, 1877–1896* (Syracuse, N.Y.: Syracuse University Press, 1969), p. 329; Dunn, *From Harrison to Harding*, 1:18.

24. William T. Hagan, "Civil Service Commissioner Theodore Roosevelt and the Indian Rights Association," *Pacific Historical Review* 44 (May 1975): 190–92; White, *Republican Era*, p. 318; Skowronek, *Building a New American State*, pp. 70–72; Sageser, *First Two Decades*, p. 160.

25. White, *Republican Era*, p. 194; Frederick E. Hoxie, "Redefining Indian Education: Thomas J. Morgan's Program in Disarray," *Arizona and the West* 24 (Spring 1982): 8–18; Dunn, *From Harrison to Harding*, 1:70.

26. Harrison to Rev. John Ireland, Sept. 1889, HP, ser. 1, reel 23.

27. Harry J. Sievers, "The Catholic Indian School Issue and the Presidential Election of 1892," *Catholic Historical Review* 38 (July 1952): 144–45; Sageser, *First Two Decades*, p. 159; Francis Paul Prucha, *Indian Policy in the United States: Historical Essays* (Lincoln: University of Nebraska Press, 1981), pp. 247–48.

28. E. W. Halford to R. S. Taylor, 10 June 1889, HP, ser. 1, reel 20; Sageser, *First Two Decades*, p. 169.

29. Morgan, *From Hayes to McKinley*, p. 325; Harrison to the following: J. S. Harrison, 13 Apr., Mrs. Lucy S. Howell, 13 Apr., J. N. Huston, Apr.—all in 1889, and to J. J. M. LaFollette, 20 Dec. 1890, and to Albert Griffin, Apr. 1891, HP, ser. 1, reels 19, 20, and 30, and ser. 2, reel 74.

30. R. Hal Williams, *Years of Decision: American Politics in the 1890s* (New York: John Wiley & Sons, 1978), p. 59; Dunn, *From Harrison to Harding*, 1:11, 86–88; Mayer, *Republican Party*, p. 221.

31. Harrison, *Speeches*, p. 202; copy of letter from Harrison to John H. Burford, 14 Oct. 1889, HP, ser. 1, reel 23.

32. Herbert S. Schell, *History of South Dakota* (Lincoln: University of Nebraska Press, 1968), p. 22; Sievers, *Benjamin Harrison, Hoosier President*, pp. 131–32; *Biographical Directory of the American Congress, 1774–1927* (Washington, D.C.: Government Printing Office, 1928). Montana and Washington had been expected to go Democratic.

CHAPTER 4
DOMESTIC PROGRAMS

1. R. Hal Williams, *Years of Decision: American Politics in the 1890s* (New York: John Wiley & Sons, 1978), p. 40; H. Wayne Morgan, *From Hayes to McKinley: National Party Politics, 1877–1896* (Syracuse, N.Y.: Syracuse University Press, 1969), p. 319; Ari Hoogenboom, *Outlawing the Spoils: A History of the Civil Service Reform Movement, 1865–1883* (Urbana: University of Illinois Press, 1961), p. 181; Richard Jensen, *The Winning of the Midwest: Social and Political Conflict, 1888–1896* (Chicago: University of Chicago Press, 1971), p. 141.

2. Marcus Cunliffe, *American Presidents and the Presidency* (New York: American Heritage Press, 1968, 1972), p. 190; Robert H. Wiebe, *The Search for Order, 1877–1920* (New York: Hill & Wang, 1967), pp. 192–93.

3. Williams, *Years of Decision*, pp. 36, 40; E. Benjamin Andrews, *The History of the Last Quarter-Century in the United States, 1870–1895*, vol. 2 (New York: Charles Scribner's Sons, 1896), p. 186; Henry Jones Ford, *The Cleveland Era: A Chronicle of the New Order in Politics* (New Haven, Conn.: Yale University Press, 1919), p. 148; Arthur Bernon Tourtellot, *The Presidents on the Presidency* (Garden City, N.Y.: Doubleday & Co., Inc., 1964), p. 240.

4. Paul Kleppner, *The Cross of Culture: A Social Analysis of Midwestern Politics, 1850–1900* (New York: Free Press, 1970), pp. 5–6.

5. Williams, *Years of Decision*, p. 20.

6. Harold U. Faulkner, *Politics, Reform and Expansion, 1890–1900* (New York: Harper & Row, 1959), p. 95; Morgan, *From Hayes to McKinley*, pp. 333–35; George H. Mayer, *The Republican Party, 1854–1964*, 2d ed. (New York: Oxford University Press, 1967), p. 224.

7. Edward Stanwood, *A History of the Presidency from 1788 to 1897* (Boston, Mass.: Houghton Mifflin Co., 1912), pp. 468–69, 473; Albert T. Volwiler, ''Tariff

Strategy and Propaganda in the United States, 1887-1888," *American Historical Review* 38 (Oct. 1936): 76-77; Williams, *Years of Decision*, p. 25.

8. John A. Garraty, *The New Commonwealth, 1877-1890* (New York: Harper & Row, 1968), p. 304; Horace Samuel Merrill, *Bourbon Leader: Grover Cleveland and the Democratic Party* (Boston, Mass.: Little, Brown & Co., 1957), pp. 129-30; Harry J. Sievers, *Benjamin Harrison, Hoosier President: The White House and After* (Indianapolis, Ind.: Bobbs-Merrill Co., Inc., 1968), p. 163; Benjamin Harrison, *Speeches of Benjamin Harrison*, comp. Charles Hedges (Port Washington, N.Y.: Kennikat Press, 1892, 1971), pp. 196-97.

9. Arthur Wallace Dunn, *From Harrison to Harding: A Personal Narrative, Covering a Third of a Century, 1888-1921,* 2 vols. (Port Washington, N.Y.: Kennikat Press, 1922, 1971), 1:46; Williams, *Years of Decision*, p. 26; Morgan, *From Hayes to McKinley*, pp. 319, 336.

10. Alice Felt Tyler, *The Foreign Policy of James G. Blaine* (Minneapolis: University of Minnesota Press, 1927), p. 185; Tom E. Terrill, *The Tariff, Politics, and American Foreign Policy, 1874-1901* (Westport, Conn.: Greenwood Press, 1973), chap. 7, "The McKinley Tariff and Reciprocity," pp. 159-83.

11. Morgan, *From Hayes to McKinley*, pp. 338, 350.

12. Ibid., pp. 167-70, 172; Dennis Alan Daellenbach, "Senators, the Navy and the Politics of American Expansionism, 1881-1890" (Ph.D. diss., University of Kansas, 1982), p. 279; Dunn, *From Harrison to Harding*, 1:44-48; Sievers, *Benjamin Harrison, Hoosier President*, pp. 165, 172; John M. Dobson, *Politics in the Gilded Age: A New Perspective on Reform* (New York: Praeger Publisher, 1972), p. 171.

13. Terrill, *Tariff*, pp. 173-74; Williams, *Years of Decision*, p. 45.

14. James Ford Rhodes, *History of the United States from Hayes to McKinley, 1877-1896,* vol. 8 (New York: Macmillan Co., 1919), p. 351; Daellenbach, "Senators," p. 280; Tyler, *Foreign Policy*, p. 187; House of Representatives, 51st Cong., 2d sess., Executive Document no. 1, pt. 1, *Papers Relating to Foreign Relations of the United States* (Washington, D.C.: Government Printing Office, 1891), p. xx; Harrison, *Speeches*, p. 287; Harrison to William M. Ivins, New York City, 17 Dec. 1891, HP, ser. 2, reel 79.

15. Morgan, *From Hayes to McKinley*, p. 353.

16. Stanwood, *History of the Presidency*, pp. 470, 474.

17. Hans B. Thorelli, *The Federal Antitrust Policy: Origination of an American Tradition* (London: George Allen & Unwin Ltd., 1974), pp. 200-201, 210, 212, 371; Morgan, *From Hayes to McKinley*, p. 347; Carl N. Degler, *The Age of the Economic Revolution, 1876-1900* (Glenview, Ill.: Scott, Foresman & Co., 1967), p. 47; House of Representatives, Fifty-first Cong., 1st sess., Executive Document no. 1, *Annual Message of the President, 3 Dec. 1889* (Washington, D.C.: Government Printing Office, 1890), p. xvi.

18. Thorelli, *Federal Antitrust Policy*, p. 371.

19. Ibid., pp. 374-77.

20. Ibid., pp. 379-80, 398; Sean Dennis Cashman, *America in the Gilded Age: From the Death of Lincoln to the Rise of Theodore Roosevelt* (New York: New York University Press, 1984), p. 85.

21. Williams, *Years of Decision*, p. 33.

22. Elmer Ellis, *Henry Moore Teller: Defender of the West* (Caldwell, Idaho: Caxton Printers, Ltd., 1941), p. 180; Davis Rich Dewey, *National Problems, 1885–1897* (New York: Harper & Brothers Publishers, 1907), p. 221; Fred Wellborn, "The Influence of the Silver-Republican Senators, 1889–1891," *Mississippi Valley Historical Review* 14 (1928): 465.

23. L. T. Michener to Elijah Halford, 5 Nov. 1889, HP, ser. 1, reel 23. The Republican platform was "in favor of the use of both gold and silver as money, and condemns the policy of the Democratic administration in its efforts to demonetize silver."

24. Robert Seward Salisbury, "William Windom, the Republican Party, and the Gilded Age" (Ph.D. diss., University of Minnesota, 1982; University Microfilms), p. 677; Rhodes, *From Hayes to McKinley*, pp. 353–54.

25. Paolo E. Coletta, "Greenbackers, Goldbugs, and Silverites," in *The Gilded Age: A Reappraisal*, ed. H. Wayne Morgan (Syracuse, N.Y.: Syracuse University Press, 1963), p. 126; House of Representatives, 51st Cong., 1st sess., Executive Document no. 1, pt. 1 (Washington, D.C.: Government Printing Office, 1890), p. xiii.

26. Ellis, *Henry Moore Teller*, p. 188.

27. Morgan, *From Hayes to McKinley*, p. 343; Wellborn, "Influence of Silver-Republican Senators," p. 462; Mayer, *Republican Party*, p. 224.

28. Dewey, *National Problems*, p. 225; Wellborn, "Influence of Silver-Republican Senators," pp. 466–67.

29. Wellborn, "Influence of Silver-Republican Senators," p. 468; Mayer, *Republican Party*, p. 227.

30. Salisbury, "William Windom," p. 680.

31. Dewey, *National Problems*, pp. 227–28; Wellborn, in "Influence of Silver-Republican Senators," p. 463, agrees substantially with Dewey.

32. Harrison, *Speeches*, pp. 288–89, in a letter of 7 Apr. 1891 to the Western States Commercial Congress, meeting in Kansas City, Mo.

33. Dewey, *National Problems*, p. 227.

34. Ibid., p. 230.

35. H. Wayne Morgan, "The Republican Party, 1876–1893," in *History of U.S. Political Parties*, vol. 2: *1860–1910: The Gilded Age in Politics*, ed. Arthur M. Schlesinger, Jr. (New York: R. R. Bowker Co., 1973), p. 1425.

36. Stanwood, *History of the Presidency*, p. 473; Williams, *Years of Decision*, pp. 12–13; Harrison, *Speeches*, pp. 197–203.

37. Richard E. Welch, Jr., "The Federal Elections Bill of 1890: Postscripts and Prelude," *Journal of American History* 52 (Dec. 1965): 511–12.

38. L. T. Michener to E. W. Halford, 1 Oct. 1889, HP, ser. 1, reel 23; George Sinkler, *The Racial Attitudes of American Presidents from Abraham Lincoln to Theodore Roosevelt* (Garden City, N.Y.: Doubleday & Co., Inc., 1971), p. 252; Ray Ginger, in *The Age of Excess: The United States from 1887 to 1914* (New York: Macmillan Publishing Co., 1965, 1975), p. 75, holds that Harrison's support for a federal

elections bill came after the 1889 elections, when certain Republicans fared badly.

39. Welch, "Federal Elections Bill," pp. 511–12; Stanley P. Hirshson, *Farewell to the Bloody Shirt: Northern Republicans and the Southern Negro, 1877–1893* (Chicago: Quadrangle Books, 1962), pp. 202–9; House of Representatives, 51st Cong., 1st sess., Executive Document no. 1, pt. 1, pp. xxx–xxxi.

40. Hirshson, *Farewell to the Bloody Shirt,* pp. 205, 214; Rhodes, *History of the United States,* p. 361.

41. Rayford W. Logan, *The Betrayal of the Negro: From Rutherford B. Hayes to Woodrow Wilson* (New York: Collier Books, 1965), p. 70; Welch, "Federal Elections Bill," p. 514; Williams, *Years of Decision,* pp. 30–32; Dewey, *National Problems,* pp. 162–73; Hirshson, *Farewell to the Bloody Shirt,* pp. 204–5.

42. Hirshson, *Farewell to the Bloody Shirt,* p. 226.

43. Welch, "Federal Elections Bill," pp. 515–18; Rhodes, *History of the United States,* p. 359.

44. Sinkler, *Racial Attitudes,* pp. 261–62, 284.

45. Hirshson, *Farewell to the Bloody Shirt,* pp. 226–28.

46. Dunn, *From Harrison to Harding,* 1:61; Wellborn, "Influence of Silver-Republican Senators," p. 475; Hirshson, *Farewell to the Bloody Shirt,* p. 233; Ellis, *Henry Moore Teller,* pp. 199–200; Louis Clinton Hatch, *A History of the Vice Presidency of the United States,* rev. and ed. Earl L. Shoup (New York: American Historical Society, Inc., 1934), pp. 79–81; Morgan, *From Hayes to McKinley,* p. 342. After the 1892 election, one journal held the Lodge bill accountable for lack of Republican inroads in the South (see *Public Opinion,* 4 Dec. 1892, p. 223).

47. Morgan, *From Hayes to McKinley,* pp. 339–41.

48. Hirshson, *Farewell to the Bloody Shirt,* p. 254; Vincent de Santis, "The Republican Party and the Southern Negro, 1877–1897," *Journal of Negro History* 45 (Apr. 1960): 71–87; Donald L. Grant, *The Anti-Lynching Movement: 1883–1932* (San Francisco, Calif.: R & E Associates, 1975), p. 56.

49. Mayer, *Republican Party,* p. 221; Welch, "Federal Elections Bill," pp. 521–26; Robert F. Durden, "Politics in the Gilded Age, 1877–1896," in *Interpreting and Teaching American History,* ed. William H. Cartwright and Richard L. Watson (Baltimore, Md.: National Council for the Social Studies, 1961), p. 182.

50. Allen J. Going, "The South and the Blair Education Bill," *Mississippi Valley Historical Review* 44 (Sept. 1957): 267; Hirshson, *Farewell to the Bloody Shirt,* pp. 192–93.

51. Going, "The South and the Blair Bill," pp. 269–74; Hirshson, *Farewell to the Bloody Shirt,* p. 194.

52. Going, "The South and the Blair Bill," pp. 275–90; Morgan, *From Hayes to McKinley,* p. 269; Dewey, *National Problems,* pp. 88–90; Terrill, *Tariff,* p. 107.

53. Leslie H. Fishel, Jr., "The Negro in Northern Politics, 1870–1900," *Mississippi Valley Historical Review* 42 (Dec. 1955): 484–85.

54. Logan, *Betrayal of the Negro,* p. 67.

55. Harrison, *Speeches,* pp. 194–203.

56. Logan, *Betrayal of the Negro*, p. 70; Sievers, *Benjamin Harrison, Hoosier President*, p. 145; Hirshson, *Farewell to the Bloody Shirt*, pp. 195–99; Going, "The South and the Blair Bill," p. 275.

57. Going, "The South and the Blair Bill," p. 275.

58. Ibid., p. 290.

59. Morgan, *From Hayes to McKinley*, pp. 269–70.

60. Logan, *Betrayal of the Negro*, pp. 196–97; Garraty, *The New Commonwealth*, pp. 243–44.

61. Stanwood, *History of the Presidency*, pp. 469, 474; Harrison, *Speeches*, p. 202.

62. 26 Stat. 10, 1103; Everett Dick, *The Lure of the Land: A Social History of the Public Lands from the Articles of Confederation to the New Deal* (Lincoln: University of Nebraska Press, 1970), p. 326; Samuel Trask Dana and Sally K. Fairfax, *Forest and Range Policy: Its Development in the United States*, 2d ed. (New York: McGraw-Hill Book Co., 1980), p. 101n. 89.

63. John Ise, *The United States Forest Policy* (New York: Arno Press, 1920, 1972), p. 115; Paul W. Gates, *History of Public Land Development* (New York: Arno Press, 1968, 1979), p. 565; Dana and Fairfax, *Forest and Range Policy*, p. 101n. 89; Dunn, *From Harrison to Harding*, 1:73–74.

64. Address of John W. Noble, Indianapolis, 27 Oct. 1908, HP, ser. 18, container 6; House of Representatives, 52d Cong., 1st sess., Executive Document no. 1, pt. 5, *Report of the Secretary of the Interior*, pp. xiv–xv. Other members of the committee from the AAAS were B. E. Fernow, secretary; E. W. Hilgard, of California; C. E. Bessey, of Nebraska; and Wm. Saunders, of Canada.

65. Harold K. Steen, *The U.S. Forest Service: A History* (Seattle: University of Washington Press, 1976), pp. 26–27; Michael Frome, *The Forest Service* (Boulder, Colo.: Westview Press, 1984), pp. 18–19; Glen O. Robinson, *The Forest Service: A Study in Public Land Management* (Baltimore, Md.: Resources for the Future, Inc., 1975), pp. 5–6; Richard C. Davis, ed., *Encyclopedia of American Forest and Conservation History*, 2 vols. (New York: Macmillan Publ. Co., 1983), 1:234; Harrison's role in suggesting the forest reserve is shown by John Spencer Bassett in *Expansion and Reform, 1889–1926* (New York: Longmans, Green & Co., 1926), pp. 139–40; Gates, *History of Public Land Development*, p. 565; William G. Robbins, *American Forestry: A History of National, State, and Private Cooperation* (Lincoln: University of Nebraska Press, 1985), p. 7.

66. Proclamation no. 6, 30 Mar. 1891; Eliza Ruhamah Scidmore, "Our New National Forest Reserves," *Century Magazine* 46 (Sept. 1893): 792–97; Davis, *Encyclopedia of American Forest and Conservation History*, p. 234.

67. *New York Times*, 27 Feb. 1893.

68. J. P. Kinney, *The Development of Forest Law in America* (New York: John Wiley & Sons, Inc., 1917), p. 245; Dana and Fairfax, *Forest and Range Policy*, p. 58; M. Nelson McGeary, *Gifford Pinchot: Forester, Politician* (Princeton, N.J.: Princeton University Press, 1960), p. 36; Robinson, *Forest Service*, p. 4; Benjamin H. Hibbard, *A History of the Public Land Policies* (New York: Macmillan Co., 1924), p. 421.

69. Letters in HP relating to the International Copyright Agreement are from Senators J. R. Hawley and O. H. Platt, 12 and 18 Nov. 1889, and from R. U. Johnson, New York City, to E. W. Halford, 15 Nov. 1889.

70. Sievers, *Benjamin Harrison, Hoosier President*, pp. 158–61; John S. Ezell, *Fortune's Merry Wheel: The Lottery in America* (Cambridge, Mass.: Harvard University Press, 1960), p. 263.

71. House of Representatives, 51st Cong., 1st sess., Executive Document no. 1, pt. 1, p. xxv, and 52d Cong., 1st sess., Executive Document no. 1, pt. 1, p. xxxv.

72. *An Address from the Workingmen of San Francisco to Their Brothers throughout the Pacific Coast (16 Aug. 1888) in Metropolitan Hall*, pp. 1–2, 10, 20, HP, ser. 18, container 4; letters to Harrison from Senator William M. Stewart, 29 June, from A. May, of LeMoore, Calif., 29 June, and from Congressman John A. Anderson, 30 June 1888, HP, ser. 1, reel 9; Harrison, *Speeches*, pp. 112, 198–99; Delber L. McKee, *Chinese Exclusion versus the Open Door Policy, 1900–1906: Clashes over China Policy in the Roosevelt Era* (Detroit, Mich.: Wayne State University Press, 1977), pp. 24–25; Homer Cummings and Carl McFarland, *Federal Justice: Chapters in the History of Justice and the Federal Executive* (New York: Macmillan Co., 1937), p. 435. Harrison, as a senator, had opposed the Chinese Exclusion Act because "he thought it would violate the Burlingame Treaty with China, and also because he thought exclusion un-American" (see Sinkler, *Racial Attitudes*, pp. 284–87).

73. Stephen Skowronek, *Building a New American State: The Expansion of National Administrative Capacities, 1877–1920* (New York: Cambridge University Press, 1982), pp. 170–71.

74. *New York Times*, 3 Mar. 1893.

75. Rhodes, *History of the United States*, pp. 371, 383; Dunn, *From Harrison to Harding*, 1:77–79; Dewey, *National Problems*, pp. 182–87; *Literary Digest*, 9 Nov. 1890 to 14 Mar. 1891; *Public Opinion*, 8 Oct. 1892 to 11 Mar. 1893.

76. *New York Times*, 1 Aug. 1892.

CHAPTER 5
PRESIDENT HARRISON ON TRIAL

1. Oscar Doane Lambert, *Stephen Benton Elkins: American Foursquare* (Pittsburgh, Pa.: University of Pittsburgh Press, 1955), p. 132; David Saville Muzzey, *James G. Blaine: A Political Idol of Other Days* (Port Washington, N.Y.: Kennikat Press, 1934, 1963), p. 389.

2. Paul F. Boller, Jr., *Presidential Anecdotes* (New York: Oxford University Press, 1981), p. 184; James Morgan, *Our Presidents* (New York: Macmillan Co., 1952), p. 229; Robert F. Wesser, "Election of 1888," in *History of American Presidential Elections, 1789–1968*, ed. Arthur M. Schlesinger, Jr., and Fred L. Israel, vol. 2 (New York: McGraw-Hill Book Co., 1971), p. 1637; H. Wayne Morgan, *From Hayes to McKinley: National Party Politics, 1877–1896* (Syracuse,

N.Y.: Syracuse University Press, 1969), pp. 328-29; Arthur Wallace Dunn, *From Harrison to Harding: A Personal Narrative, Covering a Third of a Century, 1888-1921,* 2 vols. (Port Washington, N.Y.: Kennikat Press, 1922, 1971), 1:86-87; William Starr Myers, *The Republican Party: A History* (New York: Century Co., 1928), pp. 299-300; editorial in *New York Tribune,* 18 Mar. 1891; Andrew Dickson White, *Autobiography of Andrew Dickson White,* 2 vols. (New York: Century Co., 1905), 1:224-28, 2:183.

3. E. Benjamin Andrews, *The History of the Last Quarter-Century in the United States, 1870-1895,* 2 vols. (New York: Charles Scribner's Sons, 1896), 2:225.

4. E. W. Halford, "General Harrison's Attitude toward the Presidency," *Century Magazine* 84 (June 1912): 305; Herbert Adams Gibbons, *John Wanamaker,* 2 vols. (New York: Harper & Brothers Publishers, 1926), 1:268-69; Muzzey, *James G. Blaine,* p. 387.

5. *New York Times,* 31 Aug. and 1 Sept. 1892; James A. Kehl, *Boss Rule in the Gilded Age: Matt Quay of Pennsylvania* (Pittsburgh, Pa.: University of Pittsburgh Press, 1981), p. 118.

6. Kehl, *Boss Rule,* pp. 121-22.

7. William A. Robinson, *Thomas B. Reed: Parliamentarian* (New York: Dodd, Mead & Co., 1930), pp. 160, 282-83.

8. Stanley P. Hirshson, "James S. Clarkson versus Benjamin Harrison, 1891-1893: A Political Saga," *Iowa Journal of History* 58 (July 1960): 219-24; George H. Mayer, *The Republican Party, 1854-1964* (New York: Oxford University Press, 1967), p. 231.

9. Donald Marquand Dozer, "Benjamin Harrison and the Presidential Campaign of 1892," *American Historical Review* 54 (Oct. 1948): 59; Kehl, *Boss Rule,* pp. 168-69.

10. Kathleen Prindiville, *First Ladies* (New York: Macmillan Co., 1941), pp. 188-89.

11. H. W. Morgan, *From Hayes to McKinley,* p. 343.

12. Donald L. McMurry, "The Political Significance of the Pension Question, 1885-1897," *Mississippi Valley Historical Review* 9 (June 1922): 34.

13. Thomas J. Morgan, "Benjamin Harrison: A Character Sketch," *Review of Reviews* 6 (July 1892): 676-77, 690.

14. *New York Tribune,* 24 Nov. 1890; H. W. Morgan, *From Hayes to McKinley,* p. 327; John A. Garraty, *The New Commonwealth, 1877-1890* (New York: Harper & Row, 1968), p. 296.

15. Harry J. Sievers, *Benjamin Harrison, Hoosier President: The White House and After* (Indianapolis, Ind.: Bobbs-Merrill Co., Inc., 1968), pp. 130-31.

16. "Compilation of the Ideas and Suggestions of Mrs. Harrison for Extension of the Executive Mansion, Washington, D.C.," drawn and arranged by Fred D. Owen, HP, ser. 19, container 2; Arthur Bernon Tourtellot, *The Presidents on the Presidency* (Garden City, N.Y.: Doubleday & Co., Inc., 1964), p. 114; Halford wrote to Harrison on 19 Apr. 1891, four days after the death of Halford's wife, HP, ser. 1, reel 31; Michael Medved, *The Shadow Presidents* (New York: Times Books, 1979), pp. 88-92; T. J. Morgan, "Benjamin Harrison," pp.

676-77; Bradley D. Nash, "Organizing and Staffing the Presidency," Center for the Study of the Presidency, *Proceedings* 3 (1980): 22.

17. H. W. Morgan, *From Hayes to McKinley*, p. 327.

18. Sievers, *Benjamin Harrison, Hoosier President*, p. 39; Leonard D. White, *The Republican Era: A Study in Administrative History, 1869-1901* (New York: Macmillan Co., 1958), p. 102. Tibbott served as Harrison's private secretary after the White House years, and he was mentioned in Harrison's will (see Herbert R. Collins and David B. Weaver, *Wills of the U.S. Presidents* [New York: Communications Channels, Inc., 1976], p. 149).

19. Benjamin Harrison, *This Country of Ours* (New York: Charles Scribner's Sons, 1898), pp. 159-60.

20. *Kansas Farmer* (Topeka), 4 Apr. 1889.

21. White, *Republican Era*, p. 390; Harrison, *This Country*, p. 161; Sievers, in *Benjamin Harrison, Hoosier President*, p. 39, called Dinsmore a captain; H. W. Morgan, *From Hayes to McKinley*, p. 327.

22. *New York Tribune*, 17 Mar. 1891.

23. Harrison, *This Country*, pp. 166, 169; see HP, 13 Jan. to 5 Mar. 1891, ser. 2, reel 75; T. J. Morgan, "Benjamin Harrison," pp. 682-83.

24. Sievers, *Benjamin Harrison, Hoosier President*, pp. 38-39, 130-31.

25. Ibid., pp. 54-55.

26. Margaret Leech, *In the Days of McKinley* (New York: Harper & Brothers, 1959), p. 132; Henry L. Stoddard, *It Costs to Be President* (New York: Harper & Brothers Publishers, 1938), p. 246; Sievers, *Benjamin Harrison, Hoosier President*, p. 52.

27. Letters from John A. Anderson to Benjamin Harrison, 30 June and 5 Aug. 1888, and from Harrison to Anderson, 26 Jan. 1892, HP, ser. 1, reels 9 and 10, ser. 2, reel 79; Harrison had been besieged in a lengthy series of letters by another Kansan, G. F. Little, for appointment to the Cairo position. In a bitter four-page letter to E. W. Halford, Little withdrew his application papers, 24 June 1891. Anderson telegraphed Harrison, on 27 Feb. 1891, that he was "delighted with the outlook and ever so grateful" (HP, ser. 1, reel 31, and ser. 2, reel 79).

28. Letter from Noble to Harrison, 5 Mar., and telegram from Noble to Harrison, 30 May 1891, HP, ser. 1, reels 30 and 31.

29. Robert Seward Salisbury, "William Windom, the Republican Party, and the Gilded Age" (Ph.D. diss., University of Minnesota, 1982), pp. 701-3; Sievers, *Benjamin Harrison, Hoosier President*, pp. 201-2.

30. John J. Ingalls, *A Collection of the Writings of John James Ingalls: Essays, Addresses, and Orations* (Kansas City, Mo.: Hudson-Kimberly Publishing Co., 1902), p. 441; Michael J. Devine, *John W. Foster: Politics and Diplomacy in the Imperial Era, 1873-1917* (Athens: Ohio University Press, 1981), p. 47; Richard C. Bain and Judith H. Parris, *Convention Decisions and Voting Records* (Washington, D.C.: Brookings Institution, 1973), p. 142; H. W. Morgan, *From Hayes to McKinley*, p. 401; R. Hal Williams, *Years of Decision: American Politics in the 1890s* (New York: John Wiley & Sons, 1978), pp. 61-64; Muzzey, *James G. Blaine*, p. 474; Dozer, "Benjamin Harrison," pp. 62-63; Tom E. Terrill, *The Tariff, Politics,*

and American Foreign Policy, 1874–1901 (Westport, Conn.: Greenwood Press, 1973), p. 150. Latter-day diplomat and secretary of state John Foster Dulles was a grandson of John W. Foster.

31. Williams, *Years of Decision*, pp. 57, 61–62; Mayer, *Republican Party*, p. 231; Horace Samuel Merrill, *Bourbon Leader: Grover Cleveland and the Democratic Party* (Boston, Mass.: Little, Brown & Co., 1957), p. 143.

32. Richard Jensen, *The Winning of the Midwest: Social and Political Conflict, 1888–1896* (Chicago: University of Chicago Press, 1971), pp. xii, 3. Similar trends in the same general area were found by Paul Kleppner, in *The Cross of Culture: A Social Analysis of Midwestern Politics, 1850–1900* (New York: Free Press, 1970), pp. 117–18, 125, 158; Williams, *Years of Decision*, p. 45.

33. Jensen, *Winning the Midwest*, pp. 101–15, 119–20, 138–42; Williams, *Years of Decision*, p. 47; Robert D. Marcus, *Grand Old Party: Political Structure in the Gilded Age, 1880–1896* (New York: Oxford University Press, 1971), pp. 151–52.

34. H. W. Morgan, *From Hayes to McKinley*, pp. 332, 336–37.

35. Sievers, *Benjamin Harrison, Hoosier President*, p. 77. The nineteen-page report from Surgeon General John B. Hamilton to Benjamin Harrison, 9 June 1889, HP, ser. 1, reel 20, said that one man—a kind of dictator—directed clean-up activity in Johnstown, where such work was expected to take three weeks; E. Kurtz Johnson to E. W. Halford, 15 June 1889, HP, ser. 1, reel 20. There are a dozen pieces of correspondence in HP for June 1889 concerning this catastrophe, which claimed more than two thousand lives, with property damage in excess of $10 million. The Washington relief collection amounted to $10,000.

36. Harrison to Cornelius N. Bliss, 14 Dec., to W. J. Arkell, 21 Dec., and to Thomas McDougall, 22 Dec.—all in 1891, HP, ser. 2, reel 79.

CHAPTER 6

THE STEEL NAVY AND THE NEW ARMY

1. See Peter Karsten, *The Naval Aristocracy: The Golden Age of Annapolis and the Emergence of Modern American Navalism* (New York: Free Press, 1972), pp. 284, 286 n, 288–89, 301–11; Walter R. Herrick, Jr., *The American Naval Revolution* (Baton Rouge: Louisiana State University Press, 1966), pp. 17, 29–31, 36–37; Milton Plesur, *America's Outward Thrust: Approaches to Foreign Affairs, 1865–1890* (De Kalb: Northern Illinois University Press, 1971), pp. 13, 87, 96; Walter LaFeber, *The New Empire: An Interpretation of American Expansion, 1860–1898* (Ithaca, N.Y.: Cornell University Press, 1963), pp. 60, 88, 91; John A. S. Grenville and George Berkeley Young, *Politics, Strategy, and American Diplomacy: Studies in Foreign Policy, 1873–1917* (New Haven, Conn.: Yale University Press, 1966), pp. 5–6; Kenneth J. Hagan, *American Gunboat Diplomacy and the Old Navy, 1877–1889* (Westport, Conn.: Greenwood Press, 1973), p. 56; Charles S. Campbell, *The Transformation of American Foreign Relations, 1865–1900* (New York: Harper & Row, 1976), p. 152.

2. James D. Richardson, comp., *A Compilation of the Messages and Papers of the Presidents, 1789–1897* (hereafter cited as *Messages*), 9 vols. (Washington, D.C.: Government Printing Office, 1898), 9:12.

3. Herrick, *American Naval Revolution*, pp. 23, 58.

4. "Our Diplomacy," *Nation* 49 (11 July 1889): 24.

5. Herrick, *American Naval Revolution*, pp. 37–38, 48.

6. John K. Mahon, "Benjamin Franklin Tracy: Secretary of the Navy, 1889–1893," *New York Historical Society Quarterly* 44 (Apr. 1960): 184; Rear Adm. J. G. Walker to Benjamin Tracy, 6 Dec. 1889, in Letters Sent to the Navy Department from the Squadron of Evolution, Archives of the U.S. Department of the Navy, Record Group (hereafter RG) 313, National Archives, Washington, D.C. (hereafter cited as NA).

7. Benjamin Franklin Cooling, *Benjamin Franklin Tracy: Father of the Modern American Fighting Navy* (Hamden, Conn.: Archon Books, 1973), pp. 76, 79.

8. Letterbook 2 (17 July 1889–5 May 1890), Benjamin Tracy Papers, LC, vol. 24.

9. Herrick, *American Naval Revolution*, pp. 61–63.

10. *New York Tribune*, 4 Feb. 1890, p. 1; Cooling, *Benjamin Franklin Tracy*, pp. 83–84.

11. Herrick, *American Naval Revolution*, pp. 72–76.

12. *New York Times*, 19 Nov. 1890, p. 1, and 29 June 1892, p. 1.

13. Herrick, *American Naval Revolution*, pp. 65–66, 78–81, 134; Cooling, *Benjamin Franklin Tracy*, pp. 91–98; Andrew Carnegie to James G. Blaine, 9 Mar. 1891, Andrew Carnegie Papers, LC, vol. 12.

14. Herrick, *American Naval Revolution*, pp. 52–53, 77–78n; Dumas Malone, ed., *Dictionary of American Biography*, 10 vols. (New York: Charles Scribner's Sons, 1935), 9:392.

15. Herrick, *American Naval Revolution*, pp. 75–76.

16. C. H. Davis to Lt. Nathan Sargent, 3 Feb. 1891, letters to Lt. Nathan Sargent: Naval Attache, Rome and Vienna, Archives of the U.S. Department of the Navy, RG 45, NA.

17. Cooling, *Benjamin Franklin Tracy*, pp. 103, 125.

18. Tracy Papers, vol. 27 (8 Apr. 1891 speech); Benjamin Tracy, "Our New War Ships," *North American Review* 152 (June 1891): 643–44.

19. Herrick, *American Naval Revolution*, p. 142; Richardson, *Messages*, 9:200.

20. Tracy Papers, vol. 27 (n.d.).

21. Cooling, *Benjamin Franklin Tracy*, p. 128; Herrick, *American Naval Revolution*, pp. 143–44.

22. Alfred T. Mahan to Tracy, 10 Oct. 1892 and 7 Dec. 1892, Tracy Papers, vols. 13, 14.

23. Cooling, *Benjamin Franklin Tracy*, p. 144; Richardson, *Messages*, 9:324–25.

24. Herrick, *American Naval Revolution*, pp. 175, 177–79, 212, 223, 247.

25. Lt. Gen. John M. Schofield, *Forty-Six Years in the Army* (New York: Century Co., 1897), p. 458; Robert M. Utley, *Frontier Regulars: The United States*

Army and the Indian, 1866–1891 (New York: Macmillan Publishing Co., 1973), p. 410.

26. Utley, *Frontier Regulars*, pp. 12, 16, 24, 64, 66, 267, 275–76; William H. Leckie, *The Buffalo Soldiers: A Narrative of the Negro Cavalry in the West* (Norman: University of Oklahoma Press, 1967), pp. 6, 163; Thomas W. Dunlay, *Wolves for the Blue Soldiers: Indian Scouts and Auxiliaries with the United States Army, 1860–1890* (Lincoln: University of Nebraska Press, 1982), pp. 44, 50, 55; Russell F. Weigley, *History of the United States Army* (New York: Macmillan Co., 1967), p. 267; Arlen L. Fowler, *The Black Infantry in the West, 1869–1891* (Westport, Conn.: Greenwood Publishing Corp., 1971), p. xii; Jack D. Foner, *The United States Soldier between Two Wars: Army Life and Reforms, 1865–1898* (New York: Humanities Press, 1970), pp. 7, 10, 13; Edward Coffman, *The Old Army: A Portrait of the American Army in Peacetime, 1784–1898* (New York: Oxford University Press, 1986), pp. 218, 331–32, 346.

27. See Utley, *Frontier Regulars*.

28. Ibid., pp. 26, 45; Weigley, *History of the United States Army*, p. 291; Coffman, *Old Army*, pp. 232, 274.

29. Weigley, *History of the United States Army*, p. 567; Utley, *Frontier Regulars*, p. 48; Coffman, *Old Army*, p. 282; Foner, *United States Soldier*, p. 223; *New York Times*, 12 July 1892, p. 1, 14 July 1892, p. 1, and 15 July 1892, p. 3.

30. Harry J. Sievers, *Benjamin Harrison, Hoosier President: The White House and After* (Indianapolis, Ind.: Bobbs-Merrill Co., Inc., 1968), pp. 18–19, 23; Coffman, *Old Army*, pp. 397, 403; Foner, *United States Soldier*, pp. 87, 136–37.

31. Foner, *United States Soldier*, pp. 110–11, 223; Dunlay, *Wolves*, pp. 195–96; Coffman, *Old Army*, pp. 342, 374.

32. Coffman, *Old Army*, pp. 233, 281; Utley, *Frontier Regulars*, p. 21; Weigley, *History of the United States Army*, p. 288; Allen Johnson and Dumas Malone, eds., *Dictionary of American Biography*, 10 vols. (New York: Charles Scribner's Sons, 1931), 4:490.

33. Utley, *Frontier Regulars*, pp. 413–16, 419, 422n.

34. Copy of telegram to Maj. Gen. Nelson Miles from Maj. Gen. J. M. Schofield, 2 Jan. 1891, HP, ser. 1, reel 30.

35. Sievers, *Benjamin Harrison, Hoosier President*, p. 93.

36. Copy of a letter to Benjamin Harrison from the acting secretary of war, 21 Mar. 1891, HP, ser. 1, reel 31.

37. Richardson, *Messages*, 9:167–69.

38. Foner, *United States Soldier*, pp. 112, 117, 223; Coffman, *Old Army*, pp. 225, 332, 374, 397–98.

CHAPTER 7
BLAINE AND THE STATE DEPARTMENT

1. Allan Peskin, *Garfield* (Kent, Ohio: Kent State University Press, 1978), pp. 519, 554; David M. Pletcher, *The Awkward Years: American Foreign Relations*

under Garfield and Arthur (Columbia: University of Missouri Press, 1962), p. 63; Charles S. Campbell, *The Transformation of American Foreign Relations, 1865–1900* (New York: Harper & Row, 1976), p. 91; Justus D. Doenecke, *The Presidencies of James A. Garfield and Chester A. Arthur* (Lawrence: Regents Press of Kansas, 1981), p. 74.

2. Pletcher, *Awkward Years*, pp. 62–65, 70, 73–77.

3. The post of first assistant secretary of state went to forty-one-year-old William Wharton, who had served in the Massachusetts legislature and was nominated by Congressman Henry Cabot Lodge. According to John A. Garraty, Lodge first suggested young Theodore Roosevelt for the position, but Blaine had doubts about Roosevelt. See Albert T. Volwiler, ed., *The Correspondence between Benjamin Harrison and James G. Blaine, 1882–1893* (Philadelphia: American Philosophical Society, 1940), p. 81n; John A. Garraty, *Henry Cabot Lodge: A Biography* (New York: Alfred A. Knopf, 1953), pp. 82, 103–4.

4. See John W. Foster, *Diplomatic Memoirs*, 2 vols. (Boston, Mass.: Houghton Mifflin, 1909), 2:251; David Saville Muzzey, *James G. Blaine: A Political Idol of Other Days* (Port Washington, N.Y.: Kennikat, 1934, 1963), p. 464; *American Historical Review* 41 (Apr. 1936): 555.

5. Foster, *Diplomatic Memoirs*, 2:270.

6. Muzzey, *James G. Blaine*, pp. 424–25.

7. Julius W. Pratt, *Expansionists of 1898: The Acquisition of Hawaii and the Spanish Islands* (Baltimore, Md.: Johns Hopkins Press, 1936), pp. 25–26; Walter LaFeber, *The New Empire: An Interpretation of American Expansion, 1860–1898* (Ithaca, N.Y.: Cornell University Press, 1963), p. 104; John A. S. Grenville and George Berkeley Young, *Politics, Strategy, and American Diplomacy: Studies in Foreign Policy, 1873–1917* (New Haven, Conn.: Yale University Press, 1966), p. 87.

8. Volwiler, *Correspondence*, pp. x, 1–17, and Volwiler, "Harrison, Blaine, and American Foreign Policy, 1889–1893," *Proceedings of the American Philosophical Society* 79 (Nov. 1938): 637–48.

9. Alice Felt Tyler, *The Foreign Policy of James G. Blaine* (Minneapolis: University of Minnesota Press, 1927), pp. 159, 366–67, 406–7.

10. *American Historical Review* 41 (Apr. 1936): 556.

11. Grenville and Young, *Politics*, pp. 87, 89. Volwiler had been told by Sydney Smith, Blaine's secretary, "We were always looking for lost papers both at the Department and at his home—in books, in the bathroom, in drawers— anywhere he might have put them" (see Volwiler, *Correspondence*, p. 2; H. Wayne Morgan, *From Hayes to McKinley: National Party Politics, 1877–1896* [Syracuse, N.Y.: Syracuse University Press, 1969], p. 395). Bright's disease and gout, both of which are related to kidney problems, could involve edema and hypertension.

12. Harriet S. Blaine Beale, ed., *Letters of Mrs. James G. Blaine*, 2 vols. (New York: Duffield & Co., 1908), 2:259; Blaine to Harrison, n.d., HP, vol. 73.

13. See Muzzey, *James G. Blaine*, pp. 464–65; Harry J. Sievers, *Benjamin Harrison, Hoosier President: The White House and After* (Indianapolis, Ind.: Bobbs-

Merrill Co., 1968), pp. 62–63; *New York Times*, 30 Apr. 1889, p. 1. According to Volwiler, the diary of Elijah Halford noted that Blaine had missed cabinet meetings on 23 Apr. and 25 Apr. Blaine's first illness left him disabled for at least ten days (see Volwiler, *Correspondence*, p. 59 n).

14. Blaine to Elijah Halford, n.d., Blaine to Harrison, 2 May 1889, HP, vols, 73, 76.

15. George H. Ryden, *The Foreign Policy of the United States in Relation to Samoa* (New Haven, Conn.: Yale University Press, 1933), pp. 278–79, 286–87, 343, 345–51, 371–72, 375, 413–15, 418, 443; Campbell, *Transformation*, p. 82.

16. Ryden, *Foreign Policy*, pp. 431–32.

17. Ibid., pp. 438, 467–68, 491, 501–2, 509.

18. William Walter Phelps to Whitelaw Reid, 15 Aug. 1889, Whitelaw Reid Papers, LC, box 51.

19. Beale, *Letters*, 2:262–63.

20. Edward Younger, *John A. Kasson: Politics and Diplomacy from Lincoln to McKinley* (Iowa City: State Historical Society of Iowa, 1955), p. 358.

21. Blaine to Harrison, 2 May 1889, HP, vol. 76.

22. *Washington Post*, 14 July 1889, p. 6; *New York Times*, 15 July 1889, p. 1; Sievers, *Benjamin Harrison, Hoosier President*, pp. 87–88.

23. Sievers, *Benjamin Harrison, Hoosier President*, pp. 106–7; Thomas F. McGann, *Argentina, the United States, and the Inter-American System, 1880–1914* (Cambridge, Mass.: Harvard University Press, 1957), pp. 130–31. McGann, pp. 128–64, and Tom E. Terrill, *The Tariff, Politics, and American Foreign Policy, 1874–1901* (Westport, Conn.: Greenwood Press, 1973), pp. 147–57, provide the most informative accounts of the Pan-American Conference. For details on the delegates see McGann, *Argentina*; Terrill, *Tariff*; Sievers, *Benjamin Harrison, Hoosier President*, pp. 106–9, 209; Oscar Doane Lambert, *Stephen Benton Elkins: American Foursquare* (Pittsburgh, Pa.: University of Pittsburgh Press, 1955), pp. 49–50, 104; Volwiler, *Correspondence*, p. 270 n.

24. McGann, *Argentina*, pp. 132, 134–35, 137, 163; Terrill, *Tariff*, pp. 148, 153; Sievers, *Benjamin Harrison, Hoosier President*, p. 114.

25. LaFeber, *New Empire*, p. 113; Robert L. Beisner, *From the Old Diplomacy to the New, 1865–1900* (New York: Thomas Y. Crowell Co., 1975), pp. 89–90.

26. Harrison memorandum, 22 May 1893, HP, vol. 157; Sievers, *Benjamin Harrison, Hoosier President*, p. 114.

27. *Washington Post*, 1 Jan. 1890, p. 1, 3 Feb. 1890, p. 1; *New York Tribune*, 16 Jan. 1890, p. 1; *Quarterly Journal of the Library of Congress* 27 (Oct. 1970): 338.

28. Harrison to Reid, 7 Feb. 1890, Reid Papers, box 33; Blaine to Harrison, 17 Mar. 1890, HP, vol. 101.

29. Muzzey, *James G. Blaine*, pp. 443–47; Campbell, *Transformation*, pp. 99–100.

30. Terrill, *Tariff*, p. 158.

31. LaFeber, *New Empire*, pp. 114–16; Foster, *Memoirs*, 2:4–5; Terrill, *Tariff*, p. 172.

32. Foster, *Diplomatic Memoirs*, 2:6.

33. Ibid., pp. 7-9; David M. Pletcher, "Reciprocity and Latin America in the Early 1890s: A Foretaste of Dollar Diplomacy," *Pacific Historical Review* 47 (Feb. 1978): 64; John Foster to Dr. Salvador Mendonca, 4 Nov. 1890, John Foster Papers, LC. See James D. Richardson, *A Compilation of the Messages and Papers of the Presidents, 1789-1897* (hereafter cited as *Messages*), 9 vols. (Washington, D.C.: Government Printing Office, 1898), 9:141-42, 148-55, 249-51, 253-58, 263-69, 279-83, 365-67, for texts of the reciprocity treaties.

34. Richardson, *Messages*, 9:148-52; "The McKinley Bill," n.d., Andrew Carnegie Papers, LC, box 245.

35. Terrill, *Tariff*, p. 196.

36. Blaine to Harrison, 21 and 30 June 1890, HP, vol. 108.

37. Blaine to Harrison, 19 and 24 July 1890, HP, vol. 110.

38. Sievers, *Benjamin Harrison, Hoosier President*, p. 165.

39. Blaine to Harrison, 19 and 30 Aug., and Harrison to Blaine, 29 Aug. 1890, HP, vol. 111.

40. Benjamin Franklin Cooling, *Benjamin Franklin Tracy: Father of the Modern American Fighting Navy* (Hamden, Conn.: Archon Books, 1973), p. 83; Walter R. Herrick, Jr., *The American Naval Revolution* (Baton Rouge: Louisiana State University Press, 1966), pp. 67, 77.

41. Benjamin Harrison, *Speeches of Benjamin Harrison*, comp. Charles Hedges (Port Washington, N.Y.: Kennikat Press, 1971), pp. 234-86; Morgan, *From Hayes to McKinley*, p. 355.

42. Donald Marquand Dozer, "Benjamin Harrison and the Presidential Campaign of 1892," *American Historical Review* 54 (Oct. 1948): 52.

CHAPTER 8
HARRISON'S FOREIGN POLICY

1. See Julius W. Pratt, *Expansionists of 1898: The Acquisition of Hawaii and the Spanish Islands* (Baltimore, Md.: Johns Hopkins Press, 1936), p. 25; Michael J. Devine, *John W. Foster: Politics and Diplomacy in the Imperial Era, 1873-1917* (Athens: Ohio University Press, 1981), pp. 3, 25; John A. S. Grenville and George Berkeley Young, *Politics, Strategy, and American Diplomacy: Studies in Foreign Policy, 1873-1917* (New Haven, Conn.: Yale University Press, 1966), pp. 83, 86, 90, 101; and Walter LaFeber, *The New Empire: An Interpretation of American Expansion, 1860-1898* (Ithaca, N.Y.: Cornell University Press, 1963), pp. 134-35. James D. Richardson, comp., *A Compilation of the Messages and Papers of the Presidents, 1789-1897* (hereafter cited as *Messages*), 9 vols. (Washington, D.C.: Government Printing Office, 1898), 9:180; Benjamin Harrison to James G. Blaine, 1 and 14 Oct. 1891, and Harrison to Whitelaw Reid, 21 Oct. 1891, HP, vols. 130, 131.

2. See Rayford W. Logan, *The Diplomatic Relations of the United States with Haiti, 1776-1891* (Chapel Hill: University of North Carolina Press, 1941), for the background of the negotiations. See Bancroft Gherardi to Benjamin Tracy, 7 Jan.

1891, Benjamin Tracy Papers, vol. 31, for criticism of Frederick Douglass. See Gherardi to Blaine, 31 Jan. 1891, Frederick Douglass to Blaine, 21 Apr. 1891, in dispatches from Haiti, vol. 25, for Gherardi's aggressive approach toward Haiti and details on naval strength in Haiti. All of the diplomatic material cited in this and subsequent notes is found in the archives of the United States Department of State, Record Group 59, in the National Archives, Washington, D.C.

    3. Sydney Y. Smith to Elijah Halford, 17 Mar. 1891, and Smith to Harrison, 18 Mar. 1891, HP, vol. 120; *New York Times*, 1 Apr. 1891, p. 1; Albert T. Volwiler, ed., *The Correspondence between Benjamin Harrison and James G. Blaine, 1882–1893* (Philadelphia: American Philosophical Society, 1940), p. 148n; Benjamin Harrison, *Speeches of Benjamin Harrison*, comp. Charles Hedges (Port Washington, N.Y.: Kennikat Press, 1971), pp. 289, 489.

    4. Andrew Carnegie to Harrison, 10–14 May 1891, Andrew Carnegie Papers, vol. 12; Blaine to Harrison, 22 May 1891, HP, vol. 122; *New York Times*, 31 May 1891, p. 1.

    5. Tracy to Harrison, 16 Aug. 1891, Tracy Papers, vol. 10; *New York Times*, 24 Sept. 1891, p. 1.

    6. *New York Times*, 25 Oct. 1891, p. 1; see Blaine to Harrison, 29 Dec. 1891, HP, vol. 133.

    7. Harrison to Blaine, 4 Jan. 1892, and Blaine to Harrison, 4 and 5 Jan. 1892, HP, vol. 134; *New York Tribune*, 21 Jan. 1892, p. 1.

    8. David Saville Muzzey, *James G. Blaine: A Political Idol of Other Days* (New York: Dodd, Mead & Co., 1934), pp. 461–62; *New York Tribune*, 29 Feb. 1892, p. 1; *Washington Post*, 21 Feb., p. 1, and 29 Feb. 1892, p. 1.

    9. Smith to Halford, 6 Mar. 1892, and Harrison note, 22 Mar. 1892, HP, vols. 136, 138; Volwiler, *Correspondence*, p. 243n.

    10. Muzzey, *James G. Blaine*, p. 474.

    11. John L. Gignilliat, "Pigs, Politics, and Protection: The European Boycott of American Pork, 1879–1891," *Agricultural History* 35 (Jan. 1961): 4–6, 8–10, 12; Louis L. Snyder, "The American-German Pork Dispute, 1879–1891," *Journal of Modern History* 17 (Mar. 1945): 16, 18–19, 22.

    12. Reid to Blaine, 2 Dec. 1889, and Reid to Harrison, 24 Jan. 1890, letterbook, 30 Oct. 1889–4 Mar. 1890, Whitelaw Reid Papers.

    13. Carr to Blaine, 3 Mar. 1890, dispatches from Denmark, vol. 18, and Blaine to William Walter Phelps, 15 Apr. 1890, instructions to Germany, vol. 18.

    14. Reid to Ribot, 3 July 1890, Reid Papers, box 73.

    15. Gignilliat, "Pigs, Politics, and Protection," p. 11.

    16. Reid to Blaine, 20 Nov. 1890, letterbook, 2 Aug. 1890 to 24 Nov. 1890, Reid Papers, box 144 outgoing.

    17. Richardson, *Messages*, 9:119.

    18. Jeremiah Rusk to Blaine, 9 Jan. 1891, and Blaine to Phelps, 13 Jan. 1891, HP, vol. 117.

    19. Gignilliat, "Pigs, Politics, and Protection," p. 11; Rusk to Harrison, 16 Mar. 1891, HP, vol. 120; Phelps to Reid, 18 Mar. 1891, Reid Papers, box 59.

20. Reid to Blaine, 11 Mar. 1891, letterbook, 24 Nov. 1890 to 16 Mar. 1891, Reid Papers.

21. Snyder, "American-German Pork Dispute," p. 28; see Richardson, *Messages*, 9:265–69, for Harrison's proclamations of retaliation of 15 Mar. 1892 against Colombia, Haiti, and Venezuela. All three had refused to respond to the reciprocity amendment.

22. Blaine to Harrison, 26 May 1891, HP, vol. 123.

23. Harrison to Blaine, 27 and 28 May 1891, HP, vol. 123; Reid to Blaine, 5 June 1891, dispatches from France, vol. 105.

24. William Wharton to Phelps, 15 June 1891, instructions to Germany, vol. 18; Wharton to Reid, 17 June 1891, instructions to France, vol. 22; Phelps to Blaine, 3 July 1891, dispatches from Germany, vol. 52.

25. Blaine to Harrison, 30 July 1891, HP, vol. 126.

26. Harrison to Blaine, 1 Aug. 1891, and Blaine to Harrison, 4 Aug. 1891, HP, vol. 127.

27. John Foster to von Schwarzenstein, 22 Aug. 1891, HP, vol. 128; Phelps to Blaine, 3 Sept. 1891, dispatches from Germany, vol. 52; Carr to Blaine, 8 Sept. 1891, dispatches from Denmark, vol. 19.

28. Reid to Blaine, 6 and 16 Nov. and 5 Dec. 1891, dispatches from France, vol. 106.

29. Richardson, *Messages*, 9:182, 206–7.

30. Ibid., p. 328.

31. Charles S. Campbell, *The Transformation of American Foreign Relations, 1865–1900* (New York: Harper & Row, 1976), pp. 7, 127–28; James Morton Callahan, *American Foreign Policy in Canadian Relations* (New York: Cooper Square Publishers, Inc., 1967), pp. 362–63; Robert C. Brown, *Canada's National Policy, 1883–1900: A Study in Canadian-American Relations* (Princeton, N.J.: Princeton University Press, 1964), pp. 44, 52–53; Charles C. Tansill, *Canadian-American Relations, 1875–1911* (Gloucester, Mass.: Peter Smith, 1964), pp. 277, 300–301 n.

32. Richardson, *Messages*, 9:14–15; William Windom to L. G. Shepard, 23 May 1889, HP, vol. 77.

33. Tansill, *Canadian-American Relations*, pp. 300–301 n; Edwardes to Blaine, n.d., notes from the British Legation in the United States, vol. 117.

34. Blaine to Edwardes, 24 Aug. 1889, HP, vol. 85.

35. Blaine to Harrison, 25 Aug. 1889, HP, vol. 85.

36. Julian Pauncefote to Blaine, 30 Apr. 1890, HP, vol. 104.

37. Charles S. Campbell, Jr., "The Anglo-American Crisis in the Bering Sea, 1890–1891," *Mississippi Valley Historical Review* 48 (Dec. 1961): 396–98; James T. Gay, "Bering Sea Controversy: Harrison, Blaine, and Cronyism," *Alaska Journal* 3 (Winter 1973): 13; Brown, *Canada's National Policy*, pp. 111–12.

38. Hicks to Blaine, 4 June 1890, dispatches from Peru, vol. 49.

39. Pauncefote to Blaine, 14 and 16 June 1890, notes from the British Legation, vol. 118.

40. Campbell, "Anglo-American Crisis," pp. 393, 399–402; Pauncefote to Blaine, 12 Aug. 1890, notes from the British Legation, vol. 118.

41. See Blaine to Pauncefote, 4 May 1891, HP, vol. 122.

42. Blaine to Harrison, 23 Apr. 1891, and Harrison to Blaine, 25 Apr. 1891, James G. Blaine Papers; Blaine to Harrison, 29 Apr. 1891, HP, vol. 121.

43. Harrison to Blaine, 30 Apr. 1891, Blaine Papers; Blaine to Pauncefote, 4 May 1891, HP, vol. 122.

44. Campbell, "Anglo-American Crisis," pp. 407–10; Gay, "Bering Sea Controversy," pp. 15–18.

45. Pauncefote to Blaine, 5 May 1891, and memorandum by Alvey Adee, 22 May 1891, HP, vol. 122.

46. Adee to Harrison, 22 May 1891, HP, vol. 122.

47. Blaine to Harrison, 23 May 1891, and Harrison to Blaine, 25 May 1891, HP, vol. 122.

48. Memorandum by Adee, 25 May 1891, HP, vol. 122.

49. Memorandum by Adee, 28 May 1891, HP, vol. 122; Robert Lincoln to Blaine, 30 May 1891, dispatches from Great Britain, vol. 167.

50. Pauncefote to Wharton, 8 June 1891, and Wharton to Pauncefote, 8 June 1891, HP, vol. 123.

51. Pauncefote to Wharton, 11 June 1891, and Harrison to United States Department of the Navy and Department of the Treasury, 15 June 1891, HP, vol. 124; Richardson, Messages, 9:146–47.

52. Pauncefote to Wharton, 6 June 1891, notes from the British Legation, vol. 119.

53. Pauncefote to Blaine, 29 Feb. 1892, ibid.

54. Blaine to Harrison, 6 Mar. 1892, HP, vol. 136.

55. Wharton to Pauncefote, 8 Mar. 1892, HP, vol. 137.

56. Report book 18, United States Department of State, pp. 67–69.

57. John Sherman to Harrison, 28 Mar. 1892, HP, vol. 138.

58. Report book 18, United States Department of State, pp. 74–75.

59. Charles S. Campbell, Jr., "The Bering Sea Settlements of 1892," Pacific Historical Review 32 (1963): 364–65; Callahan, American Foreign Policy, pp. 447–48; Muzzey, James G. Blaine, p. 411.

60. Benjamin F. Tracy, "The Behring Sea Question," North American Review 156 (May 1893): 532, 540, 542.

61. Fredrick Pike, Chile and the United States: The Emergence of Chile's Social Crisis and the Challenge to United States Diplomacy, 1880–1962 (South Bend, Ind.: University of Notre Dame Press, 1963), p. xxvi.

62. Ibid., pp. 56, 58–59; David M. Pletcher, The Awkward Years: American Foreign Relations under Garfield and Arthur (Columbia: University of Missouri Press, 1962), pp. 41, 73–75, 79–80.

63. Patrick Egan to Blaine, 17 Oct. 1890, dispatches from Chile, vol. 37; see Osgood Hardy, "Was Patrick Egan a 'Blundering Minister'?" Hispanic American Historical Review 8 (Feb. 1928): 65–81; see also Volwiler, Correspondence, p. 158n, on Egan.

64. Pike, *Chile and the United States*, p. 44; Egan to Blaine, 12 and 17 Jan. 1891, dispatches from Chile, vol. 37.

65. Hicks to Blaine, 24 Jan. 1891, dispatches from Peru, vol. 49.

66. Pletcher, *Awkward Years*, pp. 7, 22-25, 272, 278, 331; Walter LaFeber, *The New Empire: An Interpretation of American Expansion, 1860-1898* (Ithaca, N.Y.: Cornell University Press, 1963), p. 111; Richardson, *Messages*, 9:189; Sidney T. Mathews, "The Nicaraguan Canal Controversy: The Struggle for an American-constructed and American-controlled Transitway" (Ph.D. diss., Johns Hopkins University, 1947), pp. 85-94.

67. Egan to Blaine, 23 Feb. 1891, dispatches from Chile, vol. 37; Prudencio Lazcano to Blaine, 5 May 1891, notes from the Chilean Legation, vol. 5; see Osgood Hardy, "The *Itata* Incident," *Hispanic American Historical Review* 5 (May 1922): 195-226, for a detailed account of the circumstances surrounding the *Itata*; W. H. H. Miller to Harrison, 6 and 7 May 1891, and Harrison to Miller, 6 May 1891, HP, vol. 122.

68. Tracy to *Charleston*, 8 and 17 May 1891, and Tracy to George Brown, 9 May 1891, translation of cipher messages sent, 27 Oct. 1888-15 July 1895.

69. Pike, *Chile and the United States*, p. 68.

70. Egan to Wharton, 13 Aug. 1891, HP, vol. 128; Egan to Wharton, 7 Sept. 1891, and Egan to Blaine, 21 and 25 Sept. 1891, dispatches from Chile, vol. 39.

71. W. S. Schley to Tracy, 25 Sept. 1891, translation of cipher messages received, 3 Nov. 1888 to 14 Dec. 1897.

72. Egan to Wharton, 18 Oct. 1891, and Schley to Egan, 22 Oct. 1891, dispatches from Chile, vol. 39; Schley to Tracy, 22 Oct. 1891, HP, vol. 131.

73. Egan to Manuel Antonio Matta, 26 Oct. 1891 (includes Wharton to Egan, 23 Oct. 1891), dispatches from Chile, vol. 39; Pike, *Chile and the United States*, pp. 72-73; Egan to Wharton, 28 Oct. 1891, Egan to Blaine, 11 Nov. 1891, and Harrison to Pedro Montt, 11 Nov. 1891, HP, vol. 131. See Volwiler, *Correspondence*, p. 196n, on the brothers Montt.

74. Richardson, *Messages*, 9:185-86.

75. Tracy to Brown, 9 Dec. 1891, translation of cipher messages sent.

76. Egan to Blaine, 13 Dec. 1891, dispatches from Chile, vol. 40.

77. Egan to Blaine, 17 Dec. 1891, HP, vol. 133; Brown to Tracy, 31 Dec. 1891, Tracy Papers, vol. 31.

78. "War with Chile," 2 Jan. 1892, Alfred T. Mahan Papers, vol. 11; Blaine to Harrison, 2 Jan. 1892, and Harrison to Blaine, 4 Jan. 1892, HP, vol. 134.

79. "Naval Papers on Chile," n.d., Tracy Papers, vol. 31.

80. Pedro Montt to Blaine, 8 Jan. 1892, notes from the Chilean Legation in the United States, vol. 5; Blaine to Egan, 8 Jan. 1892, dispatches from Chile, vol. 40.

81. Egan to Blaine, 12 and 15 Jan. 1892, dispatches from Chile, vol. 40.

82. Pike, *Chile and the United States*, pp. 76-83; Tracy to Wiltse, 16 Jan. 1892, translation of cipher messages sent; Blaine to Egan, 16 Jan. 1892, dispatches from Chile, vol. 40.

83. Tracy to Brown, 17 Jan. 1892, translation of cipher messages sent; Egan to Blaine, 17 Jan. 1892, dispatches from Chile, vol. 40.

84. Blaine to Egan, 21 Jan. 1892, HP, vol. 134.

85. Tracy to John Walker, 25 Jan. 1892, translation of cipher messages sent.

86. Richardson, *Messages*, 9:216-17, 223, 225-26.

87. "The Shame of It," *Nation* 54 (4 Feb. 1892): 82.

88. Theodore Roosevelt, "The Foreign Policy of President Harrison," *Independent* 44 (11 Aug. 1892): 1-3.

89. Luis Pereira to Blaine, 25 Jan. 1892, HP, vol. 135; Egan to Blaine, 25 and 26 Jan. 1892, dispatches from Chile, vol. 40.

90. See Blaine to Egan, 29 Jan. 1892, and Blaine to Harrison, 29 and 30 Jan. 1892, HP, vol. 135.

91. Lt. Jerrold Kelley, "The Chilian Trouble," *Harper's Weekly* 36 (30 Jan. 1892): 110, 112.

92. "The United States and Chile," *Spectator* 68 (30 Jan. 1892): 157.

93. Gherardi to Tracy, 26 Dec. 1892, translation of cipher messages received.

94. *New York Tribune*, 15 Mar. 1891, p. 6; Harry J. Sievers, *Benjamin Harrison, Hoosier President: The White House and After* (Indianapolis, Ind.: Bobbs-Merrill Co., Inc., 1968), pp. 183-85.

95. Pasquale Corte to Francesco Saverio Fava, 14 Mar. 1891, notes from the Italian Legation, roll 10; Blaine to Harrison, 14 Mar. 1891, HP, vol. 120.

96. Fava to Blaine, 15 Mar. 1891, notes from the Italian Legation, roll 10; Albert G. Porter to Blaine, 4 May 1891 (includes Antonio Starabba di Rudini to Fava, 19 Mar. 1891), dispatches from Italy, vol. 24. See Volwiler, *Correspondence*, p. 192n, on Rudini.

97. Porter to Blaine, 4 May 1891 (includes Fava to Rudini, 26 Mar. 1891), dispatches from Italy, vol. 24.

98. Porter to Blaine, 4 May 1891 (includes Fava to Rudini, 27 Mar. 1891) and 1 Apr. 1891, ibid.; Sievers, *Benjamin Harrison, Hoosier President*, p. 188.

99. William Grant to Miller, 27 Apr. 1891, James G. Blaine and Family Papers, box 38.

100. Whitehouse to Blaine, 7 Sept. 1891, and Harrison to Blaine, 23 Sept. 1891, HP, vols. 129, 130.

101. Blaine to Harrison, 12 Oct. 1891, HP, vol. 131.

102. Harrison to Blaine, 14 Oct. 1891, HP, vol. 131.

103. Gignilliat, "Pigs, Politics, and Protection," p. 11; Richardson, *Messages*, 9:182-83; Whitehouse to Blaine, 29 and 31 Dec. 1891, dispatches from Italy, vol. 25.

104. Whitehouse to Blaine, 13 Mar. 1892, dispatches from Italy, vol. 25; Wharton to Whitehouse, 16 Mar. 1892, instructions to Italy, vol. 2.

105. Whitehouse to Blaine, 20 Mar. 1892, dispatches from Italy, vol. 25.

106. Blaine to Harrison, and Harrison to Blaine, 23 Mar. 1892, HP, vol. 138.

107. Harrison to Blaine, 26 Mar. 1892, HP, vol. 138.

108. Blaine to Harrison, 29 Mar. 1892, HP, vol. 138.

109. Volwiler, *Correspondence*, p. 149n.

CHAPTER 9
PRESIDENTIAL TRAVELS

1. The Harrison Papers, ser. 1, reels 18 and 19, in the Library of Congress, contain much correspondence on this activity.

2. Harry J. Sievers, *Benjamin Harrison, Hoosier President: The White House and After* (Indianapolis, Ind.: Bobbs-Merrill Co., Inc., 1968), pp. 61–71; *New York Times*, 2 May 1889.

3. *New York Times*, 29 Apr. 1889, reported that most of the president's party had boarded the train by 10:30 P.M. on Sunday night (Clarence Winthrop Bowen, *The Centennial Celebration of the Inauguration of George Washington as First President of the United States, Monday, Tuesday and Wednesday, April 29th, 30th, and May 1st, 1889* [n.p.: Committee on the Centennial of Washington's Inauguration, 1889], p. 34). The naval review lasted for two hours, beginning at 11 A.M. (Clarence Winthrop Bowen, ed., *The Centennial of Washington's Inauguration* [New York: D. Appleton & Co., 1892]). Copy 2 is part of the collection of the Benjamin Harrison Memorial Home in Indianapolis, Ind.

4. Sievers, *Benjamin Harrison, Hoosier President*, p. 64; Martha J. Lamb, "The Story of the Washington Centennial," *Magazine of American History*, July 1889, pp. 1–36. National magazines, such as *Harpers*, the *Chautauquan*, *Literary World*, and *Century*, carried feature stories on Washington's inauguration in April or May 1889, and most of the reports of the centennial observances were in the daily press.

5. Bowen, *Centennial Celebration*, p. 35; Sievers, *Benjamin Harrison, Hoosier President*, p. 66; *New York Times*, 1 May 1889.

6. *Nation*, 9 May 1889, p. 378; Sievers, *Benjamin Harrison, Hoosier President*, p. 67.

7. E. W. Halford, "General Harrison's Attitude toward the Presidency," *Century Magazine* 84 (June 1912): 307.

8. Benjamin Harrison, *Speeches of Benjamin Harrison*, comp. Charles Hedges (Port Washington, N.Y: Kennikat Press, 1892, 1971), p. 210.

9. Sievers, *Benjamin Harrison, Hoosier President*, p. 70.

10. Ibid., pp. 70–71; *New York Times*, 2 May 1889; Albert T. Volwiler, ed., *The Correspondence between Benjamin Harrison and James G. Blaine, 1882–1893* (Philadelphia: American Philosophical Society, 1940), p. 61.

11. Halford, "General Harrison's Attitude," p. 309; Sievers, *Benjamin Harrison, Hoosier President*, pp. 51–55; H. Wayne Morgan, "Election of 1892," in *History of American Presidential Elections, 1789–1968*, ed. Arthur M. Schlesinger, Jr., and Fred L. Israel, vol. 2 (New York: McGraw-Hill Book Co., 1971), p. 1703.

12. Correspondence between Benjamin Harrison and Clem Studebaker; Studebaker sought to defend himself from these political attacks (see copy of letter of 26 July 1889 to editor, *New York World*, from Studebaker Bros. Mfg. Co., South Bend, Ind., HP, ser. 1, reels 18, 19, and 21); Sievers, *Benjamin Harrison, Hoosier President*, p. 51; *New York Times*, 6 and 9 Jan. 1889 and 28 Aug. 1891.

13. Sievers, *Benjamin Harrison, Hoosier President*, pp. 57, 77; *New York Times,* 26 and 28 May and 15, 16, 18, and 20 June 1889; Arthur Wallace Dunn, *From Harrison to Harding: A Personal Narrative, Covering a Third of a Century, 1888–1921,* 2 vols. (Port Washington, N.Y.: Kennikat Press, 1922, 1971), 1:125. In 1891, Harrison declined to comment for publication on the fact that the World's Columbian Exposition in Chicago was scheduled to open on a Sunday (see Henry C. Bowen to Harrison, 3 Jan., and Harrison to Bowen, 6 Jan. 1891, HP, ser. 1, reel 30).

14. Herbert Adams Gibbons, *John Wanamaker,* 2 vols. (New York: Harper & Brothers Publishers, 1926), 2:334–35; *New York Times,* 22 and 24 June 1889.

15. Clem Studebaker to Halford and to Harrison, 2 and 12 Aug. 1889, HP, ser. 1, reel 22; Robert D. Marcus, *Grand Old Party: Political Structures in the Gilded Age, 1880–1896* (New York: Oxford University Press, 1971), p. 106; Oscar Doane Lambert, *Stephen Benton Elkins: American Foursquare* (Pittsburgh, Pa.: University of Pittsburgh Press, 1955), pp. 68, 163; Elisabeth P. Myers, *Benjamin Harrison* (Chicago: Reilley & Lee Books, 1969), p. 129. President Cleveland also used Deer Park as a summer residence.

16. *New York Times,* 5 and 6 July 1889.

17. Sievers, *Benjamin Harrison, Hoosier President*, pp. 85–89; *New York Times,* 9–20 Aug. 1889. Caroline Harrison did not go on this trip because of the illness of her father and because of her aversion to being in crowds. However, on 8 August she made a hurried journey to Nantucket Island, Mass., because of the serious illness of her sister.

18. *New York Times,* 22 Aug. 1889.

19. Harrison, *Speeches,* pp. 214–15.

20. Ibid., pp. 217–18; Sievers, *Benjamin Harrison, Hoosier President*, p. 123.

21. Sievers, *Benjamin Harrison, Hoosier President*, p. 129; *New York Times,* 5 and 6 Sept. 1889.

22. *New York Times,* 8 and 10 Sept. 1889; Sievers, *Benjamin Harrison, Hoosier President*, p. 130. Later that week, Harrison returned to Deer Park.

23. Sievers, *Benjamin Harrison, Hoosier President*, p. 130.

24. *New York Times,* 16 Nov. and 28 Dec. 1889 and 3 Jan. 1890; Jno. S. Wise to Harrison, 22 Oct. 1889, HP, ser. 1, reel 23. Originally the first duck hunt was planned for a week earlier.

25. Sievers, *Benjamin Harrison, Hoosier President*, pp. 138–39; Harrison, *Speeches,* pp. 218–22. The *Times* (London) for 10 Dec. 1891 described the Auditorium as the "finest opera-house in America" that combined a music hall, a hotel, and a theater.

26. *New York Times,* 21 and 22 Feb. and 21 and 22 Mar. 1890. The Allegheny Carnegie Library was the first of a long line of Carnegie libraries.

27. Harrison, *Speeches,* pp. 222–25; *New York Times,* 30 and 31 May 1890.

28. *New York Times,* 1 June 1890.

29. Sievers, *Benjamin Harrison, Hoosier President*, p. 155; *New York Times,* 24 July 1890.

30. Sievers, *Benjamin Harrison, Hoosier President*, pp. 156–58; *New York Times*, 24 July and 23 Sept. 1890.

31. *New York Times*, 18 Sept. 1890.

32. Harrison, *Speeches*, pp. 226–31; *New York Times*, 11, 12, and 17 Aug. 1890; Sievers, *Benjamin Harrison, Hoosier President*, pp. 166–67; Wallace Evan Davies, *Patriotism on Parade: The Story of Veterans and Hereditary Organizations in America, 1783–1900* (Cambridge, Mass.: Harvard University Press, 1953), p. 205.

33. Harrison, *Speeches*, pp. 231–34, *New York Times*, 6, 8, 14, and 25 Sept. 1890. The president departed from Cresson Springs and returned to Washington on 24 September.

34. Harrison, *Speeches*, pp. 234–86; *New York Tribune*, 8, 10, 11, and 17 Oct. 1890; *New York Times*, 4–14 Oct. 1890. Parts of this journey went through Virginia, Maryland, and Pennsylvania, but only one speech by Harrison was recorded for these states.

35. Harrison, *Speeches*, pp. 234–86; *New York Times*, 7–14 Oct. 1890.

36. Harrison, *Speeches*, p. 286.

37. *New York Times*, 15, 17, 19, and 20 Feb. 1891; James Grant Wilson, ed., *The Presidents of the United States, 1789–1894* (New York: D. Appleton & Co., 1894), p. 502.

38. *New York Times*, 12 and 13 Mar. and 3 and 10 Apr. 1891.

39. Gibbons, *John Wanamaker*, 1:334; *Thirty Days with President Harrison* (New York: J. S. Ogilvie, Publishers, 1891). This copy, in poor condition, is in HP, ser. 20; Harrison, *Speeches*, p. 490.

40. Harrison, *Speeches*, pp. 290–91; *New York Times*, 14 Apr. and 3 May 1891. The president's private secretary, Elijah Halford, did not go on this trip because of the illness of his wife. She died several days after the western tour got under way (Norman E. Tutorow, *Leland Stanford: Man of Many Careers* [Menlo Park, Calif.: Pacific Coast Publishers, 1971], p. 284). There is no doubt that Stanford had the money. In addition to endowing Leland Stanford, Jr., University, he paid Harrison the sum of $25,000 in 1894 to give a series of lectures at Stanford University.

41. Gibbons, *John Wanamaker*, 1:334–35; Harrison, *Speeches*, pp. 289–490. These speeches were also published in a separate volume: see John S. Shriver, comp., *Through the South and West with the President, April 14–May 16, 1891: The Only Complete and Authorized Collection of President Harrison's Great and Eloquent Speeches Made during the Tour* (New York: Mail & Express, 1891). The "presentation copy" of this book is in the collection of the President Benjamin Harrison Memorial Home, Indianapolis, Ind.

42. Harrison, *Speeches*, pp. 328, 397–98, 442. Harbor improvements were viewed at Galveston from a Mallory steamship. Harrison's party traveled from Oakland to San Francisco on the *Piedmont;* later they had a tour of the bay on the *Puebla*. From Tacoma to Seattle the president and his party traveled on the *City of Seattle*.

43. George Sinkler, *The Racial Attitudes of American Presidents from Abraham Lincoln to Theodore Roosevelt* (Garden City, N.Y.: Doubleday & Co., Inc., 1971), p. 276; Harrison, *Speeches*, p. 298.

44. Harrison, *Speeches*, pp. 324, 327, 386; *Harper's Weekly*, 16 May 1891, pp. 370–72; *Times* (London), 21 Apr. 1891. The *New York Times* for 24 Apr. 1891 contained an editorial that was critical of Harrison's speech at Galveston because the *Times* opposed subsidies for American shipping.

45. Harrison, *Speeches*, pp. 358, 374–75; *San Francisco Chronicle*, 26 Apr. 1891.

46. Harrison, *Speeches*, pp. 386–89; *Times* (London), 4 May 1891.

47. Paul Dorpat, *Seattle: Now and Then* (Seattle, Wash.: Tartu Publications, 1984), chap. 18. Ship names, in this quoted passage, have been italicized.

48. Harrison, *Speeches*, pp. 429, 436.

49. Ibid., p. 458.

50. Ibid., pp. 468–69.

51. Ibid., pp. 472–83.

52. Ibid., pp. 488–90; *New York Times*, 15, 16, and 19 May 1891; *Appleton's Cyclopedia of American Biography* (New York: D. Appleton & Co., 1900), p. 102; R. Hal Williams, *Years of Decision: American Politics in the 1890s* (New York: John Wiley & Sons, 1978), p. 57. Many of the souvenirs of the western tour are in the collection of the Benjamin Harrison Memorial Home, Indianapolis, Ind.; some are on display.

53. *San Francisco Examiner*, 27 Apr. 1891; Caroline Harrison to Mrs. J. R. McKee, 23 June 1891, in collection of the Benjamin Harrison Memorial Home, Indianapolis, Ind.

54. Harrison, *Speeches*, pp. 490–93; *New York Times*, 31 May and 3 June 1891. The Pennsylvania correspondent for the *New York Times* invariably depicted Harrison's visits to that state unfavorably.

55. Harrison, *Speeches*, pp. 493–509; *New York Times*, 31 July and 14–20 Aug. 1891.

56. Harrison, *Speeches*, pp. 512–48; *New York Times*, 26, 27, 28, and 29 Aug. and 1 Sept. 1891.

57. *New York Times*, 26, 27, 28, and 29 Feb. and 1, 2, 4, and 5 Mar. and 8 and 10 Apr. 1892.

58. *New York Times*, 27 and 28 Apr. 1892; *Times* (London), 28 Apr. 1892.

59. *New York Times*, 14 and 16 May 1892.

60. Ibid., 28, 29, 30, and 31 May 1892.

61. Sievers, *Benjamin Harrison, Hoosier President*, pp. 238, 241; *New York Times*, 23 June and 6, 7, 8, and 11 July 1892.

62. *New York Times*, 17 July 1892.

63. Sievers, *Benjamin Harrison, Hoosier President*, p. 242; *New York Times*, 13, 16, 20, 21, and 22 Sept. 1892.

64. The dinner card and menu for this banquet are in the collection of the Benjamin Harrison Memorial Home, Indianapolis, Ind.

65. Sievers, *Benjamin Harrison, Hoosier President*, pp. 242–43; *New York Times*, 28 and 29 Oct. 1892.

66. Robert Seward Salisbury, "William Windom, the Republican Party, and the Gilded Age" (Ph.D. diss., University of Minnesota, 1982), pp. 681–82.

67. *New York Times*, 16 and 17 Nov. 1890.

68. Herbert R. Collins and David B. Weaver, *Wills of the U.S. Presidents* (New York: Communications Channels, Inc., 1976), p. 147. Four years after Caroline Harrison's death, Benjamin Harrison married Mrs. Dimmick in New York City, with Benjamin Tracy as his best man. This marriage "estranged Harrison from his family."

CHAPTER 10

THE PASSING OF THE CIVIL WAR GENERATION

1. *New York Times*, 30 Jan. 1891, p. 1.

2. Ibid., 9 Dec. 1889, p. 4.

3. Willard L. King, *Melville Weston Fuller: Chief Justice of the United States, 1888-1910* (Chicago: University of Chicago Press, 1967), pp. 100-102, 104, 123, 148.

4. See Stephen J. Field, *Personal Reminiscences of Early Days in California (To which is added the story of his attempted assassination by a former associate on the supreme bench of the state,* by George C. Gorham) (New York: Da Capo Press, 1968); and Carl Brent Swisher, *Stephen J. Field, Craftsman of the Law* (Washington, D.C.: Brookings Institution, 1930); King, *Melville Weston Fuller,* pp. 127, 140, 222-27; Homer Cummings and Carl McFarland, *Federal Justice: Chapters in the History of Justice and the Federal Executive* (New York: Da Capo Press, 1970), p. 368; Harry J. Sievers, *Benjamin Harrison, Hoosier President: The White House and After* (Indianapolis, Ind.: Bobbs-Merrill Co., Inc., 1968), pp. 96-101; Charles Warren, *The Supreme Court in United States History,* 2 vols. (Boston: Little, Brown & Co., 1926), 2:697. Field stayed on the Court until 1897, when he was pressured into resigning because of obvious senility. He had served for more than thirty-four years, surpassing the legendary Chief Justice John Marshall in longevity.

5. Henry Dawes, "The Harrison Administration," *North American Review* 154 (June 1892): 642; King, *Melville Weston Fuller,* pp. 154-55; Preston Plumb to Benjamin Harrison, 21 Jan. 1889, HP, ser. 1, reel 16.

6. Melville W. Fuller to Harrison, 22 Mar. 1889, and Harrison to R. S. Taylor, 23 July 1889, HP, ser. 1, reels 19, 20.

7. King, *Melville Weston Fuller,* pp. 154-56; Joel Goldfarb, "Henry Billings Brown," in *The Justices of the United States Supreme Court, 1789-1969,* ed. Leon Friedman and Fred L. Israel, 4 vols. (New York: Chelsea House Publishers, 1969), 2:1555; Arnold M. Paul, *Conservative Crisis and the Rule of Law: Attitudes of Bar and Bench, 1887-1895* (Ithaca, N.Y.: Cornell University Press, 1960), pp. 42, 212.

8. Arnold M. Paul, "George Shiras, Jr.," in *Justices of the United States Supreme Court,* 2:1578-80; King, *Melville Weston Fuller,* pp. 104, 157; Paul, *Conservative Crisis,* p. 182 n.

9. Irving Schiffman, "Howell E. Jackson," in *Justices of the United States Supreme Court,* 2:1605, 1607-11; King, *Melville Weston Fuller,* pp. 155-56; Paul,

Conservative Crisis, p. 218n; Warren, *The Supreme Court*, 2:719; Sievers, *Benjamin Harrison, Hoosier President*, p. 252.

10. King, *Melville Weston Fuller*, pp. 148, 151; James D. Richardson, comp., *A Compilation of the Messages and Papers of the Presidents, 1789–1897* (hereafter cited as *Messages*), 9 vols. (Washington, D.C.: Government Printing Office, 1898), 9:42–43.

11. Paul, *Conservative Crisis*, pp. 1–3, 178–80, 182, 209, 211, 219; Arnold M. Paul, "David J. Brewer," in *Justices of the United States Supreme Court*, 2:1525, 1535–46; Irving Schiffman, "Melville W. Fuller," ibid., 2:1485; Schiffman, "Howell E. Jackson," ibid., 2:1613; Goldfarb, "Henry Billings Brown," ibid., 2:1553, 1564–70.

12. *New York Times*, 15 Feb. 1891, p. 1.

13. See Richard S. West, Jr., *The Second Admiral: A Life of David Dixon Porter, 1813–1891* (New York: Coward-McCann, Inc., 1937); Kenneth J. Hagan, *American Gunboat Diplomacy and the Old Navy, 1877–1889* (Westport, Conn.: Greenwood Press, 1973), p. 14.

14. See James M. Merrill, *William Tecumseh Sherman* (Chicago: Rand McNally, 1971). See Harry J. Sievers, *Benjamin Harrison, Hoosier Warrior, 1833–1865* (Chicago: Henry Regnery Co., 1952), pp. 247–65, for Harrison's participation in the Atlanta campaign; Richardson, *Messages*, 9:135.

15. See H. Draper Hunt, *Hannibal Hamlin of Maine: Lincoln's First Vice-President* (Syracuse, N.Y.: Syracuse University Press, 1969).

16. See Kenneth E. Davison, *The Presidency of Rutherford B. Hayes* (Westport, Conn.: Greenwood Press, Inc., 1972); Richardson, *Messages*, 9:383.

CHAPTER 11

THE END OF AN ADMINISTRATION

1. "The Formation of the Cabinet," Louis Michener Papers, box 2.

2. Chauncey Depew to Whitelaw Reid, 30 Aug. 1891, Whitelaw Reid Papers, box 19.

3. James A. Kehl, *Boss Rule in the Gilded Age: Matt Quay of Pennsylvania* (Pittsburgh, Pa.: University of Pittsburgh Press, 1981), pp. 140–44, 158–60; David Saville Muzzey, *James G. Blaine: A Political Idol of Other Days* (New York: Dodd, Mead & Co., Inc., 1934), p. 468n.

4. "Mr. Blaine's Declination," *Public Opinion* 12 (13 Feb. 1892): 471; Harry J. Sievers, *Benjamin Harrison, Hoosier President: The White House and After* (Indianapolis, Ind.: Bobbs-Merrill Co., Inc., 1968), p. 229.

5. E. W. Halford, "Harrison in the White House," *Leslie's Illustrated Weekly* 128 (3 May 1919): 685.

6. Albert T. Volwiler, ed., *The Correspondence between Benjamin Harrison and James G. Blaine, 1882–1893* (Philadelphia: American Philosophical Society, 1940), p. 245n; "The Minneapolis Convention of June 7–10, 1892," Michener Papers,

box 1; John W. Foster, *Diplomatic Memoirs*, 2 vols. (Boston, Mass.: Houghton Mifflin, 1909), 2:251.

7. James G. Blaine to Benjamin Harrison, 9 May 1892, HP, vol. 140.

8. Harrison to Blaine, 10 May 1892, and Blaine to Harrison, 11 May 1892, HP, vol. 140.

9. E. W. Halford, "General Harrison's Attitude toward the Presidency," *Century Magazine* 84 (June 1912): 310; "Harrison Prior to the National Convention of 1892" and "A Proposal to End Hostilities," Michener Papers, boxes 1, 2.

10. Lemuel Quigg to Reid, 31 May 1892, Reid Papers, box 64.

11. Blaine to Harrison, 4 June 1892, HP, vol. 141.

12. Donald Marquand Dozer, "Benjamin Harrison and the Presidential Campaign of 1892," *American Historical Review* 54 (Oct. 1948): 66, 68; Sievers, *Benjamin Harrison, Hoosier President*, pp. 228–31; Muzzey, *James G. Blaine*, p. 476.

13. Dozer, "Benjamin Harrison," pp. 75–76; Sievers, *Benjamin Harrison, Hoosier President*, pp. 237–39.

14. Harold U. Faulkner, *Politics, Reform, and Expansion, 1890–1900* (New York: Harper & Row, 1963), pp. 131, 135; Sievers, *Benjamin Harrison, Hoosier President*, p. 244; H. Wayne Morgan, *From Hayes to McKinley: National Party Politics, 1877–1896* (Syracuse, N.Y.: Syracuse University Press, 1969), pp. 423–24, 436, 441; Dozer, "Benjamin Harrison," p. 75; R. Hal Williams, *Years of Decision: American Politics in the 1890s* (New York: John Wiley & Sons, 1978), pp. 68–69; George Harmon Knoles, *The Presidential Campaign and Election of 1892* (New York: AMS Press, 1971), pp. 138, 178, 181–91, 194–98, 207–8, 216, 229–30, 236 n.

15. Ralph S. Kuykendall, *The Hawaiian Kingdom*, vol. 3: *1874–1893: The Kalakaua Dynasty* (Honolulu: University of Hawaii Press, 1967), pp. 26–30, 34, 46, 374; David M. Pletcher, *The Awkward Years: American Foreign Relations under Garfield and Arthur* (Columbia: University of Missouri Press, 1962), p. 70; Merze Tate, *Hawaii: Reciprocity or Annexation* (East Lansing: Michigan State University Press, 1968), pp. 166–67, 184, 191–92, 198, 205; Julius W. Pratt, *Expansionists of 1898: The Acquisition of Hawaii and the Spanish Islands* (Baltimore, Md.: Johns Hopkins Press, 1936), p. 36; H. A. P. Carter to Blaine, 29 Mar. and 11 Apr. 1889, notes from the Hawaiian Legation in the United States, vol. 3.

16. Sylvester K. Stevens, *American Expansion in Hawaii, 1842–1898* (New York: Russell & Russell, 1968), pp. 188–91; Merrill to Blaine, 1 Aug. 1889, dispatches from Hawaii, vol. 24; Merze Tate, *The United States and the Hawaiian Kingdom: A Political History* (New Haven, Conn.: Yale University Press, 1965), p. 99; William Adam Russ, Jr., *The Hawaiian Revolution, 1893–1894* (Selinsgrove, Pa.: Susquehanna University Press, 1959), pp. 23, 36–39; Kuykendall, *Hawaiian Kingdom*, pp. 566–67; Tate, *Hawaii*, p. 119; Pratt, *Expansionists of 1898*, pp. 41–42, 62.

17. Tate, *Hawaii*, p. 234; Pratt, *Expansionists of 1898*, pp. 47–48; Kuykendall, *Hawaiian Kingdom*, pp. 489–90, 492–93.

18. Harrison to Blaine, 14 Oct. 1891, HP, vol. 131; James D. Richardson, comp., *A Compilation of the Messages and Papers of the Presidents, 1789–1897*

(hereafter cited as *Messages*), 9 vols. (Washington, D.C.: Government Printing Office, 1898), 9:188.

19. Pratt, *Expansionists of 1898*, p. 63; Kuykendall, *Hawaiian Kingdom*, p. 521; John L. Stevens to Blaine, 8 Mar. 1892, dispatches from Hawaii, vol. 25.

20. Pratt, *Expansionists of 1898*, pp. 54, 56–57; Kuykendall, *Hawaiian Kingdom*, pp. 532–36.

21. Richardson, *Messages*, 9:316.

22. Pratt, *Expansionists of 1898*, pp. 76–77, 79, 83, 89–91; Russ, *Hawaiian Revolution*, pp. 59–60, 71–72, 77, 90.

23. Thomas J. Osborne, *"Empire Can Wait": American Opposition to Hawaiian Annexation, 1893–1898* (Kent, Ohio: Kent State University Press, 1981), p. 2.

24. Stevens to John Foster, 1 Feb. 1893, dispatches from Hawaii, vol. 25.

25. Vignaud to Foster, 3 Feb. 1893 (refers to Foster's message of 1 Feb. 1893), dispatches from France, vol. 108; Robert Lincoln to Foster, 3 Feb. 1893, dispatches from Great Britain, vol. 173; White to Foster, 14 Feb. 1893, dispatches from Russia, vol. 44.

26. Richardson, *Messages*, 9:348–49.

27. Osborne, *"Empire Can Wait,"* p. 2; Russ, *Hawaiian Revolution*, pp. 166–69.

28. Alfred T. Mahan, "Hawaii and Our Future Sea Power," *Forum* 15 (Mar. 1893): 2, 7–8, 10.

29. Faulkner, *Politics*, pp. 9–10, 12, 31, 52, 141; Williams, *Years of Decision*, pp. 72, 75–77, 81–83, 91–94; Morgan, *From Hayes to McKinley*, pp. 452–76; Dozer, "Benjamin Harrison," p. 77.

30. Sievers, *Benjamin Harrison, Hoosier President*, pp. 255–57, 264, 275.

BIBLIOGRAPHICAL ESSAY

The perception that Benjamin Harrison was an average president has resulted in neglect for this president and his four years in the White House, 1889–93. There was no war and no depression; times were not unusual. His careful appointment policy brought no taint of fraud or corruption into his administration. Although no period is tranquil and although friction between individuals and groups is part of normal relationships, the Harrison period is skipped over in many general treatments because of the absence of dynamic figures or disputes of significance. The term *colorless* has been applied to the Harrison administration. Every presidential administration has contributed to national history. Harrison's, for instance, provided extensive domestic legislation and important beginnings in foreign affairs.

MANUSCRIPTS

The basic manuscript sources for the Benjamin Harrison presidency are found in both the more complete original and the microfilm edition of his papers, housed in the Manuscript Division of the Library of Congress. Many manuscript volumes and approximately 62 reels from a total of 151 concentrate on the presidential years and contain incoming correspondence, copies of outgoing letters, clippings, speeches, and other data. The *Index to the Benjamin Harrison Papers* (Washington, D.C.: Library of Congress, 1964) makes the collection easy to use. The *Index*, p. v, says: "The story of the Benjamin Harrison Papers is largely that of Mrs. Harrison's search for a biographer." The Library of Congress first inquired about the papers in 1903, shortly after Harrison's death. By that time E. Frank Tibbott, Harrison's long-time private secretary, had abandoned an attempt to complete a biography; therefore, Mrs. Mary Lord Harrison, the former president's second wife, turned the manuscripts over to John L. Griffiths, the United States consul general in London, who agreed to serve as the official biographer. When he died a decade later, without completing a biography, Mrs. Harrison retrieved the manuscripts and approached half a dozen other potential biographers without success. The Library of Congress received some of the Harrison papers in 1915, though their use was restricted under terms of the deposit, which was converted to a gift in 1933. In the meantime, Albert T. Volwiler received permission from Mrs. Harrison to do research in the Harrison papers in the mid 1920s. He had exclusive use for almost two decades, but he also failed to produce the expected biography. Volwiler, however, received help from E. W. Halford and Louis Michener and was responsible for suggesting that E. Frank Tibbott should transcribe his own shorthand notebooks, a total of seven thousand letters. Finally, in 1945, Mrs. Harrison agreed that the Harrison Papers should be opened for public use. The Benjamin Harrison Memorial Home, in Indianapolis, Indiana, has a miscellaneous assortment of Harrison items, some of which are of interest in regard to the presidential years. At one time this collection contained personal diaries of President Harrison, which are now missing.

The papers of some of the cabinet officers and other close Harrison associates have been preserved. The most useful ones for this study include the James G. Blaine and Family Papers, Library of Congress; *The Correspondence between Benjamin Harrison and James G. Blaine, 1882–1893*, edited by Albert T. Volwiler (Philadelphia: American Philosophical Society, 1940); *Letters of Mrs. James G. Blaine*, edited by Harriet S. Blaine Beale, 2 vols. (New York: Duffield & Co., 1908); John W. Foster, *Diplomatic Memoirs*, 2 vols. (Boston: Houghton Mifflin, 1909); the Benjamin Tracy Papers, Library of Congress; the Stephen B. Elkins Papers, West Virginia University Library; the Whitelaw Reid Papers, the Wharton Barker Papers, the Louis Michener Papers, and the Andrew Carnegie Papers—all located at the Library of Congress.

DOCUMENTS, PERIODICALS, AND SECONDARY WORKS

Most of Harrison's speeches were gathered by Charles Hedges and were published in 1892 in a book entitled *Speeches of Benjamin Harrison*, which was reprinted in 1971 in New York by Kennikat Press. In 1893 the Government Printing Office published *Public Papers and Addresses of Benjamin Harrison, Twenty-third President of the United States* (reprint, New York: Kraus, 1969). A different version of Harrison's speeches, along with some of his papers, was compiled by James D. Richardson in *A Compilation of the Messages and Papers of the Presidents, 1789–1897*, 9 vols. (Washington, D.C.: Government Printing Office, 1898). Another volume, of Harrison's speeches made on his tour to the Pacific in 1891, was published under the title *Through the South and West with the President, April 14–May 16, 1891: The Only Complete and Authorized Collection of President Harrison's*

Great and Eloquent Speeches Made during the Tour, compiled by John S. Shriver (New York: Mail & Express, 1891). Published and unpublished government documents, including departmental archives and dispatches to and from foreign countries, provide insight on the Harrison administration.

Harrison prepared articles for the *Ladies' Home Journal,* which were revised and published in book form under the title *This Country of Ours* (New York: Charles Scribner's Sons, 1898) "as a modest attempt to give [his] readers a view of the machinery of our National Government in motion." After his death, Mary Lord Harrison compiled Harrison's addresses and writings of public interest after 1894, which were published as *Views of an Ex-President* (Indianapolis, Ind.: Bowen-Merrill Co., 1901).

Shortly after the Harrison Papers in the Library of Congress were opened for research in 1945, Harry Joseph Sievers began on the major work about Benjamin Harrison, a three-volume biography which was published by three different companies. These volumes are *Benjamin Harrison, Hoosier Warrior, 1833-1865* (Chicago: Henry Regnery Co., 1952); *Benjamin Harrison, Hoosier Statesman: From the Civil War to the White House, 1865-1888* (New York: University Publishers, Inc., 1959); and *Benjamin Harrison, Hoosier President: The White House and After* (Indianapolis, Ind.: Bobbs-Merrill Inc., 1968). Sievers was also the compiler of *Benjamin Harrison, 1833-1901: Chronology, Documents, Bibliographical Aids* (Dobbs Ferry, N.Y.: Oceana Publications, 1969). These volumes, especially the one on the Harrison presidency, have contributed much to this work. Personal reminiscences by Harrison can be found in Arthur Bernon Tourtellot, *The Presidents on the Presidency* (Garden City, N.Y.: Doubleday & Co., Inc., 1964).

Contemporary journals and periodicals of valued use in this study were the *New York Tribune,* 16 Jan. 1890–21 Jan. 1892, which gave a Republican perspective on the Harrison years; the *New York Times,* 11 Nov. 1888–3 Mar. 1893; the *New York World;* the *Times* (London), 10 Dec. 1891–28 Apr. 1892; the *San Francisco Chronicle,* 26 Apr. 1891; the *San Francisco Examiner,* 27 Apr. 1892; the *Washington Post,* 1 Jan. 1890–29 Feb. 1892; the *Century Magazine,* Sept. 1893–June 1912; the *Chautauquan;* the *Forum;* the *Independent,* 11 Aug. 1892; *Harper's Weekly,* 30 Jan. 1892; the *Literary Digest,* 9 Nov. 1890–14 Mar. 1891; the *Literary World;* the *Magazine of American History,* July 1889; the *Nation,* 9 May 1889–4 Feb. 1892; the *North American Review,* June 1891–May 1893; *Public Opinion,* 9 Mar. 1889–11 Mar. 1893; the *Review of Reviews;* and *Spectator,* 30 Jan. 1892.

Memoirs and biographies of the men in Harrison's cabinet provide insight on their view of Benjamin Harrison and the activities of the administration. Biographies of Blaine include David Saville Muzzey, *James G. Blaine: A Political Idol of Other Days* (New York: Dodd, Mead & Co., 1934; reprint, Port Washington, N.Y.: Kennikat Press, 1965), and Alice Felt Tyler, *The Foreign Policy of James G. Blaine* (Minneapolis: University of Minnesota Press, 1927). Material on John W. Foster, in addition to his memoirs, can be found in Michael J. Devine, *John W. Foster: Politics and Diplomacy in the Imperial Era, 1873-1917* (Athens: Ohio University Press, 1981); Secretary of the Treasury William Windom's life has been reviewed in a recent Ph.D. dissertation by Robert Seward Salisbury,

"William Windom, the Republican Party, and the Gilded Age" (University of Minnesota, 1982); specifics on Secretary of War Stephen B. Elkins can be found in Oscar Doane Lambert, *Stephen Benton Elkins: American Foursquare* (Pittsburgh, Pa.: University of Pittsburgh Press, 1955); Harrison's good friend Postmaster General Wanamaker has a two-volume biography by Herbert Adams Gibbons, *John Wanamaker* (New York: Harper & Brothers Publishers, 1926); while Benjamin Franklin Cooling, in *Benjamin Franklin Tracy: Father of the Modern American Fighting Navy* (Hamden, Conn.: Archon Books, 1973), and John K. Mahon, in "Benjamin Franklin Tracy: Secretary of the Navy, 1889–1893," *New York Historical Society Quarterly* 44 (Apr. 1960), describe Harrison's contact with his secretary of the navy.

Other political leaders of that era for which memoirs, biographies, and other materials have been published that are of some use in interpreting the Harrison presidency include Leland L. Sage, *William Boyd Allison: A Study in Practical Politics* (Iowa City: State Historical Society of Iowa, 1956); Stanley P. Hirshson, "James S. Clarkson and the Civil Service Reformers, 1889–1893," *Iowa Journal of History* 57 (1959), and "James S. Clarkson versus Benjamin Harrison, 1891–1893: A Political Saga," *Iowa Journal of History* 58 (1960); Horace Samuel Merrill, *Bourbon Leader: Grover Cleveland and the Democratic Party* (Boston, Mass.: Little, Brown & Co., 1957); Allan Nevins, *Grover Cleveland: A Study in Courage* (New York: Dodd, Mead & Co., 1933); Shelby M. Cullom, *Fifty Years of Public Service* (Chicago: A. C. McClurg & Co., 1911); Arthur Wallace Dunn, *From Harrison to Harding: A Personal Narrative, Covering a Third of a Century, 1888–1921*, 2 vols. (Port Washington, N.Y.: Kennikat Press, 1922, 1971); Carl Brent Swisher, *Stephen J. Field, Craftsman of the Law* (Washington, D.C.: Brookings Institution, 1930); Willard L. King, *Melville Weston Fuller: Chief Justice of the United States, 1888–1910* (Chicago: University of Chicago Press, 1967); Allan Peskin, *Garfield* (Kent, Ohio: Kent State University Press, 1978); Justus D. Doenecke, *The Presidencies of James A. Garfield and Chester A. Arthur* (Lawrence, Kans.: Regents Press of Kansas, 1981); E. W. Halford, "General Harrison's Attitude toward the Presidency," *Century Magazine* 84 (June 1912); H. Draper Hunt, *Hannibal Hamlin of Maine: Lincoln's First Vice-President* (Syracuse, N.Y.: Syracuse University Press, 1969); William R. Thayer, *The Life and Letters of John Hay*, 2 vols. (Boston, Mass.: Houghton Mifflin Co., 1915); Kenneth E. Davison, *The Presidency of Rutherford B. Hayes* (Westport, Conn.: Greenwood Press, Inc., 1972); John J. Ingalls, *A Collection of the Writings of John James Ingalls: Essays, Addresses, and Orations* (Kansas City, Mo.: Hudson-Kimberly Publishing Co., 1902); John A. Garraty, *Henry Cabot Lodge: A Biography* (New York: Alfred A. Knopf, 1953); Thomas J. Morgan, "Benjamin Harrison: A Character Sketch," *Review of Reviews* 6 (July 1892); Thomas Collier Platt, *The Autobiography of Thomas Collier Platt*, compiled and edited by Louis J. Lang (New York: B. W. Dodge & Co., 1910); William E. Connelley, *The Life of Preston B. Plumb, 1837–1891* (Chicago: Browne & Howell Co., 1913); Richard S. West, Jr., *The Second Admiral: A Life of David Dixon Porter, 1813–1891* (New York: Coward-McCann, Inc., 1937); James A. Kehl, *Boss Rule in the Gilded Age: Matt Quay of Pennsylvania* (Pittsburgh, Pa.: University of Pittsburgh Press, 1981); William A. Robinson, *Thomas B. Reed: Parliamentarian* (New York: Dodd, Mead & Co., 1930); Lt.-Gen. John M. Schofield, *Forty-Six Years in the Army* (New York: Century Co., 1897); James M. Merrill, *William Tecumseh Sherman* (Chicago: Rand McNally, 1971); Dorothy Ganfield Fowler, *John Coit Spooner: Defender of Presidents* (New York: University Publishers, 1961); Norman E. Tutorow, *Leland Stanford: Man of Many Careers* (Menlo Park, Calif.: Pacific Coast Publishing, 1971); Elmer Ellis, *Henry Moore Teller: Defender of the West* (Caldwell, Idaho: Caxton Printers, Ltd., 1941); *Autobiography of Andrew Dickson White*, 2 vols. (New York: Century Co., 1905); Harvey W. Wiley, *An Autobiography* (Indianapolis, Ind.: Bobbs-Merrill Co., 1930); and *The Papers of Woodrow Wilson*, vol. 6, edited by Arthur S. Link (Princeton, N.J.: Princeton University Press, 1969).

General histories of the United States that make an important contribution to interpretations of the Harrison presidency include E. Benjamin Andrews, *The History of the Last Quarter-Century in the United States, 1870–1895* (New York: Charles Scribner's Sons, 1896); John Spencer Bassett, *Expansion and Reform, 1889–1926* (New York: Longmans, Green & Co., 1926); Sean Dennis Cashman, *America in the Gilded Age: From the Death of Lincoln to the Rise of Theodore Roosevelt* (New York: New York University Press, 1984); Carl N. Degler, *The Age of Economic Revolution, 1876–1900* (Glenview, Ill.: Scott, Foresman & Co., 1967); Davis Rich Dewey, *National Problems, 1885–1897* (New York: Harper & Brothers Publishers, 1907); John M. Dobson, *Politics in the Gilded Age: A New Perspective on Reform* (New York: Praeger Publisher, 1972); Harold U. Faulkner, *Politics, Reform and Expansion, 1890–1900* (New York: Harper & Row, 1959); Henry Jones Ford, *The Cleveland Era: A Chronicle of the New Order in Politics* (New Haven, Conn.: Yale University Press, 1919); John A. Garraty, *The New Commonwealth, 1877–1890* (New York: Harper & Brothers, 1968); Ray Ginger, *The Age of Excess: The United States from 1887 to 1914* (New York: Macmillan Publishing Co., 1965; 2d ed., 1975); Matthew Josephson, *The Politicos, 1865–1896* (New York: Harcourt, Brace & Co., 1938), and *The President Makers: The Culture of Politics and Leadership in the Age of Enlightenment, 1896–1919* (New York: Harcourt, Brace & Co., 1940); H. Wayne Morgan, *From Hayes to McKinley: National Party Politics, 1877–1896* (Syracuse, N.Y.: Syracuse University Press, 1969); H. Wayne Morgan, editor, *The Gilded Age: A Reappraisal* (Syracuse, N.Y.: Syracuse University Press, 1970); James Ford Rhodes, *History of the United States from Hayes to McKinley, 1877–1896*, 8 vols. (New York: Macmillan Co., 1919); Stephen Skowronek, *Building a New American State: The Expansion of National Administrative Capacities, 1877–1920* (New York: Cambridge University Press, 1982); Leonard D. White, *The Republican Era: A Study in Administrative History, 1869–1901* (New York: Macmillan Co., 1958); Robert H. Wiebe, *The Search for Order, 1877–1920* (New York: Hill & Wang, 1967); and R. Hal Williams, *Years of Decision: American Politics in the 1890s* (New York: John Wiley & Sons, 1978).

General accounts of the presidents and their families that were of use in gaining material on the Harrison presidency include the following diverse books: Herbert R. Collins and David B. Weaver, *Wills of the U.S. Presidents* (New

York: Communications Channels, Inc., 1976); Marcus Cunliffe, *American Presidents and the Presidency* (New York: American Heritage Press, 1968); William A. DeGregorio, *The Complete Book of U.S. Presidents* (New York: Dembner Books, 1984); Louis Clinton Hatch, *A History of the Vice Presidency of the United States* (New York: American Historical Society, Inc., 1934); Margaret Leech, *In the Days of McKinley* (New York: Harper & Brothers, 1959); Stefan Lorant, *The Glorious Burden: The American Presidency* (New York: Harper & Row, 1968); Michael Medved, *The Shadow Presidents* (New York: Times Books, 1979); James Morgan, *Our Presidents* (New York: Macmillan Co., 1952); Kathleen Prindiville, *First Ladies* (New York: Macmillan Co., 1941); and Henry L. Stoddard, *It Costs to Be President* (New York: Harper & Brothers Publishers, 1938).

Republican party politics and voting records for the Harrison years can be found in Richard C. Bain and Judith H. Parris, *Convention Decisions and Voting Records* (Washington, D.C.: Brookings Institution, 1973); Franklin L. Burdette, *The Republican Party: A Short History* (Princeton, N.J.: D. Van Nostrand Co., Inc., 1968); W. Dean Burnham, *Presidential Ballots, 1836–1892* (Baltimore, Md.: Johns Hopkins University Press, 1955); Francis Curtis, *The Republican Party: A History of Its Fifty Years' Existence and a Record of Its Measures and Leaders, 1854–1904* (New York: G. P. Putnam's Sons, 1904); Donald Marquand Dozer, "Benjamin Harrison and the Presidential Campaign of 1892," *American Historical Review* 54 (Oct. 1948); Robert F. Durden, "Politics in the Gilded Age, 1877–1896," in *Interpreting and Teaching American History,* edited by William H. Cartwright and Richard L. Watson (Baltimore, Md.: National Council for the Social Studies, 1961); Richard Jensen, *The Winning of the Midwest: Social and Political Conflict, 1888–1896* (Chicago: University of Chicago Press, 1971); Paul Kleppner, *The Cross of Culture: A Social Analysis of Midwestern Politics, 1850–1900* (New York: Free Press, 1970); George Harmon Knoles, *The Presidential Campaign and Election of 1892* (Palo Alto, Calif.: Stanford University Press, 1942); Robert D. Marcus, *Grand Old Party: Political Structure in the Gilded Age, 1880–1896* (New York: Oxford University Press, 1971); George H. Mayer, *The Republican Party, 1854–1966* (New York: Oxford University Press, 1967); William Starr Myers, *The Republican Party: A History* (New York: Century Co., 1928); Albert C. E. Parker, "Beating the Spread: Analyzing American Election Outcomes," *Journal of American History* 67 (June 1980); Eugene H. Rosenboom and Alfred E. Eckes, Jr., *A History of Presidential Elections* (New York: Macmillan Publishing Co., 1979); Arthur M. Schlesinger, Jr., and Fred L. Israel, editors, *History of U.S. Political Parties,* vol. 2: *1860–1910: The Gilded Age in Politics* (New York: Chelsea House Publishers, 1973; see specific articles for the 1888 and 1892 presidential elections); John G. Sproat, *"The Best Men": Liberal Reformers in the Gilded Age* (New York: Oxford University Press, 1968); and Edward Stanwood, *A History of the Presidency from 1788 to 1897* (Boston: Houghton Mifflin Co., 1912).

Materials that made important contributions to interpreting the domestic policy of the Harrison administration include Edward Coffman, *The Old Army: A Portrait of the American Army in Peacetime, 1784–1898* (New York: Oxford University Press, 1986); Homer Cummings and Carl McFarland, *Federal Justice:*

Chapters in the History of Justice and the Federal Executive (New York: Macmillan Co., 1937); Samuel Trask Dana and Sally K. Fairfax, *Forest and Range Policy: Its Development in the United States,* 2d ed. (New York: McGraw-Hill Book Co., 1980); Wallace Evan Davies, *Patriotism on Parade: The Story of Veterans and Hereditary Organizations in America, 1783-1900* (Cambridge, Mass.: Harvard University Press, 1953); Mary R. Dearing, *Veterans in Politics: The Story of the G.A.R.* (Baton Rouge: Louisiana State University Press, 1952); Vincent de Santis, "The Republican Party and the Southern Negro, 1877-1897," *Journal of Negro History* 45 (Apr. 1960); Everett Dick, *The Lure of the Land: A Social History of the Public Lands from the Articles of Confederation to the New Deal* (Lincoln: University of Nebraska Press, 1970); Thomas W. Dunlay, *Wolves for the Blue Soldiers: Indian Scouts and Auxiliaries with the United States Army, 1860-1890* (Lincoln: University of Nebraska Press, 1982); John S. Ezell, *Fortune's Merry Wheel: The Lottery in America* (Cambridge, Mass.: Harvard University Press, 1960); Stephen J. Field, *Personal Reminiscences of Early Days in California (To which is added the story of his attempted assassination by a former associate on the supreme bench of the state, by George C. Gorham)* (New York: Da Capo Press, 1968); Leslie H. Fishel, Jr., "The Negro in Northern Politics, 1870-1900," *Mississippi Valley Historical Review* 42 (Dec. 1955); Jack D. Foner, *The United States Soldier between Two Wars: Army Life and Reforms, 1865-1898* (New York: Humanities Press, 1970); Arlen L. Fowler, *The Black Infantry in the West, 1869-1891* (Westport, Conn.: Greenwood Publishing Co., 1971); Leon Friedman and Fred L. Israel, editors, *The Justices of the United States Supreme Court, 1789-1969: Their Lives and Major Opinions,* 4 vols. (New York: Chelsea House Publishers, 1969); Paul W. Gates, *History of Public Land Development* (New York: Arno Press, 1968, 1979); William G. Glasson, *Federal Military Pensions in the United States* (New York: Oxford University Press, 1918); Allen J. Going, "The South and the Blair Education Bill," *Mississippi Valley Historical Review* 44 (Sept. 1957); Donald L. Grant, *The Anti-Lynching Movement: 1883-1932* (San Francisco, Calif.: R and E Associates, 1975); William T. Hagan, "Civil Service Commissioner Theodore Roosevelt and the Indian Rights Association," *Pacific Historical Review* 44 (May 1975), and *The Indian Rights Association: The Herbert Welch Years, 1882-1904* (Tucson: University of Arizona Press, 1985); Walter R. Herrick, Jr., *The American Naval Revolution* (Baton Rouge: Louisiana State University Press, 1966); Stanley P. Hirshson, *Farewell to the Bloody Shirt: Northern Republicans and the Southern Negro, 1877-1893* (Chicago: Quadrangle Books, 1962, 1968); Ari Hoogenboom, *Outlawing the Spoils: A History of the Civil Service Reform Movement, 1865-1883* (Urbana: University of Illinois Press, 1961); Frederick E. Hoxie, "Redefining Indian Education: Thomas J. Morgan's Program in Disarray," *Arizona and the West* 24 (Spring 1982); Rayford W. Logan, *The Betrayal of the Negro: From Rutherford B. Hayes to Woodrow Wilson* (New York: Collier Books, 1965); John Ise, *The United States Forest Policy* (New York: Arno Press, 1920, 1972); Peter Karsten, *The Naval Aristocracy: The Golden Age of Annapolis and the Emergence of Modern American Navalism* (New York: Free Press, 1972); J. P. Kinney, *The Development of Forest Law in America* (New York: John Wiley & Sons, Inc., 1917); William H. Leckie, *The*

Buffalo Soldiers: A Narrative of the Negro Cavalry in the West (Norman: University of Oklahoma Press, 1967); Delber L. McKee, *Chinese Exclusion versus the Open Door Policy, 1900–1906: Clashes over Chinese Policy in the Roosevelt Era* (Detroit, Mich.: Wayne State University Press, 1977); Donald L. McMurry, "The Political Significance of the Pension Question, 1885–1897," *Mississippi Valley Historical Review* 9 (June 1922), and "The Bureau of Pensions during the Administration of President Harrison," *Mississippi Valley Historical Review* 13 (Dec. 1926); Bradley D. Nash, "Organizing and Staffing the Presidency," Center for the Study of the Presidency, *Proceedings* 3 (1980); Arnold M. Paul, *Conservative Crisis and the Rule of Law: Attitudes of Bar and Bench, 1887–1895* (Ithaca, N.Y.: Cornell University Press, 1960); Francis Paul Prucha, *Indian Policy in the United States: Historical Essays* (Lincoln: University of Nebraska Press, 1981); A. Bower Sageser, *The First Two Decades of the Pendleton Act: A Study of Civil Service Reform* (Lincoln: University of Nebraska Studies, 1935); Eliza Ruhamah Scidmore, "Our New National Forest Reserves," *Century Magazine* 46 (Sept. 1893); Harry J. Sievers, "The Catholic Indian School Issue and the Presidential Election of 1892," *Catholic Historical Review* 38 (July 1952); George Sinkler, *The Racial Attitudes of American Presidents: From Abraham Lincoln to Theodore Roosevelt* (Garden City, N.Y.: Doubleday & Co., Inc., 1971); Harold K. Steen, *The U.S. Forest Service: A History* (Seattle: University of Washington Press, 1976); Frank Mann Stewart, *The National Civil Service Reform League: History, Activities, and Problems* (Austin: University of Texas Press, 1929); Tom E. Terrill, *The Tariff, Politics, and American Foreign Policy, 1874–1901* (Westport, Conn.: Greenwood Press, 1973); Hans B. Thorelli, *The Federal Antitrust Policy: Origination of an American Tradition* (London: George Allen & Unwin Ltd., 1974); Robert M. Utley, *Frontier Regulars: The United States Army and the Indian, 1866–1891* (New York: Macmillan Publishing Co., 1973); Paul P. Van Riper, *History of the United States Civil Service* (Evanston, Ill.: Row, Peterson & Co., 1958); Albert T. Volwiler, "Tariff Strategy and Propaganda in the United States, 1887–1888," *American Historical Review* 38 (Oct. 1936); Charles Warren, *The Supreme Court in United States History*, 2 vols. (Boston: Little, Brown & Co., 1926); Russell F. Weigley, *History of the United States Army* (New York: Macmillan Co., 1967); Richard E. Welch, Jr., "The Federal Elections Bill of 1890: Postscripts and Prelude," *Journal of American History* 52 (Dec. 1965); and Fred Wellborn, "The Influence of the Silver-Republican Senators, 1889–1891," *Mississippi Valley Historical Review* 14 (1928).

The literature on foreign affairs involving the Harrison administration has grown even faster than the literature on domestic policy. Materials important in this study include Robert L. Beisner, *From the Old Diplomacy to the New, 1865–1900* (New York: Thomas Y. Crowell Co., 1975); Robert C. Brown, *Canada's National Policy, 1883–1900: A Study in Canadian-American Relations* (Princeton, N.J.: Princeton University Press, 1964); James Morton Callahan, *American Foreign Policy in Canadian Relations* (New York: Cooper Square Publishers, Inc., 1967); Charles S. Campbell, Jr., "The Anglo-American Crisis in the Bering Sea, 1890–1891," *Mississippi Valley Historical Review* 48 (Dec. 1961), "The Bering Sea Settlements of 1892," *Pacific Historical Review* 32 (1963), and *The Transformation of*

American Foreign Relations, 1865–1900 (New York: Harper & Row, 1976); Dennis Alan Daellenbach, "Senators, the Navy and the Politics of American Expansionism, 1881–1890" (Ph.D. diss., University of Kansas, 1982); James T. Gay, "Bering Sea Controversy: Harrison, Blaine, and Cronyism," *Alaska Journal* 3 (Winter 1973); John L. Gignilliat, "Pigs, Politics, and Protection: The European Boycott of American Pork, 1879–1891," *Agricultural History* 35 (Jan. 1961); John A. S. Grenville and George Berkeley Young, *Politics, Strategy, and American Diplomacy: Studies in Foreign Policy, 1873–1917* (New Haven, Conn.: Yale University Press, 1966); Kenneth J. Hagan, *American Gunboat Diplomacy and the Old Navy, 1877–1889* (Westport, Conn.: Greenwood Press, 1973); Osgood Hardy, "The *Itata* Incident," *Hispanic American Historical Review* 5 (May 1922), and "Was Patrick Egan a 'Blundering Minister'?" *Hispanic American Historical Review* 8 (Feb. 1928); Lt. Jerrold Kelley, "The Chilian Trouble," *Harper's Weekly* 36 (30 Jan. 1892); Ralph S. Kuykendall, *The Hawaiian Kingdom*, vol. 3: *1874–1893: The Kalakaua Dynasty* (Honolulu: University of Hawaii Press, 1967); Walter LaFeber, *The New Empire: An Interpretation of American Expansion, 1860–1898* (Ithaca, N.Y.: Cornell University Press, 1963); Rayford W. Logan, *The Diplomatic Relations of the United States with Haiti, 1776–1891* (Chapel Hill: University of North Carolina Press, 1941); Alfred T. Mahan, "Hawaii and Our Future Sea Power," *Forum* 15 (Mar. 1893); Sidney T. Mathews, "The Nicaraguan Canal Controversy: The Struggle for an American-constructed and American-controlled Transitway" (Ph.D. diss., Johns Hopkins University, 1947); Thomas F. McGann, *Argentina, the United States, and the Inter-American System, 1880–1914* (Cambridge, Mass.: Harvard University Press, 1957); Thomas J. Osborne, *"Empire Can Wait": American Opposition to Hawaiian Annexation, 1893–1898* (Kent, Ohio: Kent State University Press, 1981); Fredrick Pike, *Chile and the United States: The Emergence of Chile's Social Crisis and the Challenge to United States Diplomacy, 1880–1962* (South Bend, Ind.: University of Notre Dame Press, 1963); Milton Plesur, *America's Outward Thrust: Approaches to Foreign Affairs, 1865–1898* (De Kalb: Northern Illinois University Press, 1971); David M. Pletcher, *The Awkward Years: American Foreign Relations under Garfield and Arthur* (Columbia: University of Missouri Press, 1962), and "Reciprocity and Latin America in the Early 1890s: A Foretaste of Dollar Diplomacy," *Pacific Historical Review* 47 (Feb. 1978); Julius W. Pratt, *Expansionists of 1898: The Acquisition of Hawaii and the Spanish Islands* (Baltimore, Md.: Johns Hopkins Press, 1936); Theodore Roosevelt, "The Foreign Policy of President Harrison," *Independent* 44 (11 Aug. 1892); William Adam Russ, Jr., *The Hawaiian Revolution, 1893–1894* (Selinsgrove, Pa.: Susquehanna University Press, 1959); George H. Ryden, *The Foreign Policy of the United States in Relation to Samoa* (New Haven, Conn.: Yale University Press, 1933); Louis L. Snyder, "The American-German Pork Dispute, 1879–1891," *Journal of Modern History* 17 (Mar. 1945); Sylvester K. Stevens, *American Expansion in Hawaii, 1842–1898* (New York: Russell & Russell, 1968); Charles C. Tansill, *Canadian-American Relations, 1875–1911* (Gloucester, Mass.: Peter Smith, 1964); Merze Tate, *Hawaii: Reciprocity or Annexation* (East Lansing: Michigan State University Press, 1968), and *The United States and the Hawaiian Kingdom: A Political History* (New Haven, Conn.:

Yale University Press, 1965); Benjamin F. Tracy, ''The Behring Sea Question,'' *North American Review* 156 (May 1893); Albert T. Volwiler, ''Harrison, Blaine, and American Foreign Policy, 1889–1893,'' *Proceedings of the American Philosophical Society* 79 (Nov. 1938); and Edward Younger, *John A. Kasson: Politics and Diplomacy from Lincoln to McKinley* (Iowa City: State Historical Society of Iowa, 1955).

INDEX

Reed, Thomas Brackett: and "Billion-Dollar Congress," 78; and dump Harrison campaign, 79–80; elected Speaker of the House, 48; and Lodge elections bill, 62; support for tariff, 50; travel with Harrison, 164, 169; view on silver, 58

Reed's Rules, 48

Reid, Whitelaw: and Blaine, 21, 88, 129; and Carnegie, 9; as compromiser, 79; on foreign affairs, 127; and pork sales to Europe, 132–36; and Samoan issue, 116; as vice-presidential candidate, 197; wants appointment, 22, 110

Republican defection from Harrison, 81

Republican party, and local issues, 89–90

Riis, Jacob August, 207

Roosevelt, Theodore, 40, 151–52

Rowan, Stephen C., 95, 191

Rudini, Antonio, marchese di Starabba, 153

Rusk, Jeremiah M.: Harrison's choice for secretary of agriculture, 26, 27; and pork sales to Europe, 133–34; travel with Harrison, 164, 169, 172, 179

Ryden, George H., 115

Sackville-West, Sir Lionel Edward, 13

Samoa, crisis in, 114–16

Sanger, Alice, 16, 83

Sanger, J. P., 172

Schley, Winfield Scott, 147

Schofield, John M., 103, 179

Schofield, Mrs. John M., 179

Scott, John W., 17, 85, 182, 212n. 44

Seward, William Henry, 125

Sharon, William, 186

Shepard, L. G., 137

Sheridan, Philip H., 103

Sherman, John, 47, 53, 59, 143

Sherman, William Tecumseh, 7, 87, 103, 169, 171, 185, 191, 192

Sherman Antitrust Act, 53–55, 190

Sherman Silver Purchase Act, 58–60, 207

Shiras, George, Jr., 187–90

Silent quorum, 48–49

Silver bloc, 57

Silver crusade, 55–60

Silverites, in Democratic party, 60

Sitting Bull, 104, 106

Smith, John Mott, 203

Soley, James R., 100

Sousa, John Philip, 5

South Dakota, statehood of, 44

Sparks, A. J., 70

Spectator (London), 152

Spooner, John C., 33, 61

Springer, William M., 75

Stanford, Leland, 33, 172, 179, 238n. 40

Stanwood, Edward, 88

Stevens, John Leavitt, 202–205

Stewart, William H., 56, 65

Studebaker, Clement, 33, 117, 162, 163

Tamasese, 114, 115

Tanner, James R., 34–36, 164, 215n. 13

Tariff issue, 49–52

Taylor, R. S., 33

Teller, Henry Moore, 56–58

Terry, David S., 186

Terry, Sarah Hill (Mrs. David S.), 186–87

Thompson, Albert Clifton, 166

Thompson, Hugh S., 40

Thurston, Lorrin Andrews, 204

Tibbott, E. Frank: executive clerk, 83; subsequent career, 224n. 18; travel with Harrison, 16, 172

Tilden, Samuel J., 193

Timber Culture Act of 1873, 69

Times (London), 131

Tin-plate industry, protection of, 52

Townsend, Charles Champlin, 167

Tracy, Benjamin Franklin: and Bering Sea controversy, 143; reports on Blaine's health, 129; and contributions to foreign policy, 122–23, 126; and development of navy, 97–103; and dispute with Chile, 146; and Hawaiian issue, 204; as New York's cabinet member, 24, 27–28; travel with Harrison, 164, 165, 169–70, 177, 179

Tracy, Mrs. Benjamin F., 98

Trescot, William Henry, 117, 144

Tyler, Alice Felt, 112

Victorio, 104

Volwiler, Albert T., 111, 112, 113, 229n. 13

Waite, Morrison R., 186

Walker, John G., 97, 150

Wanamaker, John: and Cape May Point cottage, 163; and efficiency in post offices, 82; Harrison's choice for postmaster general, 24, 26, 27; heads protariff committee, 10; and Louisiana Lottery, 73–74; on Platt's claim to cabinet position, 79; and postmaster